Elvis

Also by Lorraine Gibson

Robert Baden-Powell: A Biography, with a foreword by Bear Grylls, OBE
Pen & Sword History (2022)

Elvis

The King of Fashion

Lorraine Gibson

WHITE OWL
AN IMPRINT OF PEN & SWORD BOOKS LTD.
YORKSHIRE – PHILADELPHIA

First published in Great Britain in 2024 by
White Owl
An imprint of Pen & Sword Books Limited
Yorkshire – Philadelphia

Copyright © Lorraine Gibson 2024

ISBN 978 1 39904 984 9

The right of Lorraine Gibson to be identified as
Author of this Work has been asserted by her in accordance
with the Copyright, Designs and Patents Act 1988.

A CIP catalogue record for this book is
available from the British Library

All rights reserved. No part of this book may be reproduced or
transmitted in any form or by any means, electronic or mechanical
including photocopying, recording or by any information storage and
retrieval system, without permission from the Publisher in writing.

Typeset by Mac Style
Printed in the UK by CPI Group (UK) Ltd, Croydon, CR0 4YY.

Pen & Sword Books Limited incorporates the imprints of After
the Battle, Atlas, Archaeology, Aviation, Discovery, Family History,
Fiction, History, Maritime, Military, Military Classics, Politics,
Select, Transport, True Crime, Air World, Frontline Publishing, Leo
Cooper, Remember When, Seaforth Publishing, The Praetorian Press,
Wharncliffe Local History, Wharncliffe Transport, Wharncliffe True
Crime and White Owl.

For a complete list of Pen & Sword titles please contact

PEN & SWORD BOOKS LIMITED
47 Church Street, Barnsley, South Yorkshire, S70 2AS, England
E-mail: enquiries@pen-and-sword.co.uk
Website: www.pen-and-sword.co.uk
or
PEN AND SWORD BOOKS
1950 Lawrence Rd, Havertown, PA 19083, USA
E-mail: uspen-and-sword@casematepublishers.com
Website: www.penandswordbooks.com

To Steve, Molly and Matilda
Thank you, you've been fantastic

Contents

Acknowledgements		viii
Disclaimer		xii
Foreword		xiii
List of Images		xv
Introduction		xviii
Chapter 1	Clothes Encounter	1
Chapter 2	In the Ghetto	4
Chapter 3	I've a Feeling We're Not in Tupelo Anymore …	18
Chapter 4	The Lansky Effect	33
Chapter 5	Here Comes the Sun	47
Chapter 6	Part I – Prelude: Elvis Has Entered the Building	58
	Part II – Tearing Up the House	62
Chapter 7	1956 – The Year of Elvis	80
Chapter 8	Part I – My Best Girl	93
	Part II – Lights, Camera, Action!	109
Chapter 9	The '68 Comeback Special	120
Chapter 10	The Caped Crusader	134
Chapter 11	Elvis Leaves the Building	154
Epilogue: The King is Dead, Long Live The King – The Legacy		177
Appendix		
Elvis Filmography		191
Bibliography and Sources		192
Index		195

Acknowledgements

While this book is driven by the rhythm of Elvis's iconic sense of style, its heart – its backbeat, if you will – is always the man himself; his life, his dreams, his flaws, his passions, his unparalleled talent, his frailty and, above all, his humanity.

It was only possible thanks to the lasting and entirely devoted legacy created by those who loved, admired and now treasure him – some of them lucky enough to have known him, others, like me, who wish that they had.

I want to thank them all, and the many people who personally and generously shared their time, expertise, knowledge and Elvis experiences with me.

In alphabetical order:

Keith Alverson, for your magnificent Elvis photographs.

Jeanette Andrew, for recommending *A Little Bit of Elvis*, ITV's 1998 documentary about Frank Skinner's quest to find the true blue velvet shirt.

Lauren Berry at Memphis Tourism, for sharing your insider knowledge of Memphis and how best to follow Elvis's journey through it, suggesting places I might otherwise not have discovered. And for the ducky cosmos at the Peabody.

Steve Binder, the genius behind the *'68 Comeback Special*, for your time, your unique and often hilarious stories, your integrity and your humility.

And for telling Elvis that his career was in the toilet, thus rescuing him – for a while, at least.

And to your brother-in-arts, the irrepressible Spencer Proffer – thanks for your time, your knowledge, the *Reinventing Elvis* documentary reveal and invitation to the New York screening (that I missed, ironically, because of Elvis).

Ms Ardys Bell Clawson, for your incredible story (and photos) about when you met Elvis, not once, but twice, in Jacksonville, Florida, in 1955 and 1956, the first time after he'd had his clothes torn off by crazed fans. And to Trey Miller from 'Globetrotting with Trey', for allowing Ardys the time to tell her tale so beautifully.

Acknowledgements   ix

Cole Early, for the insights, the backstage tour and the historic tales at the incredible Overton Park Shell. And for being into punk rock.

Faith Eckersall for enhancing my Vegas-years' research with the full version of Ellen Willis's wonderful 1969 review of Elvis's first show at the International Hotel.

Facebook's Elvis groups, especially the marvellous Elvis in the '70s, for the insights, the cool photos and a kindness and cameraderie that Elvis would approve of.

Lonnie Fuqua, for your eyewitness account of how seeing Elvis perform his legendary *Aloha from Hawaii* live by satellite concert when you were a teenager in 1973 changed your life – and for still treasuring your two-dollar ticket after more than fifty years.

Peter Guralnick, for your time, your kindness and your incomparable, beautifully written, joyfully detailed Elvis biography. Your deep understanding of the real man behind the image was invaluable to me.

Graceland, Elvis Presley Boulevard, Memphis, for keeping his legacy so alive and for being far more moving, exciting and welcoming than I could have dreamed.

Hal and Julie Lansky at Lansky Bros., Memphis, for being my personal Elvis oracles. For meeting me, and transporting me back in time to 1950s Beale Street and allowing me inside the original Lansky store; for your time and for sharing your treasured memories, based on your family's long friendship with Elvis; for being my fashion gurus for both the past and the present. For the use of your fantastic archive photographs. And, finally, to Bernard Lansky, for, quite literally, opening the door to Elvis's fashion adventure.

Teri Hammond-Kincaid, for your charming childhood recollections of seeing Elvis live in his Chief suit at the Charleston Civic Centre in 1975, and for allowing me to use your precious photograph of him.

The National Civil Rights Museum, for such a moving and affecting journey through some of the country's darkest and most tumultuous times, and for your vision of change.

Sue Martin, for proofreading each raw chapter, moving from woggle to wiggle without a hitch, and for telling me that you loved each one of them. Also, to Peter Martin and Lesley and Vito Fereti, for encouraging me to go to an Elvis tribute show.

x   Elvis: The King of Fashion

And, speaking of which, to Jeremy and Hattie Miles, for leading me to the star of said show, an elusive Elvis impersonator I only managed to meet briefly before he had to leave the building.

Linne Matthews, my editor, for your enthusiasm, wisdom and invaluable advice. For making the process enjoyable, for making my year by telling me that my book is fabulous and for ending up more of an Elvis fan than you were when you started.

Elvis fan Jenny O'Dwyer, for the use of your calming, almost mystical message to Austin Butler fans who took to Facebook to express their anger at his being overlooked for the Best Performance by an Actor in a Leading Role Oscar for the *Elvis* movie.

Jo and Dan Paine, for alerting me to the Elvis Parapraxis theory and, therefore, also my thanks to Malcolm Gladwell for Jack White's Elvis shrine and the fascinating *Revisionist History* podcast, in which both subjects were so engagingly discussed.

Butch and Kim Polston, for your personal story, the dream answers to my relentless questions, the photos, the anecdotes and, most of all, for making outfits that I'm sure Elvis would have approved of.

Stacie Spain at the Peabody Hotel, Memphis, for the warm Southern welcome, for putting up with all my questions, and for the history. And Kenon Walker, the hotel's Duckmaster, for the insights, the ducks, for loving St Jude Children's Research Hospital – and for letting me hold the marching cane.

Billy Stallings, aka *Spa Guy*, for answering all of my questions, for the Regis Wilson prom night insights and for your brilliant YouTube channel.

Stax Museum – or 'Soulsville USA' – in Memphis, for the visual, touchable, audible journey to the birthplace of soul music. A joy, from the first steps through a reassembled 1906 Mississippi Delta church and the astonishing Hall of (vinyl) Records, to Isaac Hayes' gleaming, *Super Fly*, fur-lined, 24-carat gold-trimmed Cadillac Eldorado.

Sun Studio and Drew, for the coolest tour and allowing me to sit at the sainted Marion Keisker's desk, hold Sam Phillips's famous studio mic and stand where Elvis once did. And to Nina Kathleen Jones, for explaining the finer points of the names over the decades.

Marty Wilde, for giving the world *Teenager in Love*, and for your lifelong appreciation of Elvis and the influence he had on you. For the nostalgia trip into Britain during the 1950s teen gold rush and, of course, for the music. Rock on.

Jonathan Wright at Pen & Sword, for commissioning me to write this book and giving me the opportunity to share my passion for Elvis and his fashions with a wider audience.

Not forgetting Memphis itself, for being the unique, music-obsessed, multi-faceted, real, fascinating, historic and inspiring place where Elvis was able to find his soul.

To my husband, Steve, and daughters, Molly and Matilda, for your unending support, advice, editing, proofing, researching, encouragement, patience, opinions and love – and for listening to and watching nothing but Elvis for the past two years.

To Elvis's devoted fans, old and new – you know who you are – for keeping his light shining brightly.

And above all, to the inimitable, wonderful, fashion-loving, music-crazy, beautiful, gifted, flawed, conflicted, big-hearted, soft-hearted, weak-hearted, fragile, ground-breaking, genuine, lost, humble, visionary soul that was and will forever remain The King.

Thank you, thank you very much, Elvis – you will never go out of fashion.

Disclaimer

Some quotes or references in this book are from quotes and texts that were written or spoken in the past. Consequently, they may use some terms or expressions that were current at the time, regardless of what we may think of them in the twenty-first century.

For reasons of historical accuracy, they have been preserved in their original form.

Foreword

On my father's eighteenth birthday, his father told him, 'Son, here's the world, now go and get it.' With that advice and the $125 he was also given, my father, Bernard Lansky, started Lansky Bros., an army surplus store on Beale Street in Downtown Memphis, in 1946.

Adapting to the street, renowned for its juke joints and pawn shops, the store evolved and became ahead of its time, changing from the army surplus goods to high fashion clothing. From the start, the new offerings contrasted starkly with the clean-cut and traditional styles popular with mid-century Americans.

My father's drive and ability to hustle, in order to adjust and to change with the times, was in sync with what was a key time in history that focused on music and culture. They created vibrant window displays with bright colours and flashy designs that were intended to pop onstage. This, of course, was precisely what would catch the attention of a young Elvis Presley in 1952.

Elvis was a teenager working as an usher at a nearby theatre who liked to window-shop at Lansky's. He said to my father, 'When I get rich, I'm going to buy you out.' My dad recalled, 'I said, "Don't buy me out. Just buy from me." And he never forgot me.' When he offered Elvis credit for the outfit and styling services for his first performance on the *Ed Sullivan Show*, Elvis never forgot the kindness and showed his appreciation throughout his life.

When his fame spread, my father often opened the store at night so Elvis could avoid the crowds, and we would also take outfits to Graceland for him. Over the years, I often think about how gracious Elvis was to me and our family. He was always promoting us wherever he went. When people asked him where he got his clothes, he would often say, 'Lansky's, on Beale Street.' This generosity as an ambassador didn't stop at him mentioning our store; he would give his clothes away to people, and would even buy outfits for customers who happened to be in the store at the same time he was.

We outfitted Elvis over three decades – his iconic '50s look; his '60s continental-style suits and mid-'60s London mod looks; and in his final decade – a decade of fashion we hope never returns – his '*Super Fly* era' of furs, high stacked-heel shoes, flares and capes … For me, the Lansky Look, the one where Elvis looked his very best, was the '50s one – when he was young and innocent. At 18, he

xiv Elvis: The King of Fashion

wore a Lansky tuxedo to his junior/senior prom, and at the age of just 42, he was buried in a white Lansky suit.

As the second generation of the business that my father started in 1946, we are thankful for the relationship we had with Elvis Presley. Forty-six years after his death, his popularity and our connection with him are stronger than ever. The 2022 Baz Luhrmann movie *Elvis* created a whole new generation of fans who are now flocking to the shop that permanently changed how he – and America – dressed.

And so, from our historic, post-war beginnings, through the birth of rock 'n' roll and its most dazzling star, Elvis, to embracing modern technology, we continue to connect with customers and Elvis fans throughout the world.

Hal Lansky, Clothier to The King,
April 2023

List of Images

Black and white

1. Overall winner – Elvis in denim dungarees for Milam School's 6th-grade class photo, *circa* 1946. (*Tupelo Elvis Fan Club*)
2. Gunslingers – Elvis and his cousin Gene Smith dressed as cowboys at the Mid-South Fair, Memphis, 1953. (*Public domain*)
3. Hillbilly Cat – a still-blond Elvis dressed in two-tone suit, shoes, tie and belt for a gig at Lamar-Airways shopping centre, Memphis, September 1954. (*Opal Walker*)
4. Naked fame – Elvis with fan Ardys Bell Clawson, who came to his aid at a concert in Jacksonville, Florida, May 1955, when crazed fans ripped off his clothes. (*Ardys Bell Clawson and Jacksonville Historical Society*)
5. All shook up – Elvis in green jacket with tooled-leather, personalised guitar cover, Tampa, Florida, August 1956. (*commons.wikimedia.org*)
6. Tearing up the house – Elvis at the Cotton Bowl, Dallas, 11 October 1956. (*NGA National Gallery of Art, Washington (gift of Mary and Dan Solomon)*)
7. Mr DJ – Dewey Phillips and Elvis inside Lansky Bros. store on Beale St, Memphis, 1956. (*Lansky Bros. family archive*)
8. Key player – Elvis is presented with a guitar-shaped key to the city of Tupelo, September 1956. (*commons.wikimedia.org*)
9. He wore blue velvet – Elvis returns to Tupelo in his iconic midnight-blue shirt for Elvis Presley Day concerts at the Mississippi-Alabama Fair and Dairy Show, 26 September 1956. (*commons.wikimedia.org*)
10. Star and stripes – Elvis, *circa* 1958/9, with Hal Lansky (age 7) and siblings. (*Lansky Bros. family archive*)
11. Small screen idol – Elvis wears a bouclé jacket, statement abstract-print shirt and chunky rings for his first national TV appearance on the Dorsey Brothers' *Stage Show*, 1956. (*commons.wikimedia.org*)
12. New kid on the block – Elvis in the famous denim and cat-burglar top prison uniform for the cellblock dance scene in *Jailhouse Rock* (Metro-Goldwyn-Mayer), October 1957. (*commons.wikimedia.org*)
13. Oath of allegiance – Elvis, collar up, joins other young men to be sworn in to the US Army during an induction at Fort Chaffee, Arkansas, March 1958. (*commons.wikimedia.org*)

xvi   Elvis: The King of Fashion

14. Soldier boy – Elvis dressed in US Army uniform in Germany 1958. (*commons.wikimedia.org*)
15. Hey, baby – Elvis, Priscilla and newborn daughter, Lisa Marie, leave Baptist Memorial Hospital, Memphis, 1 February 1968. (*commons.wikimedia.org*)
16. Sensational sixties – Elvis and Priscilla at the USS *Arizona* Memorial, Pearl Harbor, Hawaii, May 1968. (*Pearl Harbor National Memorial*)
17. When Elvis met Steve – on the set of NBC's *'68 Comeback Special*, New York, with Steve Binder. (*From* Elvis: '68 Comeback: The Story Behind the Special, *Steve Binder, Thunderbay Press, 2022*)
18. Black panther – Elvis in the famous leather suit created by Bill Belew for NBC's *'68 Comeback* show, 3 December 1968. (*commons.wikimedia.org*)
19. Carny and King – Elvis with Tom Parker on Universal Studios' *Change of Habit* set, Los Angeles, 1969. (*commons.wikimedia.org*)
20. Caped crusader – Elvis meets President Richard Nixon in the White House Oval Office to offer his services in the war against drugs, December 1970. (*US National Archives*)
21. Split decision – Elvis and Priscilla leaving California's Santa Monica courtroom, arm in arm, after their divorce was finalised in 1973. (*commons.wikimedia.org*)
22. Phoenix rising – Elvis in Red Phoenix suit with matching belt and diamond Maltese cross medallion on the *Elvis in Concert* album cover. (*1977, CBS*)
23. Clothes encounter – Elvis browsing in Lansky Bros., in black shirt and trousers, striped metallic-effect waistcoat and two-tone brogues, 1956. (*Lansky Bros. family archive*)
24. Style council – Elvis with Bernard Lansky. (*Lansky Bros. family archive*)

Colour

1. Early fashionista – baby Elvis (aged about 2–3) in tweed trilby and corduroy overalls, sits with his parents, Gladys and Vernon, in Tupelo, *circa* 1937. *Elvis Country* album cover, 1971. (*RCA Victor*)
2. Hand candy – Elvis accessorises a striped, velvet-collared Lansky Bros. sports coat with chunky gold jewellery in promo shot for MGM's *Jailhouse Rock* movie, 1956–7.
3. Hollywood heartthrob – Elvis in yellow shirt with Greek keynote detail, on the set of *King Creole*. Production photo, June 1958, Paramount Pictures. (*commons.wikimedia.org*)
4. Record breaker – Elvis in white seersucker jacket, black shirt and whip-thin belt with buckle worn to the side, on the cover of his first recorded album, 1956. (*RCA Victor commons.wikimedia.org*)

List of Images   xvii

5. Mirror Man – clothier to The King, Bernard Lansky flips Elvis's collar, *circa* 1956. (*Lansky Bros. family archive*)

6. *G.I. Blues* – Elvis in Hollywood uniform for Paramount Pictures promo shot with co-star Juliet Prowse, 1960. (*commons.wikimedia.org*)

7. Little red Corvette – Elvis chills in Western-inspired cream and black-stitched outfit on the set of *Clambake*. Promo shot for United Artists, 1967.

8. That's all white – Elvis wears a dazzlingly white suit with single crimson slash of silk scarf, by Bill Belew, to sing 'If I Can Dream' on the *'68 Comeback Special*. Detail from album *Elvis*, by RCA Victor. (*commons.wikimedia.org*)

9. Hot chocolate – a shirtless Elvis in the author's favourite Bill Belew cutaway suit, with Mexican silver and turquoise belt, attends Barbara Streisand's 31 July 1969 show at the International Hotel, Las Vegas. (*Photographer Oscar Abolafia*)

10. Swinging the blues – Elvis jokes about his 'subtle' gold Hilton International belt during a press conference ahead of his Madison Square Garden concerts, New York, 9 June 1972. (*Hilton*)

11. High flyer – Elvis wears black abstract-print shirt and black suit, with burnt-orange trim detail, at Chicago Midway airport, 1972. (*Photographer Jack Baity*)

12. Aloha! – Elvis in the American Eagle suit by Bill Belew and Gene Doucette for the live satellite concert from Honolulu, Hawaii, 1973. (*Public domain*)

13. Ready to fly – Elvis in the bejewelled Pharaoh cape, Atlanta, 3 July 1973. (*From Keith Alverson's book,* Strictly Elvis; *image copyright, photographer, Keith Alverson, email eponstage@charter.net*)

14. Guitar man – Elvis in black leather suit by Bill Belew, *'68 Comeback Special*. (*commons.wikimedia.org*)

15. Life through a lens – a remarkably intimate photo of Elvis performing in his Chief suit at the Charleston Civic Centre, 1975. (Courtesy of lifelong fan, Teri Hammond-Kincaid)

16. Sun god – The King in his legendary Mexican Sundial suit, taken during his next-to-last concert in Cincinnati, 25 June 1977. (*Copyright, photographer, Keith Alverson, email eponstage@charter.net*)

17. Young pretender – actor Austin Butler in black leather *'68 Comeback* suit on a film poster for Baz Luhrmann's hit 2022 movie, *Elvis*, Warner Bros. (*wikipedia.org*)

18. Legacy – collection of B&K Enterprises Elvis-inspired jumpsuits, left to right: Peacock; Totem Pole; Mad Tiger; Chicken Bone (Black Aztec); Chief; and Mexican Sundial. (*B&K Enterprises*)

Introduction

'Elvis never had a stylist in his life. He didn't need one. The clothes didn't make the man; the man made the clothes.'

Lorraine Gibson

Close your eyes and picture Elvis, and then open them again. What did you see?

Early 1950s Teenage Elvis in an oversized jacket, splayed shirt collar, loose trousers, two-tone shoes and rocking a quiff so animated it could have had a show of its own, while belting out 'That's All Right' to hordes of screaming girls?

Or was it '57 'Jailhouse Rock' Elvis? The rubber-limbed rebel without a pause, putting his prison duds of stripy top and bold-stitched denim jacket and jeans through their paces, his hair in flight mode as he pirouettes on loafers in front of Hollywood's stylised interpretation of a cell block.

Soldier Elvis? Trademark sideburns gone, performing pompadour sheared to a crew cut, the black and white shoes substituted for regulation army boots, and yet still looking sharp in a perfectly cut army uniform.

How about Hawaiian Elvis? You know, the toned, tanned, board-shorted deliverer of cheesy tunes and even cheesier lines to swooning starlets in figure-hugging swimsuits that they'd have happily cast off to join him for a 'Moonlight Swim'.

Perhaps it was Comeback Elvis? Revitalised, rebooted and more redolent of his younger, edgier, sexually charged self in head-to-toe black leather and pacing the stage like a caged panther, growling a visceral, deeper-toned version of 'Hound Dog' at his prey – the adoring audience on NBC-TV's 1968 Christmas special.

Or maybe Angel Elvis is your look of choice? He's the antithesis of the sinuously sensual leather-clad stud, yet from the same show. An entire ensemble of purest white, right down to the shoes and the covered buttons, marked only by a dramatic, blood-red slash of silk scarf, it's a saintly look that immediately springs to mind at the first hint of the sound of the brass intro to 'If I Can Dream'.

Then there's King of Bling, the karate-kicking, strutting, jump-suited, hip-slung-belted, knicker-dodging, groin-thrusting Vegas Elvis, burning up the

Introduction   xix

stage in a flash of jewels and suggestive smiles to the world's biggest backing group – a mass of screaming women, undone by his sheer Elvisness.

Or bright sky-blue suited, floral-shirted, gold-belted, deeply tanned Madison Square Garden Elvis. A truly kingly apparition, holding court with wit and humility before a hard-bitten press corps that winds up hanging on his every word.

Or was it the slower, heavier, sweating Last Days Elvis? Flares and belts now grown exponentially larger in line with him, as he showcases ever more elaborately bejeweled onesies and continues to nail the hits – give or take a scribbled note and lyrical pun or ten – with a voice still so pure and powerful, so sincere and agile that, for a while, everyone sees only a supernova and forgets that the God of Song is really a frail and dying man whose star is waning.

We all have our own Elvis in our heads, but whichever images we conjure up, a common thread runs through them – the waft and weave of the outfits that epitomised the times and the experiences that he lived through, almost as much as did the music in which he immersed himself. They were clothes that did more than just elevate him; they narrated the eras, sometimes the exact years, even precise days in which he was living. Yet, what really makes Elvis's looks so memorable, what makes the cerebral snapshots that inhabit our minds so powerful, is the man wearing them. For he alone, the startlingly unique singer whose voice stopped a generation in its tracks way before they'd even seen him, had the balls – and let's face it, the looks – to step on a stage with defiantly wild hair, smoky eyeshadow and a bubble-gum-pink outfit, in a rowdy nightclub in the South – *in the early 1950s* – and not only avoid a beating, but actually be accepted and deemed cool.

That was back when radio, not Elvis, was king, and while you could hear him, you couldn't see him, unless you happened to be in Memphis, or thereabouts.

Even his later 1950s and '60s TV appearances were confined to US broadcasts, so it was only when he began appearing in global media and doing movies that the rest of the world got to see the actual human being from which that internationally famous voice came.

Fast-forward to the 1970s and again, only Elvis, heading into his forties, could carry off a gem-stoned jumpsuit with a huge gold belt slung around the hips. And in 1977, only he could stride on stage to a packed house of thousands, wearing his age and his declining health on his sleeve and a tad-too-snug white jumpsuit, embroidered – back and front – with huge, shimmering sunbursts, and sing a song so perfectly and with such power and emotion that it left the audience in tears – and in no doubt about who was the undisputed King of Rock and Roll.

From the get-go, Elvis instinctively knew how to dress well, both on stage and on the street. In fact, his stage wear differed very little from his streetwear,

xx   Elvis: The King of Fashion

especially in the early days. Even as a schoolkid, when painfully shy in every other way, his look was always bold, always making a statement. His appearance spoke for him. Which is why, before anyone even suspected that he could sing, Elvis didn't just stand out from the crowd, he rose above it. He looked different from everyone else, because he *was* different, and, much to the annoyance of the early bullies and critics, he looked better than everyone else, too.

This book is an homage to Elvis's personal sense of style and how it defined him through his lived experiences, long before he walked into Memphis Recording Service in July 1954 and, almost by chance, recorded a song that would profoundly change both him and the world of music forever.

Despite rarely doing press calls or personal interviews, or ever writing a book, and without music videos, social media or streaming, Elvis remains the best-selling solo performer of all time. Today, his image, as much as his music, remains as potent as it ever was.

And the Elvis I see when I close my eyes?

Reader, read on …

Chapter 1

Clothes Encounter

Memphis, Tennessee, 1952. Look: Young Pretender

'Come what may, there will always be a Beale Street, because Beale Street
is a spirit … a symbol … a way of life … Beale Street is a hope.'

Memphis Radio presenter and history teacher
Nat D. Williams, 30 November 1945

There was a reason Bernard Lansky noticed the kid who kept checking out his shop window – he stood out like a sore thumb.

This was Beale Street, Memphis, 1952 after all, epicentre of the social and cultural lives of the region's African American population and where the most conspicuous element was a constant backbeat of hard-life-lived rhythm and blues. A fusion of musical styles and field hollers, the working songs forged by plantation slaves to make their lives more bearable, R&B had filtered into the big city as a heady amalgamation of gospel, boogie-woogie, swing, jazz, ragtime, blues and more.

Among the musicians pioneering the early style were Bobby Blue Bland, Lillie Mae Glover, Muddy Waters, Booker T. White and composer W.C. Handy. Often referred to as the 'Father of the Blues', Handy's music joint, Club Handy on Beale Street, was brought back to glorious, blues- and whiskey-soaked life in Baz Luhrmann's 2022 *Elvis* movie, starring Austin Butler.

Early versions of the sound – which used the voice as an instrument as much as anything playable that the performers could get their hands on – was the mainspring of a musical revolution, now regarded as the bedrock of America's and indeed much of the world's music today.

Beale was its stage, the street where anything went, that never slept, and the hub for black communities drawn to its ethnically aligned atmosphere in the face of racial marginalisation. Its seductive, rough-hewn, at times dangerous, feel and the potent, ever-present soundtrack made every open window, doorway, bar and car a place to hang out, to forget, and to have a good time. Crowds played, loved, laughed and fought in its clandestine embrace and gathered, as though at an alternative church, where the spirited and righteous singing of their regular

2   Elvis: The King of Fashion

religious worship became amplified and more abandoned. The usual sentiments of loss, love and hope were all there, but infused with sensuality and a sense of power. Unsurprisingly, Beale was also a magnet for a procession of gamblers, pimps, hustlers and other colourful characters from around the Mississippi Delta – making it far from genteel.

Yet, among the thrift stores, pawn shops and cramped juke joints, there were flourishing businesses and a collection of on-trend fashion stores, including the Lansky Bros. shop, which the aforementioned Bernard ran with his brother Guy. Their displays of high-end, bold, unique garments, the likes of which would normally only have been found in New York or Chicago, made Lansky's a mecca for Memphis's most style-conscious shoppers. Sharp dressing was where it was at and the regular clientele, who'd pop in to chew the fat with the brothers as well as to buy new threads, read like a who's who of the era's top black musicians – think B.B. King, Howlin' Wolf, Little Richard and Ike Turner – all shrugging on the latest Lansky suits.

And so, the odd-looking boy gazing intently at the window looked markedly out of place. Yes, on account of how young he was, and of the shabbiness of his clothes and the holes in his shoes – but mainly because he was white.

'My dad saw this young man looking in his window. This was the late summer of '52 and my dad knew he was out of place,' Hal Lansky, the late Bernard's son, who still runs the clothiers with his daughter, Julie, tells me. 'Our main street was African American. Beale was famous as a rough and tough street, so my dad, he knew straight away this young man was not from there. He shouldn't 'a been there.'

After seeing him walk past – or, more often than not, stop and stare – several times, Bernard was intrigued. When the mysterious window-shopper next appeared, he opened his shop door and said, 'Come on in young man,' to which the reticent youngster replied, 'Mr Lansky, I don't have any money – but one of these days I'm gonna come buy you out.'

'My dad told him, "Young man, don't buy me out, just buy from me."'

Of course, the young man was Elvis Presley, just 17 and dreaming of one day having enough money to buy, rather than merely stare at, the finer things in life.

'Let me tell you a story,' says Hal:

Elvis was a genuine Southern gentleman, brought up saying 'yes' or 'no, sir. Yes, ma'am'. My dad would always say to Elvis, he'd say: 'Elvis, Elvis, don't call me Mr Lansky, call me Bernard,' and Elvis, with a shit-eatin' grin would say, 'yessir – Mr Lansky'. That's the way we were brought up in the South.

One can never overestimate the importance of the day Bernard Lansky invited the down-at-heel, insecure Elvis into his store, as though ushering in a king. Symbolically, that invitation was everything. It was non-judgmental, it was kind, it was encouraging and it was insightful. Bernard had sensed a certain something in Elvis that others were yet to spot, and upon talking to the boy, his modest charm and good manners merely confirmed his intuition. A life-defining moment, it was more than just access to a clothes rail; it was Elvis's first step on the road to fame, transported by a love affair with fashion that put him in the spotlight before his music ever did.

The encounter also marked the beginning of a touching friendship that would endure for the rest of their lives ... in fact, right up to the day that Bernard selected the pure-white Lansky suit and blue tie that Elvis would be buried in, far sooner than either of them could ever have predicted.

Chapter 2

In the Ghetto

Tupelo, Mississippi, 1935–48. Look: Overalled Winner

'When I was a child … I was a dreamer. I read comic books, and I was the hero of the comic book. I saw movies, and I was the hero in the movie.'

From Elvis's acceptance speech,
Jaycee Ten Outstanding Young Men of America Award,
16 January 1971

'We never had any money or nothin', but we never were hungry, you know. That's something to be thankful for.'

Elvis

Rags to riches is such a hackneyed phrase, but in the case of Elvis Presley, it is entirely justified. Most people know that he was born in a shack to poor parents, and about how, equipped only with a battered guitar and a unique voice, he took the music scene by storm, became famous and got very, *very* rich. However, to appreciate how astonishing Elvis's transformation from backwater urchin to global icon really was, it's important to consider just how disadvantaged he and his family really were. And how incredibly shy and reserved he was.

A typical product of a deeply deprived part of the Deep South, Elvis began life in a level of poverty that's hard to imagine. At the time, his young parents were so trapped in a daily struggle to survive that their main ambition was not getting ahead; it was getting through the week. Considering the childhoods they had endured, though, they had moved up in the world, relatively speaking. They were part of a low-income community, fortified by family friends and faith. Most were in some way related – if not by blood then by worship, work or woes. Women who were able to work sewed in cotton factories, men who could find work, drove trucks or toiled in the fields.

The porch – if you had one – was for down time and kids were kept amused by comics, movie magazines and music from the radio. Summers brought church revival festivals, intensifying the usual sound of gospel singing as it drifted

In the Ghetto 5

from open church windows, bathing the neighbourhood in a reassuring balm, punctuated by claps, shouts and affirmative 'Amens'.

From a very young age, Elvis would have been aware that life was anything but a bed of roses. Still, his was a happy childhood, for while he lacked material trappings, he had an endless supply of parental love. He also had an extraordinary gift ... a latent talent that would take him from rough-edged kid in second-hand clothes and no shoes to an American legend in clothes hand-made and shoes blue suede, all in what seems like the blink of an eye.

Elvis's journey began around 4.35 on the morning of 8 January 1935. After an emotionally fraught entrance into the world – a world that turned out to be no more than a glorified wooden hut on a scrap of dirt in East Tupelo, Mississippi – Elvis Aron Presley, the baby who would be King, let out his first wail. Home was far from regal, but to his parents, Vernon Elvis and Gladys Love Presley, who were as poor as a couple of church mice, the little house was a palace. A typical shotgun shack, it was narrower than it was long, divided into two rooms arranged one behind the other and dissected by a long corridor with a door at either end. The construct was to permit a cool breeze on a hot day or, should you feel inclined, for a gun to be shot clear through to the other side – hence the name.

Vernon had built the house with help from his father and his brother, Vester, when Gladys became pregnant. He bought the plot and the building materials with a loan from Orville Bean, a local landowner and occasionally his employer. And, since necessity rather than preference dictates the kingdom of the poor, it sat in a huddle of similar structures on a dirt road 'above the highway' (read as 'the wrong side of the tracks') of better-heeled Tupelo town proper. Nevertheless, Gladys loved her new home, *with its own outhouse*, and kept it as neat as a new pin.

The house at 306 Old Saltillo Road, later renamed Elvis Presley Drive, cost about $180 dollars, and it still stands. Designated an historical site by the Mississippi Department of Archives and History on 8 January 1978 – exactly forty-three years to the day that Elvis was born there – it is now a tourist attraction.

Gladys and Vernon's community was a tight-knit one, made up mainly of worshipers at the First Assembly of God – a church as humble as their own hearths and was where the couple first met. It was co-pastored by Gladys's uncle, Gains, and was a typically 'holy roller' place of prayer where God was gleefully praised, in both movement and in song, for everything they had – which in their eyes, was a lot. Gladys and Vernon, born in 1912 and 1916 respectively, came from families of impoverished Mississippi plantation workers, or 'sharecroppers'. Sharecropping was a successor of sorts to the slavery farming system where

6   Elvis: The King of Fashion

plantation owners hired workers, black and white, and paid them from crop profits. A tough, poorly paid and weather-dictated job, it was regarded as the lowest form of employment, even in the poorest parts of what was known as 'cotton country'. Extended families lived together and occasionally some married within their family groups. They camped wherever and with whomever they could, depending on where there was work. When there was no work, they had two choices – move on or sink.

As sharecroppers' children, Vernon and Gladys's lives were ones of absolute destitution, of lurching from one place to another, with families not only searching for jobs but also often avoiding debt, dodging trouble or escaping whatever blight might be upon them at the time. In his book *The Inner Elvis*, Peter Whitmer paints a bleak picture of Gladys's early years. The Smiths, a large, itinerant family group comprising grandparents, parents, cousins, aunts and uncles, and kids were constantly either moving or grafting, like a convoy of sad mules. So severe was their neediness that Gladys and her siblings chewed snuff to stave off hunger and fixed iron pig snout rings around their decrepit shoes to keep them from falling off. You could hear the Smiths before you saw them.

Gladys's mother, Doll, nicknamed for her small, pale face and fragile demeanor, had tuberculosis and was so weak that she had to be carted, prone on her bed, from pillar to post. Remarkably, she still managed to bear nine children. When their father, Bob, died, they had to beg a neighbour for a sheet in which to bury him. It is widely agreed, though contested at times, that Doll's great-grandmother was Morning Dove White, a Cherokee woman who married a Scottish-Irish settler called John Mansell. According to Alister McReynolds in *Kith and Kin: The Continuing Legacy of the Scots-Irish in America*, she was also a princess. Both McAlister and Whitmer go along with the general belief that Doll's grandmother could have been Jewish. The appearance on several Elvis family trees of Nancy Burdine, a European Jewish woman, has sparked interest in the theory. They show that Nancy's daughter, Martha, married Albert White Mansell – their daughter was Octavia, nicknamed 'Doll', aka Gladys's mother. Whatever the origins, the combination of Gladys's dark-haired, sultry appearance and Vernon's sullen handsomeness – strong jaw, ice-blue eyes and luxuriant blond hair – unquestionably shaped Elvis's distinctive looks. Looks that still see him frequently described as the most handsome/beautiful/stunning man who ever lived. And that gave Gene Nelson, who directed him in the 1964 MGM film *Kissin' Cousins*, cause to say, 'He was the handsomest son-of-a-bitch that ever walked across a screen.'

Gladys and Vernon eloped and married on 17 June 1933. She was 21 and worked in a Tupelo cotton garment factory, he was 17, out of work and dirt poor. Too young to marry legally, Vernon claimed to be 21 and Gladys said she

In the Ghetto 7

was 19. The young Presleys made a good-looking couple, he brooding, she sassy, although in photos from the time, their darkly circled eyes make them appear malnourished, which they probably were. People liked Gladys and found her fun and kindly, but most thought Vernon rather surly and unsociable. They would drink beer when they could afford it and liked to dance and sing. As a young woman, Gladys was admired for her buck dancing, which she regularly performed solo for family and neighbours. Buck is a traditional folk percussion dance, typically performed standing on a hard surface or board to amplify the beat. Usually accompanied by fiddles and other string instruments, the feet tap out an energetic, at times frenetic, rhythm to which the body succumbs. It predates clog dancing and is far earthier. Think the passion of Flamenco meets the vigour of tap. In Gladys's time, it required clearing the mind and letting oneself go. Eyes closed, as though in ecstasy, the body should be so relaxed that the hips appear to leave the – wait for this – pelvic sockets to swivel loosely and rotate. Sound familiar?

Most images of Gladys are later ones of her as the matriarch, frowning and puffy as a duvet in her sensible frocks, so it's hard to imagine the sexy young flibbertigibbet she once was. With the benefit of hindsight, her unhealthy later appearance was signposting the health issues that would lead to her death at 46. But it's wonderful to think that the establishment-offending pelvic movements that made Elvis so notorious in his early career came straight from his church-going, God-fearing mama. According to Elaine Dundy in *Elvis and Gladys*, when Gladys's old friends first saw Elvis doing his pelvic gyrations on TV, they said, 'Elvis got it honest. Gladys had rhythm.' The apple never does fall far from the tree …

Now that we have considered what made Elvis 'Elvis', it's time to return to 8 January 1935. On what very likely would have been a cold and grey, not Chicago but Tupelo morning, he made his momentous debut as Vernon and Gladys, supported by family members, a midwife and a doctor, were trying to come to terms with losing their longed-for baby, who'd arrived stillborn half an hour before. Imagine the shifting emotions that they, especially Gladys, would have felt: distress and desolation at the loss, followed by shock, then elation at the arrival of a second baby, this time mercifully alive and well. Next, the realisation that Gladys had been carrying twins, and finally, joy at being parents after all. They named their dead son Jesse Garon, and their unexpected 'miracle', Elvis Aron.

To describe this turn of events as bittersweet is too insubstantial; it belittles a deeply complex and life-changing experience that would have been both upsetting and wonderful at the same time. And surely, it represents the moment that Gladys went from being a carefree and vivacious woman who really did

8   Elvis: The King of Fashion

dance like no one was watching, to a fearful, fretful mother whose newly forged foreboding would shape the character and the future of their son.

Understandably, from the second Elvis breathed, he was adored and cherished. The loss of Jesse and being unable to conceive again left Gladys terrified of losing Elvis too, compelling her to keep him close to her over the years. He lived and thrived, cocooned in love and overprotection, while twin Jesse existed only in their thoughts and in their hearts. They never forgot him; they spoke of him often and remembered him in their fervent prayers, for they remained devout. On Elvis's birthdays, or whenever their little family unit felt the need for some divine intervention, they'd sing gospel songs and pray to Jesse. In this way, they kept him alive, just in a different place. Gladys told Elvis that he would have the strength of two men and even as a grown-up, he mentioned that he had a sense of his brother's heart beating inside him, a pace behind his own. He took comfort from the thought and believed that it made him stronger, just like his mama always said it would.

Being so aligned to their church, Elvis was absorbing music from birth. He lived to a soundtrack of harmonies and beats that formed the family's and the community's main form of entertainment. Everyone sang – in church, on their porches, at gatherings. It was mostly gospel and folk music, the kind of stuff that told stories and gave them hope but, more importantly, an outlet for their worries and their pain.

Outside of the lively services and community singalongs, though, the trio tended to keep to themselves and were now seen as a bit odd and insular, especially Vernon. Despite the perceived aloofness, Gladys was still well regarded and the young Elvis, with a politeness of forelock-tugging proportions drummed into him, was always surrounded by supportive company and limitless encouragement.

New clothes being as rare as hens' teeth, Elvis wore the same uniform of careworn hand-me-downs as all the kids around him, and from toddlerdom to sixth grade, his look barely changed. However, and perhaps it's wishful thinking, but looking at early childhood photographs of him, there's already a hint of hard-found pizzazz about him. In fact, I like to say that Elvis made his first fashion statement before he was old enough to dress himself. Maybe it's down to the privilege of knowing what lay ahead, but in the wonderful photo of an instantly recognisable Elvis aged 2 or 3 and sandwiched between his parents, whether it was Gladys or Elvis himself who thought to add a little trilby hat and then tip it at a jaunty angle, you get a feeling that this boy was never run-of-the-mill.

From an early age, he instinctively appreciated everything from blues and hillbilly to spirituals and swing, but his favourite was always harmonious gospel. Gladys liked to tell people how Elvis wriggled off her lap and ran straight down the aisle towards the choir when he was only 2. 'There he would stand, looking

In the Ghetto 9

at the choir, trying to sing with them. He was too little to know the words, but he could carry the tune.' For the rest of his life, gospel music remained his first love and he would frequently turn to it, as a child would a teddy, for comfort at the height of the madness on his rocky (and rolling) road.

When not listening to the radio, in the periods of solitude that can befall an only child, Elvis would lose himself in superhero comic books. Primarily drawn to the bold, powerful images, once he learned to read he also enjoyed the tales of bravery and benevolent superhuman powers. In a sign of things to come, he absorbed every tiny detail of how the characters looked, in particular their hair and vibrantly coloured suits. He daydreamed of being one of them, especially Captain Marvel Junior, a boy just like him – apart from the gold-trimmed blue spandex, red cape, lightning bolt and the ability to move at the speed of light – and who made the world a better place.

The innocent fantasy became a fervent desire when, in November 1938, Vernon was sent to prison for three years after being found guilty of forging a cheque. Elvis was nearly 4 and wanted to set his daddy free, but he hadn't the cape nor the superpower to do so. Little did he know that in years to come, he would have a cape, in fact several capes, and would use them to great effect. Exact details of Vernon's crime vary but the likely scenario is that he was given a four-dollar cheque in payment for a hog when, either by chance or intention, his brother-in-law, Travis Smith, and another chap, Lether Gable, became aware of it. They offered Vernon about fifteen dollars if he'd let them alter the cheque to a different amount and then cash it.

Depression-deprived, with a wife unable to work and the family surviving on next to nothing, Vernon agreed. The money would have been a relative fortune that would have kept the wolf from the door for a while. Unfortunately, the cheque was from Orville Bean, Vernon's erstwhile boss-cum-landlord, and the scam was spotted. Vernon immediately admitted his role in the affair and all three men wound up in Parchman Farm Prison, a notoriously harsh, hell-on-earth kind of place. A convict labour plantation, it maintained segregation, though black and white prisoners were treated equally when forced to run to the fields at gunpoint first thing in the morning and toil till dusk, whatever the weather. They survived on what they harvested and lived in constant dread of 'Black Annie', aka the whip.

Crime among the region's white population in general had escalated due to the Depression, and desperate people take desperate measures. Those on the receiving end of the resultant wrongdoing felt things were getting out of hand, but even so, the three-year sentence was particularly harsh. It's rumored that Bean wanted to use them as an example and the powers that be obliged; if so, then he either had a sudden pang of guilt or was harangued, as we'll find out.

10   Elvis: The King of Fashion

Gladys, now alone with a toddler and no home in which to care for him, was beside herself. Close to beaten but not quite, she sent a petition to Governor Hugh L. White, signed by many in the community, including upstanding sorts, asking that Vernon's sentence be reduced. It stated that he admitted his wrongdoing, had paid back the money and had never been in trouble in his life before. She also sent him a letter (possibly scribed for her), outlining Vernon's part in the scam and literally begging him to 'please turn him lose. I am sure God will bless you if you will.' She added that she felt that White was a just man and that Vernon's 'punishment is already enough for the little crime he did'. She continued: 'My health is bad. I have no mother or daddy and no one to lash to for a living. I have a little boy three years old. Please send him back to his wife and baby.' She signed off: 'Trusting you will hear my plea. With God's blessing on you, Mrs Vernon Presley, Tupelo, Mississippi.'

Ghostwritten or not, those words are pure Gladys. Not only is it heartfelt, it is heartbreaking. Here's a woman right on the edge, in poor health from genetically inherited maladies combined with complications from the distressing birth. She and Elvis were staying with relatives already stretched for space. Basically, she'd fallen so far backwards that she was staring her ghastly roaming childhood days right in the face.

She heard nothing …

Until a month later, when another letter pleading for leniency and an early release landed on the governor's desk – this one from Orville Bean, who explained the circumstances of Vernon's involvement and described the plight of the family, saying: 'This young man has a wife and one small child that are in financial distress, and they need him very badly. He is not a bad man and has never been.'

It worked: Vernon was released, though not until eight months later.

There's a saying that hunger can make a thief of any man – and this episode fits into the category sometimes called a 'hunger crime', one of the saddest, yet among the most common in the world today.

Before Vernon's release, Gladys and Elvis would take the five-hour bus ride to visit him on Sundays. It was no walk in the park; Parchman was the inspiration for the grim prisons in films like *Cool Hand Luke*, starring Paul Newman, and *Oh, Brother, Where Art Thou?*, starring George Clooney. It did, though, allow married couples some privacy – mainly to have sex – so Elvis would play with other visiting children whenever Gladys and Vernon made use of what was referred to as the 'Red House', a building with ten private rooms for the purpose.

Little surprise that the prison phase deeply affected all three of them, in different ways, for the rest of their lives. Vernon's failure weighed heavily on him and he was notoriously tight with money, even while living in luxury, since it was the cause of his loss of freedom and almost of his precious wife and son. Gladys internalised everything, remaining unwell and easily stressed from the indignity and hardship it wreaked. She clung to Elvis, as though he were a human security blanket, until she died. Elvis was emotionally scarred by the public shaming of his father and their inescapable poverty. It became his life's mission to ensure that they would never, *ever* be poor again – an oath he kept, even when it left him vulnerable to manipulation by his manager, 'Col' Tom Parker, who needed him to power his moneymaking machinations.

When Vernon finally got out of jail in 1939, Elvis was almost 5 years old. He was needy and nervous, haunted even, from his daddy being away and his failure to be the caped crusader who could fly to jail and break him out. They were still in Tupelo, but nomadic once more. Around 1940–1, they were living with Vester Presley, his wife Clettes (who happened to be Gladys's sister) and their daughter, Patsy. Years later, Patsy, who stayed close to Elvis all his life, described them as suffering from 'action nightmares'– sleepwalking and talking, and disturbed nights. Elvis's dreams were mainly about abandonment and lasted his whole life, causing him to fight off sleep and later to self-medicate in order to be able to sleep.

Now aged 6, he started at East Tupelo Consolidated (now Lawhon Elementary), a large school of 700 pupils from grades 1 to 12. Still very timid, it must have been overwhelming for him to find himself in such a large community. It was half a mile from home and Gladys walked him all the way, holding his hand especially tight when they crossed the highway. Deemed an unremarkable student, he was described as 'sweet and average' by a teacher and always seemed on the periphery of things. He did run around happily with a few kids out of school but Gladys was so fearful for his safety that she'd insist he came back at a set time. She banned him from going near the creek – he went anyway – and she'd fly outside to scoop him up and run to the nearby shelter in the hill at the slightest whiff of an electrical storm.

There was some rationale to that, as a deadly force 5 tornado storm – one of the worst in US history – had ripped through Tupelo the year after Elvis was born and killed more than 200 souls and injured some 700. It devastated community areas and the hospital, hampering medical care. It caused flooding and fires, and both power and water were out. It took a week to clear roads and allow proper aid to reach the town. One can only imagine poor Gladys's anxiety levels at the time. Real storms and lightning flashes, not just comic book ones, were a fact of life for young Elvis and a lightning bolt would play an important role in his later life.

By 1942, they were back in a cycle of temporary jobs and homes, now living in town in rented accommodation, where private conversations were hardly

12 Elvis: The King of Fashion

an option. Elvis would hear Gladys and Vernon discussing money troubles and try to reassure them. He'd tell his 'babies', as he called them, not to worry, because when he grew up he'd pay off the bills at the grocery shop, buy them a fancy house and 'two Cadillacs, one for you and daddy and one for me'. It was time for him to dream big. As Bobbie Ann Mason in *Elvis* so aptly put it, 'The American Dream is more urgent dreamed from near the bottom.'

Post-Parchman, there was an even deeper reticence about the Presleys when it came to socialising, though they still attended church. In 1977, Vernon told Nancy Anderson of *Good Housekeeping* magazine that the three of them created their own secret universe. From 1942, they moved around Tupelo, now with Elvis's grandma, Minnie Mae Presley, in tow. Vernon was working, though he had a reputation for being lazy and lacking drive, adding to their being labelled as poor white trash in some quarters. It was hard.

Music was their redemption and for Elvis it became an obsession, as would many things over time. All three still listened to the radio constantly and devoured the popular sounds of the day. Gladys liked Ernest Tubb's 'Mean Mama Blues' and the Louvin Brothers; Elvis was mad about Mississippi Slim, a popular hillbilly singer, and he longed to sing vocals and harmonies with the Blackwood Brothers. In truth, he lapped up everything. They tuned in to local station WELO for the *Black and White Jamboree* show, a music free-for-all, attracting performers from far and wide. Mississippi Slim worked for WELO and hosted a programme called *Singin' and Pickin' Hillbilly*. On Saturdays, Elvis would go to the radio station to hang around, study Slim and stay to see the *Jamboree*.

And what the Presleys heard, the Presleys sang – on their porch, as did most of their neighbours. This is where Elvis, naturally shy and self-conscious, really found his own voice, albeit a very quiet one; it was also likely how he found the courage to quietly enter a children's talent contest at the prompting of his fifth-grade teacher, Oleta Grimes.

The competition took place on 3 October at the 1945 Mississippi-Alabama Fair and Dairy Show, a five-day livestock and music festival, held in the Tupelo Fairgrounds. Elvis wore a pair of round glasses for the event. He didn't need glasses, so presumably he wore them to look distinctive. Could he really have been aware at that stage of the power of a sartorial standout opportunity? When asked at a press meeting in 1972 about his first performance, Elvis replied:

> They [the school] entered me in a talent show. I wore glasses. And I won, I think. It was fifth place in this state talent contest.
> I got a whipping the same day … for something, I don't know [what].

In the Ghetto   13

He then joked, 'Destroyed my ego completely.' Might it have been for 'borrowing' grandma Minnie Mae's reading spectacles?

Apart from at church, to his parents, his neighbours and a clearly impressed Mrs Grimes, Elvis had never sung in public before, so Gladys was stunned. 'Elvis had no way of making music,' she said. 'He just climbed up on a chair, so he could reach the microphone and he sang "Old Shep".' He did come fifth; 'Old Shep' was Red Foley's maudlin tearjerker about a young lad and his dying dog. Gladys made no reference to the whipping.

So, although it wouldn't have felt like it at that time, rough, tough Tupelo, still shaking off the rigours of the Depression – of which Franklin D. Roosevelt said, 'I see one third of a nation ill-housed, ill-clad, ill-nourished' – was the modest springboard for Elvis's eventual worldwide success. The place was a cultural and emotional soup of music, division, unity, loss, energy, hope and despair, and the kind of religious fervour born of a 'life's short, pray hard' mindset. It offered the sort of relentless privation that somehow, every now and then, manages to produce greatness.

Vernon told Nancy Anderson (same interview previously mentioned):

I believe Elvis's career and contribution to the world were set from the first. For during his early life, certain things happened which convinced me that God had given my wife and me a very special child for whom he had some very special plans.

Taken separately, Elvis's milestones thus far would have been insignificant: instinctively drawn to the choir as soon as he could walk; discovering music early via his parents' love of radio; doing well at the state county talent show at 10. Jointly, though, they amounted to pivotal markers on his road out of small-town obscurity.

However, 1946 saw one of the most important pin-drops. True to the usual pattern of Presley family life, there was further upheaval that year when, unable to keep up with the payments on their latest home, the family was back to square one. During this state of flux, in September Elvis started at Milam School, where he drew attention on account of his clothes – not because he looked cool, but because he was the only boy in sixth grade in dungarees, wearing his underclass status on his sleeve for all to see. As school group photos testify, Elvis, now agonisingly self-conscious and quiet, was often the only kid without a smile. Yet, he was perversely comfortable in his solitude, as though he somehow sensed (or was praying for) better things ahead.

The notable Tupelo waymarker came on his eleventh birthday, when Gladys took him to the Tupelo Hardware Co. and bought him a guitar. Now, that's the

14 Elvis: The King of Fashion

basic version, but like so many Elvis stories, it has grown arms and legs over the years … such as, he would have preferred a gun. Given that Vernon said that when he offered to get him a gun, Elvis told him, 'Daddy, I don't want to kill birds', that might well be one of those arms. Another was that Elvis would rather have had a bicycle. Possibly, but this was a boy infatuated with music, who played along to radio shows with a stick guitar. He sang at home, on his porch, in church and at school and wanted to be the musicians he was hearing. That could be a leg. I reckon he just asked his mama for a guitar for his birthday and his mama, knowing how crazy he was about music, agreed.

Let's give Elvis the final say. In an interview with director Bob Abel for MGM in July 1972, he says, 'They gave me a choice between a guitar and bicycle, so I took the guitar and learned to play it – a little bit. But I would never sing in public. I was very shy about it.'

Just ten years later, he would make his first gold record.

Uncle Vester, who played honky-tonks, showed him a few chords and Gladys's brother, Johnny, taught him some more, but it was the Reverend Frank Smith, a new 21-year-old minister and handy guitarist who'd arrived at the Assembly of God Church, who helped Elvis fine-tune his rudimentary string skills. Still, he had to be coaxed to play at the 'special singings' in church, apart from when they did Blackwood Brothers' stuff.

Later that autumn, just in case he didn't stand out enough in school, he began taking the precious guitar with him every day. Rather than impressing his peers, it opened him up to ridicule and confirmed he was a bit 'low-rent'. They called him 'redneck' and 'hillbilly'. He never retaliated nor did he try to make them like him. Unbowed, he continued to sling his guitar over his shoulder and take it to school, and on wet-weather days and in breaks, he played it and sang. It was basic crooning and string skills, so it wasn't going to blow anyone away, but some of the kids got into it.

Vernon had found steady work, so in 1947, after temporary digs opposite the Tupelo Fairgrounds, they found permanent accommodation. Despite segregation being entrenched at the time, they moved to nearby Green Street, a well-to-do black neighbourhood, part of which was known as The Hill. They were in a small row of houses occupied by equally down-at-heel white sharecropper types; otherwise, they were surrounded by respectable black families. The Presleys rubbed along just fine with their new black neighbours, including a couple of school teachers and their families and a pasture owner by the name of Bell, who grew melons, peanuts and such. His grandson, Sam Bell, became one of Elvis's friends.

'When they moved in, their backyard joined our property. It was a segregated time, so where he lived there was four houses with white families,' Sam Bell told the director Baz Luhrmann when he visited East Tupelo to research his *Elvis* movie. 'He wasn't a white kid or a black kid, he was just a kid. Elvis became friends with us kids, regardless.'

Green Street brought them close to the poetically and prophetically named Shake Rag, a lively, ghettoish area and hub for the town's African American population. Humming with the sound of commerce and social activities, it would have been where Elvis first clapped ears on the authentic and affecting sound of real, tough-life rhythm and blues, and a feast of other, previously unimagined, music that would dictate the course of his life. People on corners, groups, hawkers, schools and churches, including the revival church tents that were regularly thrown up on the dirt, all added to the kind of sounds that made him feel alive. But it was forbidden fruit and he would have been on the periphery, unseen or at least unnoticed, studying everything, his curiosity and his senses in overdrive. As he edged closer with time, he was both shocked and entranced by the unapologetic abandon of socialisers and worshipers, especially those attending the regular three-day revival tent services where the men dressed sharply and the women in vividly coloured clothes sashayed, like exotic flowers.

Their adulation was similar to the lively Pentecostal singing, arm-raising and swaying of the Assembly of God, but it was an industrial-strength version, praise on steroids. Elvis was mesmerised by how they jumped, shook and vibrated to the urgent, raw, melodic music – oblivious to the effect they were having on the so-far-unremarkable little white kid in their midst. He liked how well dressed they looked, but with neither outlet nor money, his own fancy for fashion would have to wait and he was still in the go-to denim overalls and rough shirt. Only on high days and holidays, would it be 'smart' clothes.

In a well-known and in my opinion compelling photograph taken in about 1943, Elvis, flanked by Gladys and Vernon and wearing the same scowling expression as his parents, is already giving off cool vibes. He's not in the latest fashion, far from it, but although he's in an unremarkable homespun shirt and hand-me-down trousers several sizes too big, the waistband riding high on his chest suspended by braces, the kid looks cool. At just 6 or 7, he looks straight at the lens, simultaneously proud and sullen. The flat spread collar's already in evidence, the clownish trousers sport a natty stripe and on his feet are what appears to be a pair of two-tone shoes. He would have had little or no say in this outfit and yet he wears it well; it grabs attention – well, mine at least – and here, like the mini trilby hat, there are the bones of a natural fashionista.

In his outstanding Elvis biography, *Last Train To Memphis*, Peter Guralnick describes Shake Rag Elvis as like 'Superman or Captain Marvel, unprepossessing in their workaday guises, but capable of more than anyone could ever imagine, he was just waiting for the opportunity to fulfil his destiny.'

16   Elvis: The King of Fashion

By now, the naturally blond fringe is already starting to flop over his eyes and necessitates being slicked back. And both the famous pout and the open, knowing stare are much in evidence, giving him an air of assurance that he rarely felt and the impression that he has a comprehension beyond his years. Bell says that their gang did have a fashion trend for a while where they'd all dress in the same thing – those overalls.

> We thought we was cool. We got them overalls, with the straps comin' over the shoulders and, when we was down there playin' we'd have a shirt on underneath. But when the girls came around, we'd take them off and the strap we'd throw it.
>
> 'We'd ... show out. We'd ride in front of the girls and do wheelies and jump up and down with the straps over our shoulders.

Picturing it already, Luhrmann takes note: 'One strap off, right?' Bell laughs at the memory, 'Yeah, one strap off,' he confirms.

Elvis never devised the gang's look; overalls were de rigueur after all. It is, however, highly possible that he shook things up a bit by suggesting that over-the-shoulders-strap look. Later, the way he'd elaborately spread his collar wide over a tired jacket, turn the hems of his trousers up to reveal a fancy pair of socks or fashion his naturally blond cowlick into the rebellious quiff that would come to define him, all point to someone hungry to stand out from the crowd. Someone dreaming of being something – but who just didn't yet know what.

And he'd never have realised that Shake Rag was the launch pad for rocketing him into a stratosphere, not of super heroics but of superstardom. Nor that his journey would lead him to a world that was the stuff of fairytales – literally taking him from rags to riches – but also, eventually, the stuff of nightmares. For Elvis's gift was exceptional. One that has been analysed, discussed, copied (but never equalled) and remains celebrated as widely today as it was in his lifetime. It was a voice that proved to be liquid gold, bringing him an incredibly rapid level of worldwide acclaim, unprecedented wealth and a wardrobe fit for a king, at a time when he'd barely crossed the threshold into manhood.

Achieving a degree of recognition surpassed only by Jesus, Elvis Aron Presley went from a deprived subsistence to a life of extravagance, spent in opulent mansions and designer villas that were, symbolically as well as physically, miles away from the little shack on the wrong side of the track where he took his first bow.

In 1948, citing the reason that Vernon could never shake off the stigma of his prison stint, the Presleys left Tupelo and moved to Memphis, hoping for a fresh start. Bell recalls Elvis telling him that he had to leave. He was vague about it but mentioned Memphis. 'He was always saying things like that, so we never believed him.'

Leroy Brown, a Tupelo classmate who appreciated Elvis's impromptu school performances, recalls that before leaving, Elvis, now pretty practised on the guitar, took requests for the few tunes that he knew. That evening, the Presleys loaded up their car with all the furniture and belongings they could and left in the dark of the night, without a goodbye, for reasons known only to them. Referring to it once, Elvis, never one to hide his lowly past, said, 'We were broke, man, broke.'

Sam Bell never saw his friend again.

The last song Elvis performed in his home town before leaving for good – or so he thought – was 'A Leaf on a Tree'.

Chapter 3

I've a Feeling We're Not in Tupelo Anymore …

Memphis, 6 November 1948–54. Look: Rainbow Rebel

'I don't regard money or position as important. But I can never forget the longing to be someone. I guess if you are poor, you always think bigger.'

Elvis

'In the sea of 1,600 pink-scalped kids at school, Elvis stood out like a camel in the Arctic … his appearance expressed a defiance which his demeanour did not match.'

Memphis Mafia member, Red West

Considering how judiciously he was cocooned from the day he was born, it seems fitting that Elvis evolved into a radiant butterfly. And where better for him to begin the next stage of his metamorphosis than in Memphis, the official home not just of the blues, but of all sorts of colourful characters?

For Elvis, leaving Tupelo and finding himself in Memphis must have been like Dorothy leaving Kansas and landing somewhere over the rainbow in the *Wizard of Oz*. Like her, he too was swept up from a storm-tossed, sepia-toned world and dropped into a strange and colourful new one. However, being a poor and extremely insecure 13-year-old boy, he was still very much in his drab pupal phase, so it would be quite some time before Memphis took any of notice him.

Gladys and Vernon could take the boy out of Tupelo's worst neighbourhood but it would be hard to take Tupelo's worst neighbourhood out of the boy, so at that moment, what Elvis was, was what you got. In time, he found his own yellow brick road, aka Beale Street, and a rainbow of sorts in Lansky Bros. at No 126. A sartorial emporium of cerise, emerald, ruby and yellow menswear, it helped turn his life technicolour and a new, fashion-conscious Elvis emerged – not quite fully formed, but almost ready to fly.

When they first arrived in Memphis, the Presleys could never have predicted that as well as a change of scene, it would lead to a change in their circumstances, so improbable and so far-reaching that none of them fully got their heads around it as long as they lived. So, on the face of it, Vernon's sudden decision to move,

I've a Feeling We're Not in Tupelo Anymore ...   19

whether driven by an uncharacteristic burst of ambition or by an absence of fiscal propriety, was reckless. He knew Memphis, he'd worked there for a bit during the war, returning to Tupelo on weekends, but this time there was neither job nor accommodation lined up – and they were destitute. Elvis and Gladys were hapless victims of Vernon's serial unreliability, and within their family and friends circle, and even in the wider community, he and his 'feckless' tag were never far apart. It was unintentional, possibly uncontrollable, because he loved his wife and his boy and they adored him, but somehow he was unable to commit to anything other than the pair of them.

According to Lamar Fike – Elvis's friend and member of his entourage, later dubbed the 'Memphis Mafia' by fans – Vernon wanted everything for his family; he just didn't want to work too hard for it. Fike told Alanna Nash, as detailed in her book *Elvis Aaron Presley: Revelations from the Memphis Mafia*, that after Parchman, people considered Vernon a criminal. And if he ever did find a job, he wouldn't show up. He says that Elvis once told him, 'Lamar, Daddy's had a backache for thirty years. He wouldn't work if you held a gun to his head.' Elvis could always joke with the best of them, often to conceal his pain, annoyance, call it what you will. Nevertheless, Vernon always managed to clutch on to some passing straw or other in the end.

In her book, Nash uses the Aaron spelling for Elvis's middle name. She is not alone; the double 'Aa' version is frequently used. Then again, so is the singular one, which I favour, my reason being that it is how it is spelt in the first notable recording of his name – his birth certificate – so I feel that this was his given name, the one his parents agreed on. Aron is also used on Elvis's school report, his 1953 *Humes High School Yearbook*, his Social Security card and on his marriage licence. Explanations for the duplicity abound. One is that it was a simple mis-spelling of Aaron by either Gladys or Vernon, who were not well educated and would have been in a state of grief, although people close to them have said that Aron was chosen intentionally to rhyme with Garon, the middle name given to Elvis's twin brother, Jesse, who arrived stillborn just before Elvis was born. Another explanation is that Elvis's growing fascination with religions other than his own in later years may have motivated him to change it to the more scriptural-sounding Aaron.

His cousin, Billy Smith, told Nash that one day in 1966 he asked Elvis about the spelling. 'I said, "How come you spell 'Aaron' with one 'A' when it's two 'A's in the Bible?" ... And he said, "Well, back when I was growing up, a lot of people around Tupelo didn't spell right."' Apparently, Elvis then turned to Vernon and said, 'As a matter of fact, Daddy, from now on, I want my name written with two 'A's.' Complying with his wishes, Vernon chose to have Elvis Aaron Presley on his son's tombstone in Graceland.

20   Elvis: The King of Fashion

Predictably, their dreams of a better life turned out to be a nightmare.

In Jill Pearlman's book *Elvis for Beginners*, Vernon says, 'We became slum renters … in a dilapidated house you wouldn't wish on your mother-in-law. We had one room, no kitchen and a bathroom we shared with three people.' He's referring to 572 Poplar Avenue, a long-demolished lodging house and 'home' to sixty souls living in absolute squalour. Vernon's frank description reveals a depth of privation that would have allowed Elvis little hope of being anything other than the dreamer he already was.

Gladys's brother, Travis Smith, his wife, Lorraine, and their sons, Gene and Billy, also went to Memphis in search of a brighter future; the Smith cousins would later become part of his trusted inner circle. With family nearby, perhaps it was easier to endure a further year of similarly lamentable accommodations until Vernon finally found a job packing tins at the nearby United Paint Company. Not only that, he defied all expectations by sticking with it for an unprecedented five years. This gave them a baby step up the social ladder as his wage meant that they could apply for means-tested welfare housing. To their great relief, their request was granted and in September 1949, the would-be King had an official residence – an apartment in the grandly named Lauderdale Courts, a housing authority project close to the city centre, its motto: 'From slums to public housing to ownership.'

One has to start somewhere.

To the Presleys, flat #328 at 185 Winchester was the Palace of Versailles; it had electricity, a kitchen, *two* bedrooms when they'd rarely had one, and a bathroom with a flushing toilet – untold luxury considering Elvis told future girlfriend June Juanico that as a kid he 'went' in the woods. There were catches. A condition of occupancy of the $35-a-month flat was unannounced inspections; this did nothing to dampen their spirits and satisfied Gladys's love of a tidy home. Another was that on reaching an earnings threshold of $2,500 a year, you had to leave and give someone else your hard-won rung. Despite its lowly status, at Lauderdale they were in comparable company; everyone there felt that they'd arrived. Money remained tight, yet even Gladys and Elvis eventually found part-time jobs, so it wasn't 'Tupelo tight'.

The year 1949 was a landmark for Elvis in other ways, too, for while still unremarkable to all but his doting parents, as well as the stable home life, complete with the beloved radio, he was attending Humes High School, getting noticed by girls, tentatively playing guitar for new pals and neighbours, and generally finding his groove. So deeply buried was his dream of becoming rich or famous, or both, he didn't realise that this was the start of his musical journey or that his fashion story would soon follow suit.

I've a Feeling We're Not in Tupelo Anymore ...   21

It was also a notable year for Memphis. Its thriving and diverse radio culture, including the groundbreaking radio station WDIA, was on the brink of a revolution. Over the decades, television has overshadowed the immense impact that the arrival of the radio had on the first half of the twentieth century. From literal radio silence, the USA's airwaves crackled into garrulous, melodious life from the start of the 1920s, and in 1921, five radio stations were sating a hunger in the largely immobile masses for news and entertainment. By the end of that decade, that handful of pioneering stations had grown to more than 600, confirming the human desire to connect with a world outside of its own. To put it into further perspective, in 1923, 1 per cent of US households had a radio; by 1937, 75 per cent had one. People were tuning in to a new brand of culture, commerce and comment, which, along with talking pictures, ended the print industry's media monopoly.

Born and raised on the sounds of radio's 'Golden Age', Elvis had already imbibed it virtually, but in Memphis, he could touch it, sense it, dream of being part of it. Influenced by the songs of plantations and prayers, he was naturally allied to the sentiments and sounds of the updated versions by popular black artists like Muddy Waters, Arthur 'Big Boy' Crudup et al. Yet, despite this tide of music, founded on the original songs and field hollers of slaves that flowed from the Mississippi to converge on Beale Street, black music on the radio was as scarce as a country singer without a guitar. Apart from the Presleys' beloved Saturday night *Grand Ole Opry* broadcasts from WSM Radio, the only other station in the South attracting households of all colours and creeds was WDIA. Referred to at the time as the 'Mother Station of the Negroes', it had already taken the bold step of becoming not just the South's, but America's first all-African American station; by 1949, it was positively in its stride.

Memphis and the airwaves were now jumping with the reverberations of a previously underground scene in all its raw, down-and-dirty glory. Local bluesmen like Howlin' Wolf rubbed shoulders with Junior Parker, who joined forces with B.B. King and other musicians to form the Beale Streeters collaboration. All this in one of the most fervently segregated regions in the land. Racial lines became blurred as radio rendered people colour-blind overnight. Still, imagine the coffee spills and newspaper rustlings in some quarters as the lyrics of 'I Want a Bowlegged Woman' by Bull Moose Jackson sunk in: 'She's gotta be built like an old bass fiddle, with big bow legs and plenty room in the middle' or 'I'll fall in love with her right from the start, because her big, fat legs are so far apart'. This was about sex and real life, and about grabbing them, along with a few other things, with both hands – and the young generation loved it.

Suddenly, Elvis and his 1950s peers had access to a new wave – make that tsunami – of music, a feast of definitive styles that are still regarded as iconic

22   Elvis: The King of Fashion

today. And they had money to buy it. Record companies soon took notice. However, while black fans snapped up the records played on WDIA – by then the region's number one radio show – most white adults, though also liking the new sounds, were governed by a prejudice so entrenched that they couldn't admit to it, let alone encourage their kids to buy the records.

On Union Street near Beale, Memphis Recording Service had been producing records by black musicians since its owner, radio engineer Sam Phillips, loved the music and dreamed of making it mainstream. Most other studios got around the 'obstacle' by getting white singers to record versions of blues and gospel songs. They sold pretty well alongside country and crooners, but often with little or no recognition of their original creators. These tamer, less gutsy, let's face it, less sexy versions, didn't float the kids' boats and, with their cars and pocket money, they were where the new spending power lay. If only, the studios thought, we could find a white singer who sounded like a black singer ...

Luckily, there was an upside to the situation for black musicians in that the alternative, more sanitised varieties often led people straight back to the more authentic original recordings. Now in the city centre, almost every block had its own unique style of music and Elvis was right there, soaking them all up like a parched sponge dropped in a cool river. He traversed his new hometown and hung out at Poplar Tunes and Charlie's record stores. Sometimes he would even buy something, rather than just listening on Charlie's jukebox; he relished the endless live musical events, such as WMPS studio's *High-Noon Round-Up*, where his heroes, the Blackwood Brothers and the Statesmen, would perform live. He'd quietly leave his own church to attend black spiritual services and to marvel at the voices and movements. Elvis had found the light, and much of it was neon.

Fellow Humes High School student Rose Howell-Klimek recalled:

After church on Sunday night, my friends and I liked to go to Leonard's Barbeque on Bellevue and then to East Trigg Baptist Church to listen to the spirituals.

The church had a section for white visitors. Elvis was often there and occasionally sang with the choir. I loved to watch the people who got the spirit dance and roll in the aisles.

(*Humes High 1953 Yearbook*)

At the same time, Elvis developed an appreciation of the showy styles of black performers like Waters, Little Richard and Riley B. King (aka B.B. King, the B.B. being from a shortening of his original nickname, Beale Street Blues Boy, to Blues Boy).

I've a Feeling We're Not in Tupelo Anymore ...   23

As well as the home of rhythm and blues, Memphis was the motherlode of white gospel music, too, and not just outstanding harmonisers like the Statesmen and the Blackwood Brothers, but a raft of others. Elvis had more inspiration than he could shake a leg at and boy, did he use it, eventually blending genres into an ululating, unique sound that took not just the world, but Elvis himself by storm.

Accusations of appropriation are understandably divisive and everyone has and is entitled to their own opinions. Nurtured to the sound of the radio in racially mixed neighbourhoods and an enthusiastic worshipper at both black and white music-driven churches, Elvis's preferences – gospel, country and blues – were entrenched from a young age. His style was as good as pre-ordained. According to Bobbie Ann Mason in *Elvis*, 'Rather than making black music or white music or a white imitation of black music, he was making music that was the voice of the Southern poor.' He always acknowledged his debt to black music, saying that his main influence – and love – was the black music he grew up listening to and the pioneering, exciting musicians who made it. A comment also in Bobbie Ann Masons' book (its possible source the *Memphis Press-Scimitar*) that is pure and unadulterated, suddenly famous and wet-behind-the-ears Elvis, gives a fascinating insight into the influence and his recognition of the black music that drove him in those early years.

> The coloured folks [*sic*] been singing it and playing it just like I'm doing now, man, for more years than I know. I got it from them. Down in Tupelo, Mississippi, I used to hear old Arthur Crudup bang his box the way I do now, and I said if I ever got to the place where I could feel all old Arthur felt, I'd be a music man like nobody ever saw.

When not immersed in music, Elvis watched movies, devouring every line of dialogue and studying his idols' mannerisms, clothes and hairstyles, with the same forensic attention to detail as he had done with his comic book heroes as a child.

By 1950, both Vernon and Gladys were working and Elvis had the perfect job for a teenage cinephile – part-time usher at Loew's State Theatre on Main Street. Working till 10 at night, he'd arrive home in time for late-night radio's hottest show, WHBQ's *Red, Hot & Blue*, presented by maverick motor-mouth DJ, Daddy-O-Dewey or Dewey Phillips, who broadcast live from a studio in the Memphis Chisca Hotel. Dewey ruled the airwaves when it came to exhilarating, left-field radio. A larger-than-life jokester, who as well as spinning the coolest records and calling out 'dee-gawwww' on a regular basis, would bark out adverts for local companies, including Lansky's. He'd exhort listeners (who included

24   Elvis: The King of Fashion

Elvis, who loved clothes just as much as music) to go there for the latest duds and pay for their clothes while 'wearing 'em out'. He'd end plugs with, 'Tell 'em Phillips sent you!' Elvis might well have then switched over to WDIA, where B.B. King would actually be deejaying and playing his own music live on air. Eventually, the late nights took their toll and, concerned that he was too exhausted to do his best in school, Gladys made him give up the cinema job.

In 1952, he was allowed to go back Loew's, only to lose his job over a girl. He and another usher had their eyes on the girl who manned the sweets counter. When she gave Elvis free candy, the spurned usher told Mr Groom, the cinema manager, that Elvis had *stolen* it. The boys got in a fight and were fired.

Arthur Groom is possibly the only person to have sacked Elvis Presley. Six years later, in true kingly fashion, Elvis allowed Loew's to host the premier of his third film, *Jailhouse Rock*. He also graciously posed for pictures with Groom, who held up his old uniform and joked that he was welcome to come back. Elvis laughed and politely declined, saying, 'Sir, I don't believe I'm ready to go back to my old job, yet.'

As well as fuelling his secret ambition to be a performer, preferably a gospel singer or an actor, the glamour and the drama of the movies held up a mirror to his own life, which, in comparison, seemed about as exciting as a pair of beige socks. He noted that the biggest stars, like James Dean and Marlon Brando, were deep and brooding. They didn't smile. They never joked. They were serious guys, with seriously good looks, framed by capacious hair as untamed as they were. And they always got the girls. Their perceived nonchalance and innate style made Elvis, by then dogged by teenage acne, a wayward fringe and a nervous stammer, feel both inspired and crushed at the same time. He realised that to achieve the sort of adulation and admiration that his celluloid heroes enjoyed, he'd need to get cool; he may have been in neither the movies nor in a band, but he could sure as hell look as though he were.

Although he dreaded attention, something within him conversely craved it. This dichotomy described his entire life, as though his late brother Jesse's fabled divine alter ego really was a thing. There's no doubt that Elvis was a conflicted character, man and child, extrovert and introvert, lover boy and mummy's boy, kind and selfish. However, in spite of or because of this, he faced his reflection and almost unwittingly, evolved his image. He did his hair in a way that drew attention away from his troublesome complexion and made the oil slick that was going on from the neck up work to his advantage. Instead of a typical 1950s short back and sides, Elvis created the long *front*, back and sides. A far more elaborate beast, the front was a studied quiff, constructed using the tools of his trade, namely a comb to style and Vaseline (later enhanced with Rose Oil hair tonic) to fortify and hold the luxuriant structure aloft. A 'ducktail' defined the back as he swept the hair from the sides of his face and teased it round to meet in the middle in an inverted peak. It was the hair of a superhero; now all he had to do was find his superpower.

Later, he cultivated his trademark sideburns – a pair of almost indecently mannish hairy wedges that hugged his cheeks and pointed to the mouth that would soon provide the world with the soundtrack for a raging teenage rebellion – and hormones. So controversial, so scrutinised, so photographed and so famous were the sideburns, they could have had a career of their own. When director Bob Abel asked him about them in a 1972 interview for MGM, Elvis said they were inspired by side-burned truckers he saw as a child in Tupelo.

> There were some truck drivers, believe it or not, that drove big diesel trucks and so forth cross-country … they had, I dunno, scars and they were wild lookin' guys. I sat by the side of the road and watched these guys and when I was old enough to grow sideburns, I grew 'em. I got criticized a lot for 'em.

He began wearing loud, patterned shirts and other unconventional clothes, initially second-hand or homespun, then latterly from Lansky's, where he then used to go the minute he got paid. In early 1950s conformist Memphian high school life, to say his look was a bold statement would be the ultimate understatement. Elvis's schoolmates' response was largely to ridicule and insult him, make that bully him, calling him a 'weirdo', a 'cowpoke', a 'woman', an 'oddball' … the list went on.

Marty Lacker, who joined Humes High after moving from New York, was also a bit of an unconventional dresser. He told author Alanna Nash:

> One day, I saw this kid who dressed like I did. He'd wear … black pants with chartreuse pistol pockets and chartreuse saddle stitching down the sides of his legs.
> And he'd wear a shiny black shirt or a pink one.

Marty became friends with Elvis, joined his inner circle, was a best man at his wedding, and stayed with him for twenty years.

Dwight Malone, another student, offers insight in the school's yearbook:

> Elvis was different. Most boys had crew cuts and wore tee shirts and blue jeans. Elvis would appear at school in a pink jacket and yellow pants and a duck-tail haircut. He was quiet, very courteous and largely stayed to himself.

26   Elvis: The King of Fashion

Despite the 'woman' tag, there was nothing effeminate about Elvis and in his final years, he was popular with the girls, who were less daunted by his quirkiness. They appreciated his nice manners and quiet demeanour, not to mention how he was starting to look. Betty Jean Moore-Munson, who was in his music class, recalls the time he approached her and her cousin, Dorothy Jackson:

> Whenever Elvis Presley walked by we would laugh and giggle. We both had a crush on him. One day he walked up and asked why we laughed. She [Dorothy] was so dumbfounded that she blurted out, 'It's because we think you are so good-looking'; he just broke into a grin and walked away.
>
> I often stared at him because there was something about him that I really liked. He didn't dress or act like the rest of the boys. He always had a lock of hair hanging to the side of his face.
>
> He had a serious expression … during the beginning of the school year. But, later in the year, he surprised us by playing his guitar before school several mornings. He didn't sing; he just played.
>
> I remember him driving a maroon convertible. Sometimes he wore dark pants with a stripe down the sides.
>
> (*Humes High 1953 Yearbook*)

Refusing to shave off the sideburns or cut his hair got him kicked out of the school football team, but he loved the game and played as hard as the rest of them with pals after school. Among them, Jerry Schilling, who, while a few years younger than Elvis, idolised him and became a lifelong friend, one of his closest, till the day Elvis died. That Elvis was introverted, reclusive even, yet still insisted on standing out, annoyed the hell out of his detractors. To them, he was like an alien. He was odd. His name was odd. He acted odd. He looked odd. Exciting, dangerous perhaps, but definitely odd. He made them feel infuriated and confused in equal measure, and when people don't understand something, they can become scared, distrustful or just plain hostile, all perfect triggers for an atmosphere of intimidation. Elvis experienced all three at one time or another.

Interestingly, they were even more obsessed with his hair than he was. In one of several bullying incidents, some boys ganged up on him in the toilets, wielding scissors and threatening to cut his hair. Red West, a tough, sporty student who knew Elvis by sight – presumably because he was hard to miss – walked in on the scene.

On the *George Klein Memphis Sounds Elvis Tribute* show (2011), George, another Humes High boy, who met Elvis in eighth grade and also became one of the Memphis Mafia, asked Red to explain what occurred that day.

I happened to walk in the bathroom and here were the bullies. Two guys were holding him and one was gonna cut his hair.

I said, 'What's goin' on?' and they said, 'Oh, we're just gonna give him a haircut.' I said, 'Don't look like he wants the haircut. If you cut his hair, you gotta cut my hair and I don't think you can do that.' They backed off.

In Peter Guralnick's *Last Train to Memphis*, Red West said that he felt really sorry for Elvis and that he seemed very lonely, with no real friends. Elvis never forgot Red's kindness, and he never did cut his hair. Just imagine how furious those follicular antagonists must have felt when, after scrutinising Tony Curtis, another of his movie idols, Elvis got Gladys to give him a Toni perm!

Red was later invited into Elvis's inner circle, the so-called Memphis Mafia, an entourage founded on family members and early friendships but which grew and diversified over the years.

In an interview with journalist Scott Jenkins, George Klein recalls the time their teacher mentioned their school variety talent show. Elvis raised his hand and asked if he could play his guitar and sing. 'There were a few laughs in the class because it just wasn't cool to do that in front of anyone,' says George. The following week, 27 March 1953, he got up and sang 'Old Shep' – his go-to talent showcaser – and 'Cold, Cold Icy Fingers'. 'At that moment, I was blown away because I'd never seen a kid get up in front of people and sing like that. Subconsciously, I knew there was something happening with this guy.' He also confirms that Elvis stood out, but did so in a good-natured and quiet manner, describing him as 'a velvet hammer'.

He would wear those black pants with white stripes down the sides, or pink stripes. He would wear sport coats and turn the collar up. Nobody else dressed like that. He'd wear showbizzy-type stuff to school all the time. You'd see him occasionally with his guitar singing at lunchtime too. He'd sing at class functions, so yeah, he stood out.

When Abel asks Elvis whether he really dressed differently to other kids, he answers, 'I suppose so, by normal standards, but it was just something I wanted to do. I wasn't trying to be better than anybody else.'

Humes was a working-class school, with latch-key kids and struggling families. It raised money over the year for a charity fund that was used to help poorer students. Even though most of the kids were in the same boat as Elvis socially, he was always an odd fit. Much of his reticence was a needlessly punitive sense of shame about his poverty-stricken childhood in Tupelo, and, worse, his father's imprisonment. Because he knew that they knew, he was always self-conscious.

28 Elvis: The King of Fashion

That he ignored his tormenters, maintained his unorthodox appearance and survived school armed only with a guitar and an unwavering dream of better things to come, is testament to his resilience.

Come Elvis's senior year, the Presleys had good news and bad. Their annual income had exceeded the Lauderdale Courts limit and they had to relinquish their apartment. The good news was that they could afford a new place, a whole-floor apartment in a large Victorian house on Alabama Avenue, not far from the Courts.

As school drew to an end, Elvis found some confidence and a degree of peer acceptance. He played his guitar in breaks, sang in music class and performed in a pivotal school talent show, the Annual Minstrel Show, in the Humes auditorium on 9 April 1953. In the aforementioned MGM interview, Bob Abel wants to hear about this. 'Let's go back,' he says. 'What happened?'

Elvis's reply speaks volumes. He stumbles over his words like a drunk in the dark, channelling the uncertain boy he was at the time.

> Well, uh, I wasn't, like I said, I wasn't popular in school, I wasn't dating anybody at that school. Uh, I failed music … the only thing I ever failed.
>
> And, uh, they [mainly his teacher, Miss Mildred Scrivener] entered me in this talent show, and I came out and I did my two songs. And when I came onstage I heard people kind of rumbling and whispering and so forth, 'cause nobody knew I even sang, really.

Shrewdly, he adds that it was amazing how popular he became in school after that. Asked what he sang, he mumbles, 'Uh, let me see. "Till I Waltz Again With You" by Teresa Brewer.' He makes no mention of 'Old Shep', though others who were there say he sang that, too, and yet others say it was at a later Christmas show.

Abel wants more. 'Hang on a second,' he says, 'You've never sang in public before, and you got up there and you're scared pissless and everything, and you start to sing. *What* happened?'

'Well, uh, about the same thing that happened later on, at the Shell,' says Elvis.

He's referring to the shell-shaped stage at Memphis's Overton Park, where the following year he'd perform his first major public gig to an ecstatic audience. The school homeroom once had a picnic there and, in later years, Miss Scrivener described him sitting alone, plucking his guitar, when the other students stopped dead and began to gather around him.

> There was something about his quiet, plaintive singing which drew them like a magnet. It wasn't the rock 'n' roll for which he later became famous, more like 'Love Me Tender'. He went on singing his young heart out.

I've a Feeling We're Not in Tupelo Anymore … 29

Continuing the Overton Park Shell talk with Abel, Elvis says, 'The kids got wild … I got ten or eleven encores, that type of thing. It just kind of halted the show. … And it, it scared me but then I got happy too.'

Of the April school performance, George Blancett, also performing that night, says that Elvis offered to warm up for him.

> When that night came, he did warm them up! After a couple of songs, the audience demanded he … sing more. The show really finished when Elvis did, but we went on and performed our act without much distinction.
>
> It was at that Humes Talent Show in April, 1953 that I realized Elvis could really sing. … The ovation was thunderous and long.
>
> (*Humes High 1953 Yearbook*)

Whatever occurred, Elvis had had his first, addictive taste of fame, of affirmation, of adulation. They liked him. No, they loved him, and they hadn't wanted him to stop. Something in the Elvis Presley firmament had shifted and it wouldn't be going back. Nor would he.

Despite this fleeting brush with celebrity, where he was listed on the programme as Guitarist – Elvis *Prestly*, he defaulted back to his quiet self that final year. He volunteered at the library and was in the Reserve Officers' Training Course (ROTC) educational military programme, and wore his uniform as often as possible – an early costume change – but otherwise, he went largely unnoticed. Nuggets of detail from the few who did remember him merely add to, rather than solve, the mystery of how he suddenly leapt from nowhere to everywhere just a couple of years later.

Elvis took his last bow at Humes on 3 June 1953 with decent grades, including an A in Language (those hours spent reading comic books paid off). His music grade was not an F but a C. His proud parents got his diploma framed, while Elvis went to the employment office and got a job, starting the following day, at M.B. Parker Machinists' shop.

Now 18, he took 14-year-old Regis Wilson, a girl he'd been double-dating with his cousin Gene and his girlfriend for some weeks, to his school prom at the Peabody Hotel on Union Avenue. The dance was in the Continental Ballroom and, if Elvis had looked out of place at Humes High, then the prom took his quest for individualism to a whole other level. While the other boys were clean-shaven, Elvis's hair was now unapologetically even longer, a flawless peak/DA (duck's ass) combo flanked by sideburns sharper than a pair of Sabatier knives. As was tradition, all the guys wore white tuxedos – aside from Elvis, who was in a sharp, dark-blue Lansky suit, which, according to Regis, he'd teamed with blue suede shoes.

30   Elvis: The King of Fashion

In an interview with YouTuber and engaging Elvis historian Billy Stallings, aka Spa Guy, Regis Wilson (now Vaughan) confirms this non-conformity:

Elvis wore a blue suit to the prom and … the other guys had on tuxedos with a white coat. I think he was the only one there in blue. And he wore blue suede shoes … I kinda chuckle when I think about that.

Coincidental or strangely prophetic footwear? Despite a rigorous search, I've only unearthed one photo of Elvis and Regis that night; it's grainy and it's black and white, so it's impossible to tell whether the shoes really were blue or even suede. I'm trusting Regis and saying they were. And I can confirm that, whatever the colour, the slip-on loafers looked very cool – as did he.

He'd certainly been on a spending spree that week, since he collected Regis from her home in a hired Chevrolet – also dark blue – and gave her a corsage that matched her sweet, pink strapless taffeta dress and pink shoes. Wilson recalled:

He rented a nice car for the night because the car that we usually went out in was his dad's car and it was a really old, broken down car.

It was the most exciting thing I had ever done. I felt like Cinderella getting ready to go to the royal ball.

In the photo, however, Elvis seems to be glowering, or perhaps he's just trying out his brooding Brando look. Regis is sort of smiling, though it looks a little forced. Perhaps their apparent lack of cheer is because the night was a Cinderella story, in that it didn't turn out as Regis had expected. According to Regis, everyone blanked Elvis, which, coming from a different school from him, shocked her. She already knew that he hadn't been very popular at high school, but she was taken aback by the hostile behaviour of his peers. Elvis quickly told her that he wouldn't dance as he didn't know how to and suggested that they sit down, promising Regis that they'd have fun afterwards with his friends at Leonard's Barbeque, then go to a party.

Regis's eyewitness account, during the 2022 Spa Guy interview, of just how badly Elvis was snubbed at his last school event is immensely sad.

Not one, no one, came over and said 'hello' to him, and I felt kinda bad. We sat at a table and drank Coca Cola by ourselves and just talked to each other. …

I thought it kinda strange that nobody, absolutely nobody, not one person, came over and said 'Hi, Elvis, how are you?'

I've a Feeling We're Not in Tupelo Anymore ...   31

Regis also suggests that some of those dismissing him would later become part of Elvis's inner circle.

> It's amazing to me that those people – I'm familiar with some of the names of the people that he probably went to high school with – became part of his entourage, or they call it the Memphis Mafia, and these guys wouldn't have anything to do with him when he was in high school. And yet, boy, when he got famous ...

She says that to her, it therefore didn't 'ring like true friendship, cos, if you're friends, you're friends, you know? Good times and bad times.'

With the luxury of hindsight, it's clear to me that Elvis refusing to dance was out of fear of being ridiculed, more than any lack of ability.

Nobody spoke to him. Not one single person.

Spa Guy sums up Regis's take on the event:

> Not one person spoke to them at the prom. That's [future Memphis Mafia members] George Klein, that's Red West, none of them. Elvis was really a loner and that's the real truth of the matter. Once he became famous, then all those people knew him. Oh, the difference a little bit of fame can make.

So, on that less-than-magical night, it was a little less action, a little more conversation and instead of tripping the light fantastic, poor Regis wound up sitting on the sideline with Elvis all evening, paradoxically, something his fans would have later killed for, while other couples happily swanned around them on the dance floor. Despite Regis describing him as 'all boy' and having 'a kind of swagger', the situation screams of him being overcome with inhibition in the face of his antagonistic and judgmental peers, making Regis's experience all the more poignant.

Standing in the empty and silent Continental Ballroom in 2023, I am struck, not simply by its elegantly sumptuous burnished gold and ivory décor, but by the scale of the space. Jokingly referred to by the hotel staff as being 'as big as Lake Michigan', it is vast. I close my eyes and picture Regis, gliding across its gleaming oak dance floor, like a pale rose, held in the arms of Elvis, her handsome Prince Charming, and feel sad that they never got to dance – that she never even had the chance to step on his blue suede shoes.

In the end, even the promised BBQ pals were a no-show and there was no party either, so Elvis had no choice but to drop Regis home. A few weeks later, she and her family were forced to move to Florida as they were struggling financially. Ironically, she was too embarrassed to tell Elvis they were broke, so

32   Elvis: The King of Fashion

she never said goodbye to him. It wasn't until he called at her house some days later that he discovered she'd gone.

Not long after, and settled in Florida, Regis's mother showed her a teen magazine article about a boy from Memphis who'd become a rock and roll heartthrob and a national phenomenon – known for his unique dance moves …

Chapter 4

The Lansky Effect

Memphis 1953. Look: Superstar in Waiting

'They ask me why I wear the clothes I do. What can I say? I just like nice clothes, that's all. I like colour and such. Is there something wrong with that?'

Elvis

Being poor did not sit well with Elvis. Let loose on an unsuspecting world after graduating in 1953, he was more naval-gazing than trailblazing. Still affected by the memory of Vernon's time in prison, the resulting humiliation and hardship that he and Gladys suffered and, worse, his inability to do anything about it, he was fixated on becoming famous. As far as he could see, movie and music stars didn't need fancy qualifications or certificates to make money, they just needed to be great at entertaining people and then it just rolled in anyway. Ironically, this consuming preoccupation was driven by neither greed nor vanity, but by circumstance. It was no vainglorious pipedream, for, despite his youth, experience had already taught him that poverty, the root cause of his family's misfortunes, was only ever a few paychecks away. He craved the blanket of reassurance and protection that wealth could offer and, recognising that his parents were unable to provide that, he accepted that it was down to him to do so.

Elvis held on to the promise that he'd made in Tupelo, and most likely again at their horrible Poplar Avenue doss house, that one day he'd make enough money to ensure that the Presleys would never, ever be poor again. Blissfully unaware of the unique talent that he possessed, all he had to do was work out how. To say that he was desperate to achieve this goal is no exaggeration. It was a quest that became the main driving force of his life and, in part, of his death.

The previous year, while he still had the job at Loew's, he contributed towards the household finances, the first small step in his parental support mission. What little he had left he put towards his second most important undertaking, that of being a fashion icon. Luckily, this came naturally. There he was, hair drenched in enough oil to run a small generator, in gaudily patterned, wide-collared shirts

34   Elvis: The King of Fashion

under wider-collared jackets – sometimes of the bolero persuasion – and pleat front, or 'pegged', trousers with neon trim down the legs and around gunslinger pockets. Oh, and hats. Remember that shot of the trilby-toting toddler Elvis with his mamma and daddy? He loved a bit of headwear.

Whatever he put together, he looked good in it. Once he was earning, he'd go to Lansky's and purchase the best duds he could stretch to, and the bolder the better. Loud they may have been, but they were smart, too. His style gradually became intuitively elegant and, apart from in some of his movie roles and on his ranch, Elvis rarely wore jeans, because as a child, they were often the only things he had to put on. In teen photos with pals, cousins and even with girlfriends, he stands out every time, not just because the baby face has gone, replaced by more linear features that make him strikingly handsome, but because of what he's wearing and how he wears it. Although light years away from monetary security, what clothes Elvis could afford to buy, he wore with a natural, easy panache.

Early photos also show that, fashion-wise, he was ahead of his time; in fact, he was in a time of his own. It's no exaggeration to say that he was pioneering and many of his outfits – then deemed outlandish – wouldn't look out of place today. Gender-neutral in his attitude towards dressing, long before the phrase was even invented, he was wearing stuff that flew right in the face of prescribed 'male style', and that earned him that early reputation of being a weirdo. He layered jewellery and wore soft pastel shades usually associated with womenswear; occasionally he used eye make-up and wore what looked like women's blouses. Perhaps some of them were. Sheer lace, florals, citruses, glossy satins, frills and transparent chiffons – you name it, Elvis wore it. Texture, as much as colour, was his thing. As if that wasn't daring enough, on hot summer nights, he'd undo the buttons of his shirt down to his navel or hitch the tails up and tie them in a knot under his chest, baring his midriff for all to marvel at. A stranger to the word 'clashing', he often went for unconventional colour combos: think hot pink with apple green, scarlet with cornflower blue, claret with banana yellow. They should never have worked, but on him, they did.

Considering the deprivation of his Tupelo days and the restricted choice of garments within his home radius in Memphis, the international playboy-style vibes he was giving off were impressive. Perhaps it was poring over the celebrity magazines he loved so much, or watching the cool musicians doing their thing, whatever his inspiration, he owned every outfit he wore. For example, a picture of him with his friend Luther Nall, taken inside Loew's around 1952, shows both boys dressed to the nines, and although Luther looks spruce in his sports jacket, shirt and jazzy kipper tie combination, Elvis, looking at the camera like he rules the world, is in a different league. In his tailored jacket and fitted turtleneck sweater that could be cashmere though probably wasn't, he looks so

The Lansky Effect   35

suave and self-assured that he could be a leading man who's just stepped out from the big screen. He was 17.

Much of the time, though, the only shopping the young Elvis could stretch to was of the window variety – a punitive game of look, but don't touch. All those hours spent gazing hungrily at the clothes in Lansky's window had been his way of working out how to afford them, so it seems apt that this was where his road to riches began to be tinged with gold. Bernard and his brother Guy took a shine to the careworn lad from the wrong side of Tupelo who didn't know a tweed from a twill or that brocade or bouclé were even a thing. In what became a bit of a project, they proved that you really could make a silk purse out of a pig's ear, provided it happened to belong to a best-in-show, prize-winning beauty – ensuring that Elvis was suitably dressed to take on the world.

Today, the store is still going strong and remains in the family; Hal Lansky, Bernard's son, now runs it with his daughter, Julie. It has relocated from its original Beale Street site to the grand lobby of the nearby Peabody Hotel, the scene of Elvis and Regis's bittersweet prom date. All lofty ceilings, carved panels and glittering chandeliers, the Peabody is a paean to old-world, Southern comfort and charm, and when it comes to Memphis and indeed Elvis's history, it has pride of place. As well as the location of his school prom, it's also where he collected his bonus payment on signing to RCA Victor on 21 November 1955, after being released from Sam Phillips's Sun Record Company. The deal was another major waymarker on his career path, yet legally, he was too young to sign the paperwork, so Vernon, still shell-shocked at his son's sudden fame, obliged.

The sheet of Peabody-headed stationery used to record the $5,000 bonus (less 25 per cent fees for his recently materialised manager Colonel Tom Parker) sold at auction in 1999 for a reported $65,000, almost fifteen times the amount of the original transaction.

When I called Hal, now 72, in July 2022, he was in great demand, so it's a measure of the man and his affection for Elvis that he still made time to talk to me about how his dad helped make him the King of Fashion. The global heatwave wasn't the only thing that was hot that July. Researching online ahead of the interview, Hal was everywhere. Vlogs, blogs, the press, glossy magazines, social media, radio and a conveyor belt of studio sofas from where he regaled TV hosts with Elvis-related anecdotes. You name it, he was in it or on it.

In fairness, given the nature of his business, he talks a lot about Memphis's most famous son. However, the reason he was doing it far more than usual was the release of the new Warner Bros. movie, *Elvis*. Only a few weeks before, film director Baz Luhrmann's dazzling and unexpectedly affecting film bounded onto the world's cinema screens and blew everyone away, just as the teenage Elvis did when he sprung from the wings of the Overton Park Shell stage on 30 July

36 Elvis: The King of Fashion

1954. It would be impossible to shoehorn Elvis's entire life story into a movie, for although tragically short, its scale is huge. The man was huge. A king, no less. Still, Luhrmann got a lot in and, thanks to its quirkiness, spectacularly detailed costumes, his decision to tell the story through the rheumy old-man's eyes of Colonel Tom Parker, a goliath of the music industry's most loathed villains and, most of all, its sheer humanity, *Elvis* was an instant success. Costing $85 million to make, it swivelled past hot favourite *Top Gun: Maverick*, starring Tom Cruise, and took first place in the debut box office race by grossing more than $30 million on its first weekend alone and, at the time of writing in February 2023, had grossed $287 million worldwide.

Watching Hal on a chat show, sandwiched twixt Austin Butler, the actor who plays Elvis, and the Peter Pan-esque Luhrmann, I had to smile at the irony of how the intense media attention that he was experiencing stemmed from the part his family played in putting Elvis in the spotlight. And so, when we speak, the world and his wife, the die-hard fans, unmatched in their devotion and many of whom were lucky enough to have seen Elvis when he was alive and some when he was live on stage, plus a whole new audience of hitherto Elvis virgins, were all talking about The King's clothes.

Lansky's contribution to the fashion iconography of Elvis cannot be overestimated. I asked Hal about the famous Elvis-meets-Bernard moment and the mention of his dad's name brings an instant anecdote. Thankfully, from an author as well as a story-lover's point of view, he has many – and in a soft, Mississippi-Delta roll of an accent he elaborates on the tale everyone kind of knows:

> My dad saw this young man looking in his window and knew he was out of place. Not just because he was hanging around a lot, nor that he was a glaringly obvious white boy in what was, at the time, an almost exclusively black neighbourhood, but also because he was just so damn shabby looking.

We talk about the mutual regard Elvis and his father had for one another from the start. How, despite him being an obviously low-rent, worn-out-shoes kind of a kid, Bernard treated Elvis with as much respect as Elvis showed him. They introduced him to the newest, trendiest threads that side of the Mississippi, which they'd sourced straight from New York and California when they had needed something new to replace the post-war army surplus and uniform items they'd been selling since opening in 1946. In a world of beige, tan, and yet more beige, they eschewed the innocuous, clean-cut look that epitomised the era and stocked more flamboyant but good-quality garments in bright colours. Pieces in pineapple, orange, green and pink were teamed with base colours of

The Lansky Effect 37

black, white and, occasionally, blue. Window displays were show-stopping with shades that were popping. It was a brave move – but it paid off as performers were quick to recognise that the outfits would make them the focal point when they were on stage – and off.

It was quite the palette, but their unconventional combos appealed to Memphis's black community – and to Elvis. Some other white artists, too, were drawn to the allure of Lansky's couture. Carl Perkins and Jerry Lee Lewis bought their gear there through the fifties and sixties, and Johnny Cash was a regular, although he ditched the bright colours early on and bought his first all-black suit from them; it became his definitive look for the rest of his career. To Elvis, a fashion junkie on a mission to stand out from the crowd, the place was pure catnip, fitting since one of his earliest nicknames was the 'Hillbilly Cat', and it's hardly surprising that, come payday, he headed straight there.

On their first auspicious meeting, Bernard, as mentioned in chapter one, told Elvis not to buy him out but to buy from him and, being a polite Southern boy who always listened to his elders, Elvis did. In an interview courtesy of Memphis Tourism, Bernard explains:

> That Friday, he came in and bought a shirt for five dollars, the next week he came in and bought another five-dollar shirt. I mean, he didn't have no money. That young man, he had nothin', but he was a nice young man.

Hal elaborates:

> Since Elvis was in high school and working around the corner as an usher in the theatre, he'd come in every week. He started buying small items, a shirt one week, maybe a pair of pants, a cap, just little purchases; he'd come in whenever had some money.
>
> When he started shopping with us, it was for, as you would say in the UK, off-the-peg stuff. Eventually, when he became more famous we did have some of his clothes specially made for him.

Later, as Elvis progressed from nerve-jangling performances in small venues to touring, albeit still quaking in his shoes, larger ones around the South in 1954 and '55, his increased income funded the fine-tuning of his look.

True to form, and clearly undeterred by the awkward Regis Wilson prom date, Elvis escorted his first serious girlfriend, Dixie Locke, to *her* junior prom on 6 May 1955, wearing yet another conspicuous outfit. He'd clearly lost some of his self-consciousness, if the photograph of their enthusiastic snogging on the hotel sofa is anything to go by. Black and white photos of the night show

38   Elvis: The King of Fashion

Dixie in a sweet, tulle frock, her corsage pinned at the centre of her décolleté. However, yet again, Elvis steals the show in a bespoke outfit and two-tone shoes. A quote from Bernard adds colour to the picture: 'He had the tailor create an ensemble set of black pants, pink coat and pink-and-black cummerbund for the prom. He always wanted to be the belle of the ball.'

Imagine the balls, or plain steely determination it would have required to make a statement like that in a sea of traditional white tuxedos.

Just a few years after buying his first Lansky shirt and with his career starting to take off, Elvis walked into the store and made an announcement.

'Elvis came in one day with a piece of paper, saying "Mr Lansky, Mr Lansky!" I said, "What's happenin', Elvis," and he said, "Man, I'm goin' to New York this week and I gotta have some clothes."'

He was referring to his first appearance on *The Ed Sullivan Show*, the topical, variety TV show, which, after *I Love Lucy*, with Lucille Ball and Desi Arnaz, drew the country's second highest ratings. Elvis had already made some TV appearances, including on the Dorsey Brothers' *Stage Show* (CBS) and on the *Milton Berle Show* (NBC), but Ed Sullivan – that was the big time.

Aware of what a huge opportunity that performing to a national audience would be for Elvis, Bernard hotfooted it to New York's Garment District and selected some black pegged trousers, brightly coloured shirts, even though the show would air in black and white, and three distinctive sports coats. Back in Memphis, he laid the clothes out on the store counter for Elvis to see. 'I told him how much it was and he said, "Man, that's a lotta money." I said, "Don't worry, Elvis, we'll take care of you."'

They really did. He looked great in the outfits, which are now as legendary as is their wearer.

When the show went out on the Sunday night, Bernard was still working in the Beale Street store.

We had the TV set on. He'd teamed the black pants with the pink plaid coat and sang 'Don't Be Cruel', 'Love Me Tender', 'Ready Teddy' and 'Hound Dog'. And as soon as Elvis had finished, we knew he was on his way.

As did the entire nation – they just weren't sure where.

Lansky Bros. also provided the clothes for his appearances on all the other TV shows and his regular, live *Louisiana Hayride* gigs. Elvis continued to shop at Lansky's from those heady early performances up to his final days at Graceland. They would open at midnight or at times during the odd hours that he kept, so that he could shop without being mobbed. They knew his size and his tastes so well, that if he were too busy, they'd deliver selections of clothes to

The Lansky Effect   39

Graceland for him to try. When he did go into the store during opening hours, he'd often buy clothes for other shoppers, whether he knew them or not – an early indication of the breathtaking levels of generosity that he demonstrated throughout his life.

When Bernard delivered, Gladys would greet him at the door and invite him to stay for a meal.

> They [Elvis and his entourage] used to stay out all night on gigs. They'd eat breakfast at four o'clock in the afternoon. Gladys would tell me to take the clothes up to Elvis's bedroom and come back down and eat with them.
>
> He bought Graceland when he was 22 years old. He got good and did a lot of concerts. Memphis had a lot of pimps, gamblers at the time and we had high fashion in the window. I'd do tailor-made mohair, silk and wool. Flare leg, no back pockets. Twenty-six-inch knee, 14-inch bottom drape. Then I made thinner legs.

The trousers became Elvis's go-to stage choice as the loose fit allowed him to move easily. When he cut his shapes, they also had the unexpected habit of billowing out, making it look as though he was gyrating his groin. And we all know the effect that had on his audience.

Ironically, it was during a shopping trip to Texas that Bernard learned of Elvis's death. He was with Hal and they flew home. 'I went out to Graceland,' said Bernard. 'He was a heck of a nice guy. I put him in his first suit, and I put him in his last suit.' Bernard outlived Elvis by thirty-five years, dying peacefully on 15 November 2012. He was 85.

Hal made a natural heir to his father. He'd grown up in the shop, helping out and meeting the cool and famous clientele; it's easier to name the famous artists who didn't shop there when he was a kid, than those who did. All the big names went there, but the guy Hal remembers so fondly is Elvis. He shows me a 1958 photo of his 7-year-old self, wearing, to coin a Hal phrase, a shit-eatin' grin on his face as he and his siblings stand next to Elvis, who has his hand resting on young Hal's shoulder. Behind them is a rack of what looks like wide-boy ties. The Lansky children look excited about just being in his company, while Elvis stares at the camera in full brooding Brando mode. He appears to be wearing a smidge of dark eyeshadow. The picture's a tad blurry but his outfit, a bold-striped sports coat, white pocket kerchief, velvet-looking trousers, white open-necked shirt with dark t-shirt underneath shirt, and a patterned silk cummerbund, is pure, unadulterated, head-to-toe Lansky and he looks cooler than a polar bear on a block of ice.

40   Elvis: The King of Fashion

When Hal took up the measuring tape on behalf of his late father, who was known as the 'Clothier to The King', he needed a title of his own.

> I guess I was 'Delivery Boy to The King'. I delivered stuff out to Graceland, too. You know, Elvis loved clothes and a lot of times he'd say, 'I'll take it all.'
>
> You have to remember the Lansky Look, as we called it, was not traditional and it was always on the edge.
>
> He was interested in being different. Anything that was different and didn't blend in with the traditional items in the marketplace, he liked.
>
> Of course, in the early fifties the fabrics were natural – silk, wool, cotton, even velvet was made from cotton; we had bouclés, jacquards and shiny silks.

Hal loves talking fashion and we consider the fact that his family informed Elvis's chameleon-like style choices for more than thirty years, from the early 1950s until the early '70s – Hal's least favourite fashion phase.

> You know, the seventies was a decade of fashion that I hope never comes back. All the black exploitation movies were out, like *Shaft* and *Super Fly*. In fact, it's the fiftieth anniversary of *Super Fly*, but all that dressing with the long, leather coats …
>
> We were probably the only store in America that had a full-time furrier putting mink collars and mink cuffs on things. Yeah, I hope that never comes back.

I daren't mention that Elvis was the proud owner of at least nine of those '*Super Fly*' coats, including one made by IC Costumes, where a certain Bill Belew worked. Bill would also play a crucial role in the shaping of Elvis's image in later years by designing the stunning wardrobe for his 3 December 1968 *Singer NBC-TV Christmas Special* TV show, now the stuff of showbiz legend and known as the '*68 Comeback Special*.

One of the so-called 'pimp' coats was in full-length black leather, complete with mini shoulder cape, another two, in red and in camel-coloured wool, were trimmed with chocolate-brown fur collars, pocket flaps and capelets. The camel-coloured version sold at a recent auction for almost $50,000. These elaborate coats for fly (or trendy) guys have had a comeback or two since, but they were an acquired taste; even so, Elvis got away with wearing them – just.

'Now, the sixties,' says Hal, 'that's a different story. The continental style.' Bernard's hand can be seen all over Elvis's Beatle-era statement pieces; they were sharp, slim-fitting, glamorous and a little edgy at the same time. Even now, they look classy.

The Lansky Effect   41

When we get on to the Vegas years and the second star of every Elvis concert, the jumpsuit, also designed by Belew, Hal says:

> I would call his jumpsuits costumes. Lansky's did not do any of his jumpsuits. When we were doing research for our history book (*Lansky Brothers: Clothier to The King*) and Graceland let us go through his clothing, we discovered a few sixties jumpsuits. They were very plain and did not have any embellishments. We do not take credit for the Vegas jumpsuits.

The early, unadorned jumpsuits to which he's referring are among my favourite outfits. Based on Elvis's obsession (of which he had many) with karate, they were precursors to his more elaborate stage versions.

Hal makes no bones about when he believes that Elvis was at the top of his style game: 'Elvis shopped with us for over three decades and I tell everybody that the Lansky Look was when Elvis looked his best, when he was young and innocent.'

Nowadays, the store sells contemporary fashions under slogans like 'Dress Like a Rockstar'. In a nod to tradition, they're pretty flamboyant and, as in the early days, attract many celebrities. They also stock reproduction heritage pieces, directly inspired by Elvis, including the famous black-and-white-striped sports coat worn in *Jailhouse Rock* (when not in prison gear) and his beautiful black brocade wedding coat. Hal continues:

> You know, being a clothier to Elvis is a two-sided sword, because a lot of people, when they come in our store, they expect it to be like the '50s, you know, like a time tunnel. But to stay in business, we have had to zigzag with the times.
>
> So, yes, a two-sided sword, but I wouldn't trade it for anything. It's a great legacy to have and I keep my dad's legacy, and also Elvis's legacy, going.

Part of my research involved poring over hundreds of photos of Elvis, most of them in black and white, aside from some early film studio and occasional TV promotional shots, until you get to the later 1960s and the '70s. While details like the stitching, the buttons, the cut, those sorts of things are there, the colour is not and, as anyone knows, since humans first wrapped fabrics about themselves to indicate status, personality, culture or taste, colour is everything.

It was frustrating, since his famously and unapologetically bold colours even had a nickname. 'My dad used to call them his Lifesaver colours, like the little candies in a roll. Your reds, your greens, your yellows,' says Hal.

42   Elvis: The King of Fashion

Yes, it was Elvis's music that made him an industry colossus. After all, when he first grabbed people's attention, they had no idea what he looked like. In fact, because his sound was so influenced by the poor, black and sub-working-class white communities in which he grew up, many listeners simply assumed that he was an African American singer. However, once he stepped out from behind those radio speakers and greeted the world, it was about the look, too.

'It was about both – the look and the sound – that's what made him,' says Hal. 'If he'd showed up wearing plain jeans and a flannel shirt, he couldn't have put it over the way he did. It was unbelievable.'

On learning that Lansky's was still going, was still called the 'Clothier to The King' and sold Elvis-style clothes, Luhrmann had to visit. He sought out Hal and Julie and visited so that they could advise him on the costume designs. Luhrmann's wife, the award-winning fashion and interiors designer Catherine Martin, created the meticulously detailed wardrobe for *Elvis*, including Butler's outfits, which were based on early Lansky originals. Hal says:

> You know what, Catherine Martin is a genius. Her and her husband, Baz, they did an excellent job. I don't know anybody that could have done as good a job as they did – even myself.
>
> I mean, on a skill of one to ten, I would say they're a hundred! They twisted it, but they know what they're doing and they did an awesome job.

They certainly did, because not only were the costumes stars in their own right, but suddenly I had an instant source of full-colour, close-up, beautifully shot, cinematic answers to the questions that had been spinning around my head, like: 'What colour were those trousers?' 'Was that one of the pink jackets?' 'Were those suede shoes actually blue?'

Hal confirms that the black lace shirt that Butler wears in the film is an authentic interpretation of ones that Elvis wore a lot. 'We did sell those in the '50s, so yeah, I know he wore a pink one, he did wear them.' Martin's version of the shirt enjoys an especially high profile in the movie's fairground scenes, where Elvis encounters 'Col' Tom Parker (played by actor Tom Hanks) in the Hall of Mirrors and then joins him on the Ferris wheel. Teamed with impeccably cut, high-waisted cream trousers, the flimsy, sheer black shirt is defiantly feminine in style; however, Butler wears it in a louche, open-fronted, lounge-lizardish way that adds balance with an almost insolent masculinity. In another scene, in the Memphis Recording Service studio, Butler clearly likes the style as much as Elvis did, as he's wearing a burgundy version, this time with pink trousers – which should clash, but don't. Elvis would have thoroughly approved.

Judging by the obvious kick that Hal and his daughter Julie get from sourcing, displaying and suggesting Elvis-inspired outfits, one can't help but feel that, in the same way, Bernard had as much fun dressing Elvis as Elvis did being his mannequin, muse, model, advertisement, call it what you will. Bernard guided him and taught him to appreciate the quality, textures and cut of garments; to understand the power of clothes and, crucially, for a performer who wants to literally steal the show, of looking confident, even when you don't feel it. He immediately recognised Elvis's flamboyant side and encouraged him to make choices to which, while some might say 'What the hell?', most would say, 'I want to be that guy.'

We get back to the *Elvis* movie. I was writing this book when it premiered and we'd both seen it – several times. We rave about how great it was. Hal says:

I've seen it four times now. I tell everybody, my daughter Julie and I, we sleep, eat and breathe our business which is in the Elvis world – and other things, too – but I have two other daughters who could [*sic*] care less about what we do.

I took them to the premiere and after that, they really got into Elvis. Now they want to know about Priscilla, they want to know about everything! So, it's bringing the new generation into the fold, which is great, great.

I'm glad this movie is out to show the younger generation the impact Elvis had, not only on Memphis or even music but on the world. It's amazing how much power Elvis still has today.

I confess that when the news came out that Austin Butler would play Elvis, I couldn't see it. Trying to capture the essence of The King is like trying to capture starlight. I think I even said something flippant like, 'I look more like Elvis than Austin does.'

And then … I watched the film.

Willingly, I ate humble pie, as he became Elvis before my very eyes – a triumph of his fine and intuitive acting and the wizardry of Luhrmann, who fused reality, virtuality and surreality to produce a cinematic fireworks display of a movie that's also a love letter to the indefinable spirit of Elvis.

We met both Baz and Austin in September 2019. They met us in the store at the Peabody. Austin was quite timid and was a great listener. Baz was interested in how my father met Elvis and about the African American culture vibe of Beale Street in the fifties. He was amazed how Beale Street influenced Elvis at an early age.

44   Elvis: The King of Fashion

Julie and I spent a lot of time with Catherine Martin and her team in Memphis. We also have many back and forth emails discussing colours of the fifties and sixties and the various styles we sold Elvis.

The brothers were the first to outfit customers in pink. Men in the fifties and sixties did not wear pink. It was too feminine for the day. We would also like to take credit for the fifties black and pink trend. Elvis loved this colour combination – you can tell by his outfits and even his automobiles.

In 1955, as promised to Gladys in leaner times, Elvis bought a pink Fleetwood Series 60 Cadillac. It remains on permanent display at Graceland's car museum.

The black and pink sport coats and suits and the Milton Berle two-tone sport shirt [so called as he wore it on Berle's TV show] were prominent in the movie.

We sent Catherine Martin many photos of the store on Beale and a lot of other photos, so her set designer could bring fifties Beale Street back to life. She nailed everything she set out to do. She is a real pro and I hope she wins an Oscar for wardrobes and set design.

I ask whether they suspected how big the film would be and whether they'd go to the Oscars.

We knew this movie would be a blockbuster. With Baz and Catherine involved, we knew it would be an international hit, and it has been.

I would love to go to the Oscars; however, we would have a better chance of buying a 300 million dollar lottery ticket.

The amount of attention the film has brought to this historic stalwart of Memphis commerce might just make it feel like they already have.

As it happens, on 12 March 2023, the night of the Oscars (or the 'Scars', as I call them, on account of the agony that unsuccessful nominees must go through when the camera zooms in on their faces, and they have to look not disappointed but thrilled at not winning), *Elvis*, although nominated for a raft of well-earned top awards, including Best Costume Design for Catherine Martin, Best Picture, and Best Actor for Austin Butler, no little gold men came its way. Nothing. Zilch. A surprise, but in the lead-up, Baz and the team had already won a slew of other awards, including a Best Actor Golden Globe for Butler.

Fans were fuming, with many saying that they felt the Oscars had become too 'woke', and others, that the academy favoured older male actors; yet more called the shock result an intentional, elitism-based snub, citing that Elvis,

The Lansky Effect   45

too, had experienced similar condescension in his music career. Despite selling hundreds of millions of records and holding the world record for the greatest number – make that 299 – of Gold, Platinum and Multi-Platinum records, he only received three GRAMMY Awards. All three were in gospel categories, including Best Inspirational Performance in 1974 for a live version of 'How Great Thou Art'.

Facebook really was shaking all over with comments like, 'It's a major disrespect to not only Elvis Presley's legacy, but to all those involved', 'The true honor is not to be awarded with this prize. Things are changing …' To soothe things, fan Jenny O'Dwyer posted a rather mystical message about both Elvis and Austin, saying:

> Think not of him [Elvis] as dead – his soul and spirit are very much alive, especially when listening to his music. That feeling of goosebumps you get when you hear a certain song – or watch 'his' latest movie, called *Elvis* – is when he is with you. Remember, at the end of this movie, Baz swaps the footage of Austin for the live footage of Elvis singing 'Unchained Melody', just after the scene of him as a little boy – everyone has said they cry when that happens. That is because he [Elvis] is there with us, I feel.

This calmed that particular group a little, but for days afterwards, comments like 'Austin was robbed!' and 'Catherine Martin's great outfits should have won!' proliferated on social media.

So, of the many wonderful outfits that Elvis wore – and Martin replicated – over the years, which is Hal Lansky's favourite? Having met him, a man as stylish and as dapper as one would expect the Clothier to The King to be, I feel sure he'll flag up the aforementioned two-tone striped sports coat with velvet collar, shirt and pegged trouser ensemble.

Bingo. Without hesitation, he says:

> It would be the *Jailhouse Rock* outfit – in my opinion that's the most iconic. Of course, people have different ideas, some like the jumpsuits. Some, the gold lamé.
>
> It come from us. He wore that in the movie and he liked it so much, he also wore it as street dress, too.

In early 1953, though, all that was yet to come and, aside from getting his first car – a fifty-dollar 1942 Lincoln Zephyr Coupe from his parents as an eighteenth birthday present – and graduating, Elvis didn't do much more than work a couple of mediocre jobs and sing wherever and whenever he could.

46   Elvis: The King of Fashion

Music-wise, he was still infatuated with myriad genres, especially the all-pervading blues and country. Spiritual churches and all-night gospel sessions were his entertainment; neighbourhood gatherings and parties, his singing outlets. He even did the odd small gig with pals in empty car lots and at small events, and he came second in a talent contest in Mississippi. And still, Memphis didn't notice him. Which wasn't surprising, since, despite his maverick appearance, his intense shyness had not abated and he came across as timid and physically nervy. Even Dixie Locke, whom he'd meet the following year and who adored him in the unconditional manner of a besotted teen, once said that Elvis Presley was the most easily embarrassed boy she ever saw. He was twitchy and jumpy – but this was not all down to nervousness.

Throughout his childhood, although outwardly quiet in public, Elvis was a bundle of energy. Now older, he was positively hyperactive, like a coiled spring, and was still sleeping badly. Constantly in motion, he would drum his fingers on surfaces, tap his feet, hum and move his head and his legs, even when sitting down, to the beat of some subliminal soundtrack playing in his head. He was at his most relaxed when immersed in the city's music scene, especially on Beale, popping into Lansky's or milling around the local record stores, talking to anyone willing to answer his endless questions, and on Saturdays he'd be at the WMPS studio for DJ Bob Neal's *High Noon Round Up*, where the Blackwood Brothers would sing. He harvested insight like a farmer preparing for a storm, seeking advice from the likes of Jake Hess, the incredible singer from the Statesmen with the tempered vibrato. Hess first noticed him in Tupelo.

> We didn't know Elvis Presley from a sack of sand. He was just a nice, nice kid, this bright-eyed boy asking all kinds of questions. …
>
> He wanted to know if he'd be handicapped if he couldn't read music … you know, he just looked important, even as a kid.'

Clubs frequented by predominantly black musicians and customers were Elvis's clandestine playgrounds and their patrons got used to seeing the young, underage white boy hanging around, digging their music and longing to join in.

A stranger to the concept of 'clashing', he was now even more into unconventional colour combinations. Think hot pink with apple green, scarlet with baby blue or claret with canary yellow.

Finally, Elvis had become the butterfly; in fact, he was the whole goddamn rainbow.

Chapter 5

Here Comes the Sun

Memphis 1953–4. Look: Rockabilly Pioneer

'All of a sudden, I just got an urge to go in this recording studio with Mr Sam Phillips at the Memphis Recording Service.'

Elvis

'I don't sound like nobody.'

A yet to be discovered Elvis, 1953

'Elvis opened the door so I could walk through. I thank God for Elvis Presley.'

Little Richard

In July 1953, with his look progressing from trucker to rocker, Elvis walked through another doorway of destiny – one that would be even more life-changing than the last.

Memphis Recording Service, at 706 Union, had only been in business for four years, but word on the street was that its owner, Sam Phillips, was producing songs by the unlikeliest of people in his studio there, and they were selling well. In fact, they were becoming hits.

A pioneer of racial decency with a musical heart, Phillips set up the studio in 1949 to record the raw, straight-from-the-gut type of singers that only the underprivileged and the undermined – white or black, but mainly black – had the experience to do with conviction. Like the Statue of Liberty for music, he held his mic aloft and invited the tired, the poor and the huddled masses to set their voices free. He'd lease recordings to record labels, who'd subsequently release them, and in 1951 he produced 'Rocket '88' (Chess Records) by Jackie Brenston and his Delta Cats (actually Ike Turner and his Kings of Rhythm), which is now considered one of, if not *the*, first ever rock 'n' roll records.

Unsurprisingly, with unashamedly open segregation being the norm, Phillips's modus operandi brought indignation, ostracism and pressure to desist, and he became known as the guy who produced 'them race records'. However, the more his business was denounced, the more determined he was to continue, and the longer he did, the more records he sold. So, taken with the sound of one black doo-wop harmony group, Phillips arranged for them to come to the studio for

48 Elvis: The King of Fashion

a recording session. The Prisonaires were real, hard-time-serving inmates of the Tennessee State Penitentiary, where, luckily for them, the warden embraced prisoner rehabilitation. And so, they were permitted to go to Memphis, escorted by an armed guard and a trustee paid for by Phillips. They started at 10.30 in the morning and worked until 10.30 at night – wearing leg chains throughout. From this remarkable and historic moment, came their hit song 'Just Walkin' in the Rain', and its success saw them signed to the Sun Records label with a view to producing more singles.

Phillips was a talented radio broadcaster, engineer and producer who left high school when his father died, shelving plans to be a lawyer, to take a paying job in radio to support his family. Like Elvis, he was a dreamer who was crazy about music, especially African American music. The son of a tenant farmer, he too grew up surrounded by gospel and spiritual music, his source being the songs of the black field croppers and their church hymns. Even as a boy, he sensed the inequity between white and black people and would ponder what his life would be like, had he been black. As time passed, his unease grew, particularly in church, where the morality of the preaching seemed hypocritical to him.

In a 2001 interview, Phillips, then 78, told Alex Halberstadt, 'When I was growing up, I wanted to be a criminal defence lawyer, because I saw so many people, especially black people, railroaded.' As an adult, he mused on how he could use his audio skills to give black musicians the same opportunities as white ones. Yes, it was magnanimity, but it was also a desire to expose the American public to the sounds that excited and entertained the fringes of society, while rarely reaching the ears of those beyond.

'All he wanted to record was black artists. That was where his heart and soul lied [sic],' says Sam's son, Jerry Phillips. 'He really did feel that they were not getting the attention they deserved.'

Despite having a young family and a job at WREC radio, located in the Peabody Hotel's Skyway Ballroom, Phillips, never one to let an idea simmer when it could boil, shared his vision with his assistant, Marion Keisker. Also a talented radio writer, producer and broadcaster, whose voice was known all over Memphis, Keisker loved his idea, but then, it's widely agreed that she also loved Sam. Encouraged, he searched for a way to make the dream a reality and found it in the shape of an odd little building close to WREC, where they worked. As soon as Phillips clapped eyes on the place, he knew he had to have it. He also knew that he could make it work as a studio but that it would likely mean quitting his job. It was a risk, but it was also a sign that it was time to leap into the unknown – ideally while holding Marion Keisker's reassuring hand. With a tin ceiling and irregular walls, it didn't exactly lend itself to a pioneering experiment in sound recording, but they raised funds and set about transforming

Here Comes the Sun   49

it. They ripped out the roof and, working to Sam's exacting criteria, applied acoustic tiles to crucial areas.

Peter Guralnick, in his book *Sam Phillips: The Man Who Invented Rock 'n' Roll*, writes:

> Over and over he paced the studio, starting in the corners, working his way toward the center, clapping his hands and listening to the reverberation until he was certain that there was enough 'liveness' in every square inch of the room, 'to where it [would] sound real—R-E-A-L—when it went into the microphone'.

On 3 January 1950, with neon signage in place, venetian blinds to lend an air of mystique and the acoustics as close to perfection as he could get, the Memphis Recording Service opened for business. Two years later, having leased his recordings to various music distributors, Phillips launched his own label, Sun Records, and changed the studio name to match.

Today, it is still a recording venue, and to music pilgrims, especially those of the rock 'n' roll persuasion, it's one of the holiest of shrines. The preserved inner sanctum still lies within the original, small, redbrick building that had previously been a car repair business. Its awkwardly shaped, vaguely triangular façade hides a treasure trove of artefacts, ephemera, modern merchandise and original recording-studio gadgetry that's the stuff of dreams for vintage technology fans. Listen carefully and you can almost hear the lingering voices of its earliest stars – the industry's mightiest practitioners of rhythm and blues and of the formative rock 'n' roll that was the soundtrack of the '50s kissing goodbye to bland balladeering. As well as Howlin' Wolf, B.B. King and Little Milton vibes, there's an echo of Carl Perkins' 'Blue Suede Shoes', Johnny Cash's 'Cry, Cry, Cry' and of Elvis telling his mama 'That's All Right'.

While working at WREC, one of Sam Phillips's jobs was to pre-record live swing band performances to be broadcast later. Being an out-and-proud sound geek, he was less interested in what the concerts sounded like than he was in creating exquisite recordings of them. Now, at last, he had his very own studio, which he frequently referred to as his 'laboratory'.

The 'race' records sold well, although mainly to black fans and not well enough to make a living. Entrenched prejudice thwarted his efforts and, under pressure to survive, he became fixated on breaking down the barriers and attracting white music fans – who had all the money, after all – to his artists. As he racked his brain for the answer, the then-unknown Mississippi teen with a dream walked in.

Elvis had no doubt heard or read in the local paper that Sam Phillips's Memphis Recording Service ('We Record Anything – Anywhere – Anytime')

50   Elvis: The King of Fashion

had been recording 'strange visitors', including The Prisonaires, so he decided he'd fit right in and drove past in his truck a few times to have a look. He would also have known that, for a few dollars, anybody could go to the studio and record a song or a special message for someone. When he finally found the courage to go inside, he told them he was there to record a birthday song for his mum.

Gladys's birthday had been a few months before, so perhaps it was a calculated move. What he longed to make was a *real* record, but he hadn't enough confidence to say so. The 'birthday treat' was a foot in the door, with a glimmer of hope that maybe Mr Phillips would be there and would hear him sing and be instantly blown away. Instead of Phillips, it was Marion Keisker who looked up from the desk and greeted him. She noticed that he was a bag of nerves, gripping his child's guitar like grim death. Factor in his poor complexion, lank hair and scruffy work attire, he would have hardly come across as a star in waiting. Keisker later said that he looked like a boy who'd worked all day. To be fair, right then, that's exactly what Elvis was.

So much for the butterfly effect …

As well as the song for his mother conversation, at some point Elvis asked Marion whether she knew of anyone who needed a singer. The exchange that followed is now carved deep into the face of Rock 'n' Roll History Mountain, but let's revel in it anyway. In an interview more than thirty years after the event and featured in Channel 5's documentary *Elvis: The Man Who Shook Up the World*, Marion relates the legendary exchange:

> The thing I always notice first about a person, first I notice the eyes, mouth and the hands, and of course, Elvis's remarkable eyes and that strange little half smile hovering there and his hands – very tense around his guitar.
>
> The conversation, as best I recall it, was, 'You know anybody looking for singer?' and I think I said, 'What kind of singer are you?' and he just said, 'Well I sing everything.'
>
> I said, 'Who do you sing like?'
>
> 'I don't sing like nobody.'
>
> And I just thought, oh dear.

One can almost feel Keisker's eyebrow arch.

This was no cockiness on Elvis's part – he was hard-wired to be indecently respectful – it was genuine humility. Regardless of his then eclectic, small gig music repertoire, he believed that the road to success lay in crooning – a touch of Nat, a smidgen of Dean, possibly some Bing; however, he'd never have dared suggest that he sounded like any big stars. The other reason was because he really *didn't* sound like anyone else, although that would have been impossible

Here Comes the Sun   51

for him to articulate. How could one so timid explain that what he sounded like was eighteen years of insanely diverse musical influences, all shook up to form a uniquely expressive voice, the likes of which had never been heard before?

So, Elvis paid his four dollars and recorded an acetate of two songs, 'My Happiness' and 'That's When Your Heartaches Begin'. When he was done, Keisker typed his name and the song titles on the blank reverse side of a used Sun label and stuck it on. Elvis left with the pressing, without having caught a whiff of Sam Phillips.

Keisker made a note of his name and phone number and after he'd left, either on a whim or with Lansky-style insight, she added the words 'Good ballad singer. Hold' to it.

Elvis took the freshly minted disc to his friend Ed Leek's house to play it on his record player and, clearly unimpressed with his own efforts, left it there. According to Leek's niece, Lorisa Hilburn, her Uncle Ed had kept it safe and in perfect condition for decades; when it was discovered after his death, it was still playable. 'We didn't know he still had it,' she said. 'It just sat in the safe. Nobody in the family ever saw the record.'

Hilburn put the extraordinarily rare dubplate into an auction at Elvis's last home, Graceland, in January 2015. 'I'm hoping that somebody who loves Elvis Presley and is a huge Elvis Presley fan and who can appreciate the record … ends up with it,' she said.

That the record sold to an anonymous bidder for $300,000 is notable in itself, considering its original $4 price tag. However, what makes the story even more interesting is that the mystery shopper turned out to be musician Jack White, formerly of The White Stripes and a huge Elvis fan.

Elvis's voice on the record is disarmingly earnest and hopeful, achingly naïve and tremulous. Hearing it recently at Sun Studio, formerly Memphis Recording Service, the building where it was created and where Sun Records remains an active label to this day, caused the hairs on the back of my neck stand up. It's truly affecting. Sort of melancholic, like listening to a wistful ghost (similar to the sound of his later, though still early, Sun recording of 'Blue Moon'), and heavy with longing and unfulfilled dreams. The fragility reminds one of just how young and inexperienced he was when, come the following year, he'd be catapulted directly into a spotlight that would never switch off, placing his life in the public domain until his dying day – and beyond.

As raw as both song and singer are, there's clear evidence of the startling vocal dexterity that would define him and, since being deeply analysed, has been deemed highly unusual. Of course, at the time Elvis had no idea he possessed this natural gift. On 'That's Where Your Heartaches Begin', the spoken bridge is delivered in a deep baritone that sounds like someone else entirely. However,

52   Elvis: The King of Fashion

it's when he switches to tenor, then to high falsetto without pause, that the chills happen.

At the time of the 2015 auction, Jayne Ellen Brooks, PR director at Sun Studio, said of the record, 'As far as the song choice goes, it's really interesting. It sort of sums up Elvis, pre-fame.' White cherishes the priceless acetate, the holy grail of Elvis memorabilia, and keeps it cocooned in a vault at his Nashville recording studio. While being interviewed there by author and podcaster Malcolm Gladwell, for the *Revisionist History Podcast*, White asks Gladwell if he'd like to hold it. He declines, admitting on the podcast that he was too terrified to say yes.

A month after acquiring it, White took it to music archivist Alan Stoker at Nashville's Country Music Hall of Fame, who digitally transferred the rare recording. During the process, they noticed the makeshift, typewritten paper label was peeling away from the record. White gingerly prised back the loose edge with a knife and there, on its underside, was the yellow Sun Records label, still bright and printed with the title 'Soft and Tender' by The Prisonaires – a poignant reminder of the studio's vision and diversity – and an early example of Marion Keisker's fiscal efficiency, aka recycling skills.

For Elvis, nothing came of that Memphis Recording Service session, but he took to hanging around the studio anyway, digging the music, watching performers record and, as always, soaking up everything. He hadn't found fame, but in January 1954, he found love, in the shape of Dixie Locke. They met at church and he was sure he'd marry her. Her friends found him odd, *she* found him odd, with his fidgety ticks, long greasy hair and black-and-pink outfits. Still, she was intrigued. 'He was just so different – all the other guys were replicas of their dads,' she said. Imagine the conservative early 1950s skate rink crowd's reaction when, having heard Dixie loudly announce that she was going there, Elvis unexpectedly turned up rocking a bullfighter's bolero jacket, black trousers with pink stripes down the sides and a ruffled shirt.

Mainly through Dixie, since Gladys and Vernon had somewhat fallen away from church, he also found new and exciting forms of worship. They attended the fire-and-brimstone-fuelled First Assembly Church at McLemore Avenue, with the Blackwood Brothers on tap, and would often steal away to East Trigg Baptist Church for the rousing prayers and to hear the Reverend Harper Brewster tell his congregation, 'When grace is in, race is out,' and without fail, they went along to the monthly all-night gospel sessions at Ellis Auditorium, close to Lauderdale Courts.

Come April that year, Elvis found a permanent job at the Crown Electric Company on Poplar Avenue. In *Elvis in His own Words*, he told Bob Abel:

Here Comes the Sun   53

I got outta school and was driving a truck. I was training as an electrician because they made three dollars an hour. I was very serious about it. I [only] made that first record as a personal thing for my mother.

In May, Dixie was taken aback when Elvis announced that he was going to the Hi-Hat Club to try out as a singer for a guy called Eddie Bond and he needed her to go with him. She would have been flabbergasted had he said he was auditioning with a gospel group but the Hi-Hat Club? That was an African American blues joint! Dixie was terrified someone would see her going in and tell her parents. However, love conquers all, so she agreed to go.

Dressed in his bolero outfit with a pink frilly shirt, he was more nervous than she'd ever seen him. They cowered in a corner and drank Coke; she was mortified at how much Elvis was twitching and drumming his hands. Finally, he talked to the band leader, got up on stage and sang two songs. Although Dixie thought he was brilliant, Bond did not. He told him he should stick to driving a truck, because he couldn't sing. When he was a big star, Elvis often thought about what Bond would say then. En route to California to make *Jailhouse Rock*, less than three years since the brutal post-audition advice, he told his pal George Klein, 'Man, that sonofabitch broke my heart.'

Back at Memphis Recording Service, Keisker had grown fond of Elvis, as he seemed so childlike and unaffected. She'd seen beyond his strange look and seemed to get him; they'd talk about this and that and he even recorded two further acetates. Sam Phillips, however, was still too preoccupied to notice him, probably because he was under pressure to make Sun Records work. Although he'd scored a hit with Rufus Thomas's gloriously bitchy, cat-screech intro'd 'Bear Cat' single (the blues singer's male response to Big Mama Thornton's 1952 'Hound Dog'), and had potential winners lined up with The Prisonaires and Little Junior Parker's 'Feelin' Good', sales still weren't cutting it. Unfortunately for Phillips, 'Bear Cat' was so similar to 'Hound Dog', that the legal powers behind the latter's writers, Jerry Leiber and Mike Stoller, won a lawsuit claiming that it infringed copyright.

Good things come to those who wait, though, and almost a year after his first recording, as had been written in the stars, Elvis and Sam's worlds finally collided. After a mix of pestering and nudging from Marion, Sam had found a song he felt would suit the kid's pensive style and decided to give him a try. Elvis said:

That same company [Memphis Recording Service] called me a year later and said, 'We got a song that you might be able to do.'
It was twelve o'clock. They said, 'Can you be here by three o'clock?'
I was there by the time they hung up the phone.

54 Elvis: The King of Fashion

In later years, Elvis always joked about how he became an overnight success – after a year. Sam later said, 'Elvis was probably as nervous as anybody, black or white, that I had seen in front of a microphone.'

Song and singer did not gel, but now paying attention and sensing something indefinably unusual about the boy, Sam threw him a lifeline. He called guitarist Scotty Moore and upright bass player Bill Black, local musicians and members of the Starlight Wranglers band, and asked them to audition Elvis then let him know their thoughts. Sam warned them that the kid was a bit odd. Moore and Black said that when they heard his name, they assumed it was made up.

Scotty Moore called Elvis and invited him over for a trial at his house on Belz Avenue. No doubt hoping to make an impression, he turned up in pink trousers, with trademark stripes down the sides, this time in black, a black shirt and black-and-white two-tone shoes. Despite the showy appearance, he was beyond nervous and came across as painfully shy throughout. Still, he played his guitar and sang a selection of songs by the likes of popular country singer Hank Snow, and jazz and pop singer Billy Eckstine.

His outlandish get-up did not impress Scotty and Bill, nor did the singing much. Reporting back to Sam, Scotty said, 'Elvis had a good voice, but he didn't knock me out.' As non-committal as the comment was, they didn't hate him and that was enough for Sam to ask the three of them to come to the studio and try recording something.

On 5 July, Elvis finished work at Crown Electric and went to the studio. A series of unfruitful tryouts of an endless stream of potential songs ensued, with Elvis enthusing neither Sam nor Scotty and Bill, seasoned players who could make just about any song fizz. They all agreed his voice was good, but everything they tried just felt lacklustre, pedestrian, familiar. Attributes that Sam had hoped the timid youngster might have had buried within him – grit, rage, something wild, anything – failed to materialise. He'd wanted primal, untamed, fresh. What he got was ballads. 'No', 'Nope' and 'Try again' were frequent comments.

As Elvis's despondency increased, so too did Sam's frustration. Nevertheless, like a dog with a bone, he remained patient with his potential apprentice. He held his tongue and at one point looked the youngster right in the eyes – possibly searching into his soul – and quietly reassured him that he was doing just fine. During a particularly draining episode, Sam called a break and fiddled around in the studio while Scotty and Bill let off steam and messed around with Elvis, who jumped up and down like a hyperactive genie released from a lamp. Out of the blue and in a bolder, higher, more erratic, hitherto unheard voice, he began belting out lines from one of his favourite blues songs, 'That's All Right', recorded by one of his musical heroes, Arthur Crudup, back in 1946. Scotty and Bill fell in behind with guitar and tonal-slap bass.

Here Comes the Sun   55

Sam stopped dead. He may even have stopped breathing. He asked Elvis how the hell he knew the obscure Big Boy Crudup number, which he himself loved, and then told all three of them to rewind and start again. So they did. And right then, all of them knew that the real Elvis, the one Phillips had always felt was there, had entered the building.

As Scotty Moore recalled much later in the liner notes on RCA's *Sunrise* album:

All of a sudden, Elvis just started singing this song and acting the fool, and then Bill Black picked up his bass and he started acting the fool, too, and I started playing with them.

Sam, I think had the door to the control booth open, and he stuck his head out and said, 'What are you doing?' And we said, 'We don't know.' 'Well, back up,' he said, 'try to find a place to start, and do it again.'

That almost accidental interpretation of the song was transformative. It changed things, it changed Elvis, exposing his true character – as much to himself as to others.

Listening to the original recording today, from the galloping guitar intro and his first proclamation that 'that's all right', to the final defiant stroke of the strings, it sounds dynamic and fresh, unlike anything that had come before. And there's a muffled fury to it, which I can't help but feel is aimed at everything and everyone who'd ever suppressed, misunderstood or belittled him.

Suddenly, Sam Phillips had something unique on his hands, something bright and multi-toned, young and pure one minute, sultry and knowing the next. With an almighty roar, Elvis's dream had moved closer to becoming a reality. He didn't know that at the time, though, and 'conscientious' being his middle name, he went back to work as normal the following day.

Sam was convinced that he had found vocal nirvana, though he was uncertain about how others would react as Elvis's sound was just so damn unusual. He decided to go straight for the acid test. On 7 July, he took a freshly pressed copy to Memphis's best-loved disc jockey, Dewey Phillips (no relation), who ruled the airways with his madcap banter and deranged jokes and was considered the god of cool sounds. A frontline radio pioneer in his twenties, he was obsessed with music. On his hugely followed late-night WHBQ show, *Red, Hot & Blues*, live from the Hotel Chisca, he played a mix of black and white, but predominantly and unapologetically, black blues records. Live studio guests regularly included B.B. King and Muddy Waters. Defiantly transracial, he could go anywhere, anytime and be welcomed with open arms and he was a hero to Beale Street's black community. Rufus Thomas, then a DJ at the WDIA radio station, said

56   Elvis: The King of Fashion

that Dewey was a man who just happened to be white. Even Sam Phillips called him a genius – not a word he used lightly.

Dewey needed to personally love a record before he'd even consider playing it and was known to tear discs off the turntable mid-play and smash them on the floor if he tired of listening to them. He and Sam were friends, they admired one another, but Sam knew that Dewey never pulled his punches when it came to music, so he was anxious about how he'd react to 'That's All Right'. His conviction that he'd found the key to tearing down entrenched barriers – a singing wrecking ball who transcended race, who crossed the line and who would appeal to all music fans – was all very well. However, he knew that if Dewey didn't rate Elvis, it would be a lost cause. He also knew that if he liked him, it could be the making of his new artist and, more importantly, it might just save his business.

Dewey played the record a couple of times in silence, which was highly unusual. To Sam, this meant that he either hated it but was working out how to tell him that his protégé was crap, or – just maybe – that he loved it.

It was the latter.

Dewey played it on his show that night and the phones lit up like Beale Street on a Saturday evening. He spun it a few more times – in fact, altogether he played it an unheard of fourteen times, and things went crazy. He phoned the Presleys and told them to get their boy Elvis into the studio immediately for an interview. Having been warned by Sam that his song might get played that night, Elvis was so anxious that he went to the cinema rather than tune in. Gladys hotfooted it down there and got him out, telling him, 'Dewey wants you on the radio – right now!'

When Elvis arrived, he said, 'I don't know nothin' about doing interviews.' Dewey told him, 'Just don't say anything dirty,' then suggested they could talk between records. What he didn't tell Elvis was that the mic was on 'live' the entire time. Blissfully unaware and although stuttering and speaking quietly, he was relaxed answering Dewey's rapid-fire questions. When asked which high school he'd gone to and Elvis replied 'Humes High', the world stopped. It being the time of segregated schools meant that in every home, car, bar and café tuned into Dewey Phillips's show that night, people, regardless of colour or creed, looked at one another in disbelief and said something along the lines of, 'Wait, Elvis Presley is *white*?'

Attempting to sum up Elvis's unique and derivative sound at the time, Sam Phillips said, 'He sings Negro songs with a white voice which borrows in mood from, and emphasis from the country style, modified by popular music. It's a blend of all of them.' In other words, it was exactly what he'd had been praying for and although Elvis couldn't' have put it into words himself, it was exactly how he naturally sang. They were going to get along just fine.

Sam's son, Jerry Phillips, said, 'Sam and Elvis were kindred spirits because Elvis was into all the records my dad was recording, B.B. King, Howlin' Wolf, Roscoe Gordon, Ike Turner ... Elvis was listening to all that stuff.'

Having found their mojo, things moved like an express train. They'd already recorded a fast-paced, rockabilly version of Bill Monroe's bluegrass song 'Blue Moon of Kentucky' – a perfect flipside to 'That's All Right'. On 11 July, studio house drummer Johnny Bernero joined them and they recorded a sublimely evocative version of Junior Parker's hypnotic 'Mystery Train'. In the middle of all this, a shell-shocked Elvis and his similarly stunned parents signed a one-year contract with Scotty Moore. He, Elvis and Bill Black were now a trio of sorts.

On 19 July, 'That's All Right'/'Blue Moon of Kentucky' was officially released and promptly sold 20,000 copies. It was time for Sam to unleash his secret weapon on an unsuspecting world.

Chapter 6

Part I
Prelude: Elvis Has Entered the Building

Overton Park Shell theatre, Memphis, 30 July 1954.
Look: Hillbilly Cat

'Rock and roll music, if you like it, if you feel it, you can't help but move to it. That's what happens to me. I can't help it.'

Elvis

After walking onto Overton Park Shell's vast stage and taking in the size of the crowd, Elvis stood still for once in his life.

His appearance on that hot July night in '54 was momentous. Not just because it was his first truly professional gig, but because the course of music history had hung in limbo while Elvis, crippled with an extreme case of stage fright, had almost refused to go on. Despite frantic reassurances from Team Gladys, Vernon and Dixie, and sundry other family members, his anxiety levels had been so bad that he shook from head to toe and he couldn't face going on stage. It was only after a fraught, make that desperate, pep talk from Sam Phillips, who arrived late to find Elvis quaking on the back steps of the Shell building, that he was finally convinced to perform. Even then – barely three weeks since 'That's All Right' had hit the airwaves and been released – as an inexperienced lad who'd only played to small, mainly supportive or even vaguely ambivalent audiences around town, it would have been overwhelming.

Sharing the bill with a raft of seasoned and idolised performers, including a headlining Slim Whitman, yet, being so little-known that he was listed as *Ellis* Presley, couldn't have helped his imposter syndrome either.

And the crowd was big. Really big.

As he approached the mic, his mouth was bone-dry and the shaking had kicked in again with a vengeance. Scotty Moore was only half kidding when he said that Elvis's knees were knocking so loud they could almost hear them. Sam held his breath, they all did. He hadn't the slightest idea how his new prodigy would perform. Sure, he knew that the kid could sing, but that was about it, and

Part I Prelude: Elvis Has Entered the Building 59

he'd only managed to get him on stage by saying, with no basis for it whatsoever, that the crowd would love him. Later, he admitted that telling Elvis that was a bit like knowing someone's mother is sick but telling them everything is going to be all right, even though it's quite possible the mother might die.

DJ Bob Neal, who would be Elvis's manager by the following year, introduced Elvis, Scotty and Bill, none of whom had ever experienced such a daunting venue as the Shell, with its amphitheatre-like construct. There are very few images of Elvis that night. Of those that do exist, none is of him on stage, and all are black and white. However, in a shot of him backstage with 4-year-old fan Charlie Torian Jr., who's wearing a little cowboy outfit, we get an idea of Elvis's stage wear. He's dressed to impress in what's said to have been a pale pink ensemble. The first thing that stands out is the two-tone tie with its bold vertical stripes, and stars running down the centre. It might have been fashioned from a scarf, since the end is straight, wide and looks frayed; it hangs loose round an open-collared white shirt that's under what looks like a fine wool or cotton jacket with unusual – read as Lansky-style – gathered, buttoned-back sleeves. In another shot, he's holding his guitar with his leg on a chair, so his trousers, which would soon cause a motion-based commotion, have ridden up to reveal jazzy diamond-patterned socks, which would no doubt have matched the colours of his outfit.

In a poignant twist of fate, when Charlie Torian grew up, he actually became a Memphis police officer, and on 17 August 1977, was one of the honour guard sergeants who watched over Elvis's coffin while he lay in rest at Graceland the day after he died.

But at that moment, in Overton Park, Elvis was young and full of hope, as well as fear, and so, with sideburns sharp, hair still it's original dusty blond colour – slightly curling in the heat – and greased into a ducktail, or DA, he certainly looked ready to roll, even if he didn't feel it. Grasping the mic tight enough to whiten his knuckles, he stood on the balls of his feet in an attempt to stop his legs from trembling. All it did was make them shake some more.

'We were all scared to death,' said Scotty. 'Here we come with two funky little instruments and a whole park full of people … and Elvis, well he was kind of jiggling.'

Suddenly, 'That's All Right' burst out of Elvis like fizz from a shaken bottle, and once it was out, he was unstoppable. At turns high-pitched and wailing, at others languorous, he moved to the beat and, wait for it, he looked *confident*.

And then things got crazy. Scotty explained, 'Those old loose britches that he wore … they had lots of material and pleated fronts, you shook your leg, and it made it look like all hell was going on under there.'

60   Elvis: The King of Fashion

To the crowd, it must have seemed like an alien had landed in Memphis. There was no backstory to this odd boy. They didn't understand what they were seeing, let alone the strange sound they were hearing, but they understood that they liked it – especially the women. It wasn't white, it wasn't black, and it sure as hell wasn't crooning. It was the nebulous but unmistakable reverberations of juke joints and desire, of having sex and loving it.

Then Elvis, legs bent and spread wide apart in the manner of a labourer about to raise a lump hammer in a chain gang, rather than an acoustic guitar on a stage, began to move. Although he was unaware that anything was happening and that the wild gyrating going on in the trouser department was as much to do with the nature of the cloth as the nature of the boy, to the audience, it was absolutely, gloriously scandalous.

Was it rockabilly? Was it country? Was it what would be called rock and roll? Whatever it was, his uncontrollable twitching looked sensual and dangerous and had much the same effect on the teenagers as an overdose of catnip on felines. This was something new, something forbidden, something normally kept behind closed doors – and it represented a moment of awakening that pressed buttons they never knew they had.

That's when the screaming started.

Elvis's rebellious manifestation was further compounded by a completely involuntary lip curl, which although he'd later adopt it as a trademark, was then yet another of his ticks, a visual sign of fear. Whatever. A line had been crossed; some called it innocence lost, others, paradise found.

In his musical abandon he didn't notice the reaction at first, though when he did, his fears became manifest and thoughts raced through his mind as to why they were hollering at him. Was it Humes High all over again? Were they making fun of him? Were they trying to drown him out, make him look stupid? Did he sound terrible?

Sam and Marion Keisker, who'd joined the crowd, were both gobsmacked. Apart from a bit of rocking to the backbeat during recording sessions, there had been no hint of the wild shapes that Elvis was now throwing. Not a hip had swiveled, nor a leg shaken in their studio sessions. That was because he was relaxed at the studio and comfortable in their company; history had not yet taught them that Elvis's wiggling was down to abject terror. It was no unsteady hand; it was an uncontrollable, full-body quake.

Mirroring the crowd, Elvis was also shocked and confused – but by the girls' loud hollering. When the trio performed the next song, 'Blue Moon of Kentucky', with its fast-rolling train rhythm and Elvis's vocal gymnastics, they got the same reaction. Panicking, he asked Scotty and Bill why the hell they were all shrieking at him, but they were as baffled as he was.

Standing on that stage recently, with my husband and Cole Early, Archives Manager at the Shell, it was easy to imagine how daunting it would have been for Elvis, Scotty and Bill. A magnificent piece of engineering it may be, but, with only three of us, it felt huge. Cole offers an insight into why the screaming was particularly unsettling and confusing for Elvis and the boys:

> The concentric circle design of the stage naturally projects well out to the audience, but it also super-concentrates sound coming into it from the audience.
>
> So the spontaneous uproar of the crowd screaming would have been heightened for Elvis on stage by the acoustics of the stage design itself.
>
> My understanding is that the Greek root *amphi-* in the word amphitheatre roughly means both ways.

Elvis told a reporter, 'I came offstage, and my manager told me that they was hollering because I was wiggling my legs. I went out for an encore and, the more I did, the wilder they went.'

Later in the show they returned to the stage and performed the same two numbers again, along with 'I'll Never Let You Go (Little Darlin')', a new number they'd been trying out for size.

Now aware of the power of the trouser effect, Elvis continued to do his thing and do it brilliantly, safe in the knowledge that the screams were ones of approval.

Part II
Tearing Up the House

1954–5. Look: Stripped Back

'I never even thought of singing as a career. Ah, in fact, I was ashamed to sing in front of anybody – except my mother and daddy.'

Elvis

Barely had the echoes of Overton's noisy ovations drifted into the ether, than Elvis was back driving his truck, being Dixie's boyfriend and playing small venues, while dreaming of playing big ones. Meanwhile, Sam Phillips sustained the momentum of Elvis's performance by travelling miles across the South, his car stuffed with the latest Sun Records releases, including 'That's All Right', to sell to distributors, record store owners, jukebox suppliers and DJs – anyone who'd spread the sound of Elvis far and wide. Having now seen him perform as well as heard him sing, Sam had decided Elvis was perfect – unheard, unseen and unspoiled, like a diamond accidentally found in the dirt and which, after a good buffing, would be ready to shine.

Small-fry stuff and Overton aside, Elvis had never played anywhere, other than in his own bedroom with his old guitar, before he had walked into Memphis Recording Service. Navigating the South's high streets and hinterlands, Sam decided that it was Elvis's innocence that was so compelling. He wasn't that eloquent, but when he said things in his own, unaffected way, Sam knew exactly what he meant. And he knew that it came from a bright intelligence, somewhat lost in the depths of poverty.

Sam's trade patch being home to entrenched country and western, hillbilly, bluegrass and swing fans, the responses to Elvis's record ranged from hostility, through bewilderment to mild curiosity. His contacts trusted him, though, so he spoke honestly to them, telling them that he believed Elvis was special and that his unconventional sound was where – like it or not – music was heading. It paid off and most of them agreed to give him a spin.

Talking to the *Memphis Press-Scimitar*, Marion Keisker reported, 'We've just gotten the sample records out to the disk [*sic*] jockeys and distributors in other cities … we [already] got big orders from Dallas and Atlanta.'

Part II Tearing Up the House   63

Also keeping the ball rolling post-Overton was Scotty, who'd got them further bookings under their new name, The Blue Moon Boys. The best of these was a regular spot at Memphis's Eagle's Nest, a small and lively nightclub on Lamar Avenue, near the airport, and overseen by a promoter called Sleepy-Eyed John. It was atop (hence the name) the Clearpool leisure and pool complex and was favoured by white middle-class country and swing band crowds.

Their first appearance on the tiny stage was on 7 August 1954, a mere month after Dewey smashed up the airwaves playing 'That's All Right' on a loop. It would have been all the sweeter, knowing that the record had just received a glowing review in *Billboard*:

Presley is a potent new chanter who can sock over a tune for either the country or the rhythm and blues markets. On this new disc, he comes through with a solid performance on an r & b and blues type tune and then on the flipside does another fine job with a country ditty. A strong new chart talent.

Having only heard this new kid on the block, little did the reviewer on the sacred commenter on music of the day realise that, underpinning Elvis's hip new take on popular genres was a deep-rooted foundation and passion for an altogether more fervent musical style – gospel. Nor could they have known that the physical manifestation of said influence had already been witnessed, albeit by a small Memphian minority, in the startling moves that accompanied his singing – moves that would cast a shadow of controversy over his early career, but would ultimately accelerate him to unprecedented levels of fame, unmatched by any solo performer before or since.

Asked by Bob Abel, in his 1972 interview, what he thought of those controversial moves when he later saw the recordings, Elvis laughed nervously and said it was embarrassing. Presumably looking at a photo of himself, he says, 'Here it's like I was having an epileptic fit – they just happened to film it.'

Asked how old he was, he says, 'about 19'. And on what happened to all his movements, he replies, 'I guess I learned better after a while.' Which, sadly, seems to mean that he'd no longer, or perhaps never had, fully appreciated the wonder of his younger self.

Playing the Eagle's Nest most weekends, the trio gained confidence and, despite Elvis's outré, some called it 'pretty boy' appearance, the comprising willfully flamboyant outfits and anything but red-neck-friendly make up, they attracted a strong following, drawn to their unique sound and underground feel. Gladys, Vernon, Dixie and other family members would go to see the boys play.

64   Elvis: The King of Fashion

At one August performance, maybe that first one, Gladys's sister, Clettes, wife of Vernon's brother, Vester, took photos of a young-looking Elvis outside the club. He's 19, with the world at his feet. 'That's All Right' is all over the radio and is selling like ice-cold Coke on a sweltering day. Dirty blond hair slicked back, face tanned and hands on hips, he's leaning against the Eagle's Nest sign looking relaxed, the shyness seemingly gone. There's already a hint of continuity to his style – two-tone shoes, two-tone polo shirt, collar up, of course. The pale (I'm guessing pink), cropped jacket with revere collar pays lip service to his favourite bolero style but it's nipped in at the waist, blouson style. The trousers are dark and baggy, freedom of movement is all, the waist outlined by a skinny belt. It's a daring look for the era, not quite rock star, but certainly no longer truck driver. At later gigs, he'd wear the striking black-and-white striped coat with black velvet collar, the one that Hal Lansky described as a favourite Elvis look and which Elvis would later wear in some pre-prison scenes in his 1957 movie *Jailhouse Rock*.

Guy Lansky, Hal's uncle, recalled the time Elvis asked him to cash a cheque for him as he didn't have a bank account:

> I think it was $500, from Sam Phillips. Elvis asked me to cash it, then bought some clothes [including the coat], and some new jewellery.
>
> I was wary about it because of his appearance, and remember running to the bank to see if the cheque was good.
>
> Years later, after he got Graceland, I used to take my kids out there and I remember he showed me the sports coat from years before. Boy, he loved that coat, it was still in his closet.

Elvis's unusual appearance even came up when he was job-hunting. Before Jim and Gladys Tipler, who owned Crown Electric, interviewed him, they were pre-warned by the employment agency to ignore what he looked like, because he was 'a nice boy, really'. When he turned up, they didn't like what they saw, but they did like his polite manner, so they gave him the job anyway – and suggested a hairdresser he might like to try. They began to go along to the Eagle's Nest, too, and took friends and business associates with them. In the end, they were proud of Elvis and savoured being part of his fledgling success.

Throughout that August, Elvis would pop into the Memphis Recording Service office to see Marion Keisker to find out how his record was selling and talk about this and that. Marion was fond of him in a maternal way and, like Sam, believed that he was special; that he had a 'magical quality' that cocooned him and brought out the best in others. This indefinable characteristic, evident from a young age, has been mentioned by many who knew Elvis.

Part II Tearing Up the House   65

'He was like a mirror in a way,' said Marion. 'Whatever you were looking for you were going to find in him. It was not in him to say anything malicious. He had all the intricacy of the very simple.' By this, she meant simple as in refreshingly uncomplicated, not in any derogatory way. Elvis remained grateful to her all his life and frequently credited her with giving him his first break.

Sam, an anxious, driven worrier who had experienced bouts of mental illness, also saw his own reflection in the insecurity that motivated Elvis. He described him as being imbued with the essence of the poor South, and in *Last Train To Memphis*, Peter Guralnick, said of him, 'He conveyed his spirituality without being able or needing to express it. And all these adults with their more complicated lives and dreams and passions and hopes looked for themselves in his simplicity.'

Whatever Elvis had, others wanted a piece of it; they still do. He is often described as having been extraordinarily engaging, saintly, a king, even godlike. Although he earnestly searched throughout his adult life for an explanation for the fame that came to him, Elvis was very modest and humble. In his Vegas years, on spotting a fan at a concert who was holding up a sign calling him 'The King', he acknowledged it and thanked her, but said, 'I'm not the King. Jesus Christ is the King. I'm just an entertainer.'

Back to the summer of '54, and sales of 'That's All Right' were booming, eventually hitting 20,000, taking it into the national charts. *The national charts!* For a boy often too shy to talk, let alone sing, in front of people, this had huge implications. And, often, it was the flipside, the wildly catchy 'Blue Moon of Kentucky', that drove the sales. As well as the positive review, *Billboard* ran an article about a new upstart label in Memphis called Sun Records and its hot young artist, Elvis Presley. This piqued the interest of major record producers and distributors, many of whom knew Sam Phillips and all of whom had an eye on what was suddenly going on in that little corner of the South.

Brad McCuen, an RCA field salesman covering mid-Tennessee into Virginia and the Carolinas, kept hearing the name Elvis, and in Knoxville, where the record was flying, visited record shop owner Sam Morrison, whose store was in the market place. He had a loudspeaker over the door that piped music into the crowd, who would then come and buy his records. He told McCuen that something weird was happening and put the Elvis record on. Immediately, customers started arriving. Morrison told him that he was selling at least a box a day.

McCuen was baffled. 'But it's just a normal rhythm 'n' blues record, isn't it?'

'No,' replied Morrison, 'it's selling to a country audience.'

McCuen bought two copies. He sent one to Steve Sholes, an RCA big wig and also their country and western promotions director who had signed the

66 Elvis: The King of Fashion

likes of Jim Reeves and Elvis favourite, Hank Snow, to the label. Sholes seemed to get Elvis – his bosses did not. This random series of events turned out to be twists of fate and while not rolling, the ball was definitely rocking.

Back in Memphis, on 9 September 1954, The Blue Moon Boys were about to perform at the opening of Lamar-Airways, a local shopping and leisure centre near the airport. Elvis's style dial had turned up a few notches, as photos taken in the car park by a fan, Opal Walker, before the show, demonstrate. 'Elvis had that one record out, and it was a smash locally, and I loved it,' Opal told a local paper, likely the *Memphis Press-Scimitar*.

I had a girlfriend who was a friend of Dewey Phillips, the first deejay to play him. My girlfriend and I went down and sat in with Dewey while he did his show, and he told us all about Elvis and where he went to church.

You can bet we were at First Assembly next Sunday, and he was there with a friend. After church we flirted with them. He teased me about my long blond hair.

This show at Lamar-Airways shopping centre came up and I went along and took my camera. I rode a streetcar, I believe, and waited for Elvis to arrive. They all came up in that Chevy, and I asked him to pose and he seemed happy to.

There were a lot of people there, but few besides me seemed to know who he was. I had him all to myself. I could have shot a whole roll.

But I didn't know then what I know now. He went on stage and started singing and shaking … the girls went wild. Me, too. That was the first time I saw Elvis perform, but I didn't miss any opportunities in the future.

In the photos, you can see why he caused a sensation before singing a note. He is dressed to kill. The pose where he's leaning on a Chevrolet, guitar case on the floor, hands on hips and looking like he owns the world, is undiluted Elvis and joyfully era-defining. It's one of those shots where those who know him well could pinpoint the occasion; the year, the month, the day – some even the actual time of day. Again, he's in a cropped, blouson jacket, but the style has already progressed from the day he 'accidentally' bumped into Dixie at the Rainbow skate rink. One eyewitness described the colour as 'grey', so, for the sake of fashion, let's say it's slate, or charcoal; a set of pink epaulette stripes across the shoulders give it a certain military vibe. The shirt, too, is pink and he's wearing the tie – vertical bold stripes, with stars running down the centre – he wore for the Overton Park Shell appearance. Perhaps he'd decided it was lucky? The loose trousers have the trademark matching stripes down the side and are just

Part II Tearing Up the House   67

short enough to reveal his usual, colour-coordinated, diamond pattern Argyll socks and gleaming white-and-black two-tone shoes.

Make no mistake; this was a well-planned killer look, it being unheard of for men to wear non-neutral colours, let alone girly pink, in 1954. At that time, fathers and sons pretty much wore the same things, in shades of fawn, fawn and more fawn, give or take a wisp of white or black or a pair of jeans or two.

Elvis may have been suited and booted and their record may have been riding high, but their auditorium was a car park, their stage, a flatbed truck in front of the Katz drugstore. It was no Overton, but it didn't matter; it was a paid booking and it was clear that everyone there was there for Elvis. Enter the teenager, a newly forged variety of super child, an adult-in-waiting with leisure time, spending money and rampant hormones. By the time Elvis was due to go on, the car park was rammed with them.

Elvis's former L.C. Humes High classmate, George Klein, was emceeing and immediately recognised that the star of the show was the awkward kid from school. He gave The Blue Moon Boys a big build-up and when Elvis leapt onto the 'stage', the place erupted.

'That was the first time we could see what was happening,' said Scotty. All three knew something had changed. Bill fooled around, twirling and riding on his bass, and Elvis began to shake, this time not in terror but from a mix of adrenalin and intent. Still, it was the sound, this new, pulsating, energetic beat, that got the kids going. According to Scotty, they went crazy, getting so out of control that it was almost frightening. Some guys in the audience, jealous of their girlfriends' patently lust-based reactions to the singing tornado tearing up the truck, used the only weapon they had – they criticised Elvis's appearance.

The girls, pony tails now fully perked, couldn't give a damn. Unable or unwilling to repress his natural primality now that he'd found his groove, this Elvis Presley, with his exotic-sounding name and dark, knowing glances, was a different and exhilarating type of boy. Memphis's males didn't stand a chance as the 'Hillbilly Cat' in candy pink, wild hair sticking up and, wait, wearing *actual* eye shadow, belted out his songs, swivelled his hips and blew their conservative little minds.

Watching from the side, Dixie was proud but also astonished at the new Elvis. Apart from at church or serenading her on the porch, he'd shown no desire to perform or sing like that in public. She hadn't even known he'd cut a record until a DJ named him as the singer of 'Blue Moon of Kentucky' on the car radio while she was heading home from a family holiday. She left a mild trucker and returned to a wild rocker. That she, his peers and even Vernon and Gladys were flabbergasted at his instant showmanship underlines just how deeply Elvis guarded his ambitions. So much so, that even he was taken by surprise and, just

68 Elvis: The King of Fashion

like them, was woefully unprepared for what was happening. Dixie wanted to be happy for him, but it would have been a bittersweet moment as she realised how happy Elvis seemed in his new world. She has since said that that was the time she realised that she would unlikely be part of his life for much longer.

Also watching Elvis's every move was a young singer who *would* feature in Elvis's future.

> The first time I saw Elvis, singing from a flatbed truck at a Katz drugstore … two or three hundred people, mostly teenage girls, had come out to see him.
>
> With just one single to his credit, he sang those two songs over and over. That's the first time I met him.

The singer was Johnny Cash. Just three years older than Elvis, he approached him at the end and was invited to his next Eagle's Nest gig. They would eventually perform together. In *Cash: The Autobiography of Johnny Cash with Patrick Carr*, he says, 'Elvis was so good. Every show I did with him, I never missed the chance to stand in the wings and watch. We all did. He was that charismatic.'

After a touring hiccup, when they went down more of a light wind than a storm, playing to a die-hard country and western crowd at their first – and last – appearance at the Grand Ole Opry in Nashville on 25 September, things took a turn for the better with the release of 'Good Rockin' Tonight'/'I Don't Care if the Sun Don't Shine' and a confirmed booking at the *Louisiana Hayride* radio show on KWKH, which aired across the South from Shreveport's Municipal Auditorium every Saturday night.

Around this time, Elvis drove past the Humes High football team boarding a coach for an end-of-season game. Among them was Red West – hero of the hour in the attempted hair-cutting incident in the school toilets – who spotted him and congratulated him. He invited him to watch the game, which Elvis did. Afterwards, he invited Red to his next show. From then on, Red went to their shows with them whenever he could. The Memphis Mafia apprenticeship had begun.

The Blue Moon Boys performed on the *Louisiana Hayride* show on 16 October and, helped by the first impressions of people who had hitherto only heard and not yet seen Elvis, they immediately blew away the crowd. While Scotty and Bill opted for intricately embroidered Western-themed shirts, his look was pure and unapologetically 1954 Elvis. His nerves may have been jangling, but he was meaning business. The ubiquitous bolero had been swapped for a loose drape jacket, a jazzy bowtie as a pop of colour on his jet-black shirt and white baggy trousers that accentuated his beloved two-tone shoes.

Part II Tearing Up the House   69

Introducing him, emcee Frank Page said:

Just a few weeks ago, a young man from Memphis, Tennessee recorded a song on the Sun label and in just a matter of a few weeks, the record has skyrocketed right up the charts. It's really doing good all over the country.

He's only 19 years old, he has a new, distinctive style; Elvis Presley, let's give him a nice hand. He's been singing his song around here for weeks and weeks and weeks.

Elvis, how are you this evening?

'Fine, thank you sir.'

You all geared up with your band there to let us hear your songs?

'Ah, well, ah'd like to say how happy we are to be out here, it's a real honour for us to get a chance to appear on the *Louisiana Hayride* and we're gonna do a song for ya …

Elvis stops, looks at Page and asks: 'Have you got anythin' else to say, sir?'

'No, a'hm ready.'

'We're gonna do a song for you we got on Sun Records 'n it goes summin' like this …'

Suddenly, there's that saddle-rise, rocking intro then Elvis comes in, voice as pure and clear as a sudden raindrop, singing the first line of 'That's All Right'. There is no known footage of the performance, but there are recordings and there is no mistaking the moment, a few lines in, when he starts to move, for that's when the screaming starts …

Elvis just carries on through a mix of stunned silence, punctuated by screams every time he moves, and finishes with the line, 'any way you wanna do …'

The crowd loved it. Elvis was in the building.

They continued to perform at the *Hayride* over the autumn and Elvis became so popular, they wound up with a one-year contract.

It was after his final *Hayride* appearance, later in 1956, that announcer, Horace 'Hoss' Logan, advised the fans of his departure with the immortal line, 'Elvis has left the building.'

* * *

1955

Moving not too far forward from 'That's All Right', Elvis had become a local sensation and it wasn't long before he, Scotty and Bill and their new drummer,

70 Elvis: The King of Fashion

D.J. Fontana, were burning up the stage in just about every town in the Deep South. Within the year, they'd played almost 200 dates.

He kicked off January by releasing 'Milkcow Blues Boogie'/'You're A Heartbreaker' and played in Texas, where Buddy Holly saw him perform in Lubbock and was inspired to play rock 'n' roll. By the time young Buddy graduated that year, he was already a popular performer on the local music scene.

Free as a bird, and touring with the band and other musicians, for Elvis, just 20 and who'd hardly spent a night away from his parents his whole life, it was like being on holiday. Where in Memphis he was self-conscious about being recognised and, ever aware of his original outcast status, never sure if he was being laughed at, on tour he could start over. He could create a whole new persona. He was by far the strangest but also the best-looking guy in every town they went to. With his soulful, ice-blue eyes, knowing smile and cool hair – now getting darker – he was living every heterosexual boy's dream. From a young age, he'd always preferred the company of girls and now he could flirt with them all with nobody warning him not to take things too far, which the girls didn't seem to mind.

Conscious that his lower-body swivels and perceived or real double-entendre-laden lyrics were what had sent the imaginations of Memphis's adolescents into warp drive, he was ready to share them with the rest of South's teens. The pelvic-gyrating, leg-splaying, lip-curling act (which could hardly be called that, since it was just the real Elvis – a seething mass of pent-up sexual energy) was honed to girl-magnet perfection and suddenly given an outlet on stage. And off, since he was constantly encircled by star-struck and occasionally accommodating females. Brought up to be a polite young man, he was disinclined to turn them down and, according Bobbie Ann Mason's book *Elvis*, Scotty Moore said that after the shows Elvis hovered by the stage door like a young stud at a rodeo.

Paul Yandell, guitarist for one of his mother Gladys's favourite groups, The Louvin Brothers, said, 'The girls would swarm, and he'd kiss every one and run his hands all over them, and they'd giggle.' Photos of Elvis with women over the years, of which there are many, confirm that Yandell's comment holds water. While researching this book and poring over endless such images, two things in particular struck me, two things that literally went hand in hand. The first was that even his hands were good-looking. I'd made a mental note of this before, and studying such a variety of photos confirmed my opinion. They were smooth with long, slender fingers and perfect nails long before he'd have encountered a manicurist, let alone could afford one. Second, was the reason I noticed them in the first place. Those hands were everywhere. They were as busy as he was and, considering Elvis's unrelenting touring schedule, that's saying something. Apparently making the most of endless opportunities to get a feel for what lay

Part II Tearing Up the House   71

beneath the frocks of the besotted females who threw themselves at him and melted in his presence, he was in his hormonally rampant element. And – while it could be accidental – he seems to have had a preferred technique: arm around the back of breathless girl and circling, not the waist, but further up the ribcage, so his hand happened to linger just under, and occasionally on, the breast. With two women, it could be an arm round each of them and activating the rib/lower breast combo on girl one, while slinging an arm over girl two's shoulder, allowing his fingertips to brush just above – or on – the target, aka a heaving bosom.

Sometimes, though, that sense of his own power of attraction backfired. Legend has it that on spotting a gorgeous girl talking in a phone box, Elvis pulled open the door and sent his hands to work. According to Paul Yandell, who was touring with him at the time: 'He opened the door and grabbed her by her breast.

'She slapped him silly!'

Most fans, however, were utterly in awe of Elvis and, music, gyrations and bad boy good looks aside, the reason was simple – he could whip them into a frenzy during a show simply by teasing them, thus leaving them begging for more. One minute he'd be coming across as the shy boy next door, which to some fans, he actually was; the next, he'd be toying with them in a fairly overt sexual manner. He'd throw a sexy move and when they started to squeal, he'd stop dead, go completely silent and give them a knowing, some might say leering, grin. Once they'd calmed down, he'd do it all again. As his self-assurance grew, whenever the audience shouted out requests, he'd say, with blatant innuendo, stuff like, 'I'm gonna do what I want first, and then I'll do what you want me to do.' Cue louder squeals of outraged delight. On it would go. The playful pelvic teasing (in later years, likened to the machinations of a cheap stripper by one unenamoured reviewer), the suggestive chat and the freeze-framing that exercised his control over masses of frenzied, hormonal girls suddenly faced, for the first time, with an openly sexually provocative man.

Scant footage exists of Elvis playing live in those early, post-pupal stage days of his transfiguration from down-at-heel teen to incandescent megastar, but eyewitness accounts consistently mention how shockingly crude and coarse his first performances were. Quiet, polite and shy he may have been offstage, but once he hit the boards, Elvis was an uncontrolled explosion of suppressed energy, fuelled by nerves, excitement and rampant hormones. He allowed even his most awkward twitches and ticks a free rein. Sometimes he'd spit, or belch, and would often start laughing mid-song; the latter was likely a nervous response to the ferocity of the audience's reaction initially, but it continued through all his years of performing. He'd tell off-colour jokes and make lewd gestures, most notably groin-located and later, do the famous finger wiggle, which was Elvis's

72 Elvis: The King of Fashion

way of giving the bird to the 'suits' who told him not to move so much and also just to add a further splash of carnal connotation for good measure. He'd even writhe around the floor and fondle his microphone like an objectophiliac, while whispering risqué nothings into it.

In Florida, Mae Axton, at the time a teacher and freelance country music writer and publicist, including for some of Elvis's tours there, met a former student at his 7 May Daytona Beach concert. The student, along with all the other young girls, was in full-on, exuberant Elvis crazy mode. When Axton asked, 'Hey, honey, what is it about this kid?', the girl replied, 'Aw, Miz Axton, he's just a great, big, beautiful hunk of forbidden fruit.'

In Alanna Nash's book *Elvis Aaron Presley: Revelations from the Memphis Mafia*, Lamar Fike, a Memphis friend who became one of the most enduring members of Elvis's entourage, says: 'Elvis was a gunslinger. You meet a gunslinger without his guns on and he's just as normal as everybody else. But when he puts his guns on, you better watch your ass!' Fike questions Elvis's claim that he was unaware of his leg shaking in time to the music: 'He was no fool, he found out what worked and made it work again.'

And so, the world of music was turned upside down and, despite the protestations of parents, preachers and politicians, there would be no resetting of its axis. Prior to all of this, in 1954, a man called Oscar 'The Box Office Baron' Davis, a successful and colourful music entrepreneur, was in Memphis on a music tour and caught up with Elvis's manager, DJ and tour promoter Bob Neal, who'd invited him to see his young new singer, Elvis, perform at the Eagle's Nest. Davis was impressed and invited Elvis to see his country and western show at the Ellis Auditorium in downtown Memphis. Elvis went along, and – in a sign of things to come – was instantly recognised at the box office and handed the tickets set aside for him.

Performers included Eddy Arnold, one of the biggest country singers at the time, and chipper hillbilly songster Eddie Hill, whose backing group, a quartet called the Jordanaires, instantly caught Elvis's forensic musical ear with their silky-smooth harmonising. He was in his element. But it got better. Davis invited him backstage after the show and introduced him to Hoyt Hawkins, of the Jordanaires. Elvis told him how much he'd liked their singing and, to his amazement, Hoyt said that he'd heard his record when they were in California and reckoned he sounded like a quartet singer. Elvis was abashed but thrilled and, in a prophetic moment of rare bravado, told Hoyt that if he ever got as famous as Eddy Arnold, he'd like a group like the Jordanaires to sing on his records. Going a step further, he even asked Hoyt whether he thought that could happen.

As always, the boy dreamed big.

Part II Tearing Up the House   73

Hoyt's parting shot was that they'd love to work with him one day ...

As Davis ushered him away, Elvis briefly locked eyes with a hulking man in a crumpled suit, chomping on a cigar. When he asked Davis who he was, he told him, 'Colonel Parker'. The name was an alias, the military prefix unfounded. It was partly to make him sound important; partly to cover up his reputed illegal immigrant status. As someone once said: 'He wasn't a colonel, he wasn't a Tom, he wasn't even a Parker.' But he *was* an important cog in the music business wheel, a canny impresario associated with country music artists and touring shows and with a string of contacts in major recording studios.

Davis had previously enthused about Elvis to Parker but he'd appeared ambivalent. However, he eventually watched him in the *Louisiana Hayride*. He liked what he heard and, more to the point, he liked what he saw, in particular the almost feral reaction of the audience. His business radar detected potential in the strange kid from nowhere, a possible star in the making, ergo, a serious money-making prospect. Forbidden fruit, indeed.

It's now common knowledge that Parker's past – and often his business methods – were cloaked in mystery and littered with red herrings. Almost universally reviled, he's considered by many to be the man who helped make Elvis, but who also steered his career on a path that would ultimately be the unmaking of him. Details of his early life are still conflicted, but he's generally seen as a shyster and a huckster who'd fled Europe, ditched his real Dutch name, Andreas Cornelis van Kuijk, to escape who knows what – he intentionally kept everything vague – to join the circus and forge a new life in America.

What is known is that he was adept at doing deals that were a bit tricksy, a bit one-sided (always on his side), persuading the other party into relinquishing more than they'd intended and leaving them feeling satisfied, yet also as though they'd been hoodwinked in some way. Armed with a shiny new name and a rusty old accent, he worked a series of jobs on the carnival circuit, where, often by means of fakery and cheating, he'd fool the public with side shows that promised unbelievable sights to separate them from their money. A well-recorded example was his claim to having 'dancing chickens'. To prove it, once the audience had paid of course, he'd place the poor birds on a mini 'stage', which happened to conceal a hotplate, where they'd automatically flinch and jump in a grotesque dance to avoid the heat.

Parker was ruthless when duping gullible 'rubes', as he referred to them, and eventually made enough money – or, as he liked to call it, 'snow' – to become a showman – or, as he liked to say, 'snowman' – of a more respectable kind. By the time he zoned in on Elvis in early 1955, he'd worked his way up from the spit and sawdust and was a self-serving, confident and, at times, belligerent mover and shaker in the music business, promoting recording artists like country and

74 Elvis: The King of Fashion

western idol Hank Snow (oh, the irony – that his artist's surname was Parker's raison d'être made flesh). He and Snow became partners and ran the Hank Snow Enterprises and Jamboree Attractions shows.

So, let's cut straight to the money shot where, with a mix of quirky promotional ideas, powers of persuasion and an in-depth knowledge of the industry, Parker met with Bob Neal and Elvis and convinced them to let him facilitate lucrative bookings and to negotiate the fees. As Elvis and the boys were performing as part of a matinee and an evening concert at Memphis's Ellis Auditorium on 6 February, Neal, with Sam Phillips, Parker, Tom Diskin (Parker's right-hand man) and Oscar Davis, decided to meet at a café across the street to discuss Elvis's next career move. Between shows, Elvis, Scotty and Bill joined them for part of the meeting. It was a tense affair, as Parker, a stranger to finesse, pointed out to Sam that he had the sort of connections that could take Elvis further than a small label like Sun Records could. Unsurprisingly, Sam, who'd discovered Elvis and put in endless hours making him the success he was already, was royally pissed off by this. Davis, however, soothed things somewhat by telling Sam – who was constantly juggling finances – that if Parker got Elvis more bookings around the country, it would get Sun Records into more stores than ever. The less than genial talks led to success for Parker, because, to a man, and for varying reasons, all of them wanted Elvis to do well. And to give Parker his due, Elvis did just that.

By August, Sam had finally accepted that the scale of management Elvis required was too much for Sun Records so, with his blessing, Elvis, who was in awe of the enigmatic, shambolically dressed Parker's exciting plans for him, and Bob Neal agreed to his promoting and negotiating deal. Parker drew up a one-year promotion agreement and was soon literally running the show. He had inveigled himself into the Presley family, where he prepared them for the next step of his master plan – becoming Elvis's manager.

As is well documented, the terms were weighted in Parker's favour, awarding him generous expenses, $2,500 upfront for his expertise and as good as ownership of Elvis's actual talent. It also required Elvis to perform a hundred concerts, for which he'd get $200 a time, to be shared with his band. Oh, and Parker could revise the agreement whenever he liked. The result, though, was Elvis being in constant demand, working further afield as a professional artist and earning not just admiration, but money the likes of which he'd never seen. Playing on the Presleys' working-class insecurities, Parker bombarded them with ways in which he could get their boy the success he deserved and assured them that they would never have to worry about money again. In this, at least, he was being truthful and it was all that Elvis had dreamed of. Now he was the superhero of those comic books of old.

Part II Tearing Up the House   75

Over the months, as Parker involved Elvis in Hank Snow's touring show and bagged ever-more profitable bookings, insisting on top rates of pay and conditions, the cash poured in for both him and 'his boy'. And as Elvis's fame grew, even though Gladys considered Parker a 'fast-talking bullshooter', she couldn't argue with his logic. The carny, the ultimate snowman, had struck and the rubes (in Parker's gimlet eyes), Elvis and his parents, who signed the contract on his behalf because he was too young, were none the wiser.

Parker hadn't really hoodwinked them, though. They would have suspected that he was fleecing them, but they were smart enough to realise that without him, they couldn't open closed doors or negotiate with the kind of business people that he could. And, having lived through the Great Depression while not even on the bottom rung of the economic ladder, being told that Elvis's earnings could be in the thousands, the hundreds of thousands, even the millions, whatever Parker's slice of the cake was, it was almost irrelevant.

In a precursor to what lay ahead, early 1955 turned into a whirlwind for The Blue Moon Boys. In March, they recorded 'I Got A Woman'; in April, they shook the firmament with the release of 'Baby, Let's Play House'/'I'm Left, You're Right, She's Gone', as the former appeared to allude to pre-marital sex and that same month, Elvis bought his first pink Cadillac. A 1954 model with white trim, they used it as the band's transport vehicle until June, when it caught fire on the road in Arkansas.

The concerts continued apace, as did the one-night stands, late nights and long drives, often overnight, to get to the next venue. As an adoring mother, Gladys missed Elvis terribly and was worried sick when he was away. She was proud of his success and would tell everyone how well he was doing. However, being intensely protective and having witnessed some of the extreme responses of fans, and having heard the negative comments from those who had begun to condemn him, she was torn. Much as his fancy outfits would be before long.

As well as feeling fearful of Elvis being hurt, like Dixie, who would gradually fade from the picture, Gladys knew in her heart that the special relationship she had with her 'Baby', or 'Boobie', had shifted. The tight bond, formed the day he was born and reinforced in their darkest Tupelo hours, when he clung to his 'Satnin', was loosening. (Satnin was the pet name he used for his mother throughout her life and he also used it for certain women that he was particularly fond of, including his wife, Priscilla.) Having always been his best friend, best girl, chief adviser and confidant, now she was feeling less needed as he navigated his way, not just around the South, but through the start of his adult life. Her worries over the emotional cost of Elvis's fame were largely unnecessary, for having never been away overnight from home before, and although it was a nuisance at times, he called her every day when he was touring. On the other hand, Gladys's concerns over the physical cost were warranted after an event in

76 Elvis: The King of Fashion

Florida in May after he'd been interviewed by Mae Axton for publicity ahead of his show at a ballpark.

Perhaps it was the date – the show was on Friday the thirteenth – but an extraordinary photo of Elvis, taken that day, at Wolfson Park in Jacksonville, shows him standing dazed and semi-naked after a fanatical mob of girls had ripped the clothes off his back. Next to him stands a young woman wearing a neat, floral dress and demure choker necklace. She's smiling up at him, her outfit and cheerful expression in stark contrast to his shocked and dishevelled appearance. She is Ardys Bell Clawson, now 85. Her brother took the photos, with Elvis's permission, directly after the attack, and he and Ardys stayed with him in the aftermath.

She was *not* one of the crazed fans. She liked Elvis, she says, but she was never a screamer, as she puts it. In a fascinating eyewitness account, Ardys tells Trey Miller on his YouTube channel, *Globetrotting with Trey: The ELVIS Travelogues*, how they just happened to be backstage when things kicked off:

My brother always carried a camera and Elvis was there. Now, he was almost a nobody then; he was the opening act … for the big dogs.
    When he got through, he told them [the audience], on stage, 'Girls, I'll see you all backstage.'

On previous tour dates, audiences had already been going wild, with some girls trying to rush the stage and grab Elvis, so the ballpark was prepared. Or, so they thought. Of the 14,000 inflamed spectators, it's been suggested a few hundred took Elvis's invitation seriously. Ardys said, 'They [the organisers] thought that they had secured everything back there, to where the crowds couldn't get to him, well!' She laughs at their misplaced optimism.

In what's been called the first rock 'n' roll riot in history, mayhem broke out. Fans poured from the stands and chased Elvis into his dressing room. Some even crawled through a ceiling vent or window, while he clung for dear life to overhead pipes in the shower area. They tore at his clothes, ripping off his jacket, shirt, socks, boots and even the belt from his trousers, before they were eventually dispersed and evicted by security.

'My brother and I just happened to be there,' says Ardys.

Trey Miller asks, 'So they pulled his clothes off of him?'

'Absolutely, and that's what I witnessed. Afterwards I asked Elvis's permission [about taking the photo].' Then she explains Elvis's odd expression. 'He was eating ice straight out of an old drink box. He didn't even answer [me] – he was worn out.'

Apparently, Parker, now always around, was at the concert but was elsewhere tallying up, when he heard what had gone on. Asked if she and her brother

Overall winner – Elvis in denim dungarees for Milam School's 6th-grade class photo, *circa* 1946. (*Tupelo Elvis Fan Club*)

Gunslingers – Elvis and his cousin Gene Smith dressed as cowboys at the Mid-South Fair, Memphis, 1953. (*Public domain*)

Hillbilly Cat – a still-blond Elvis in two-tone suit, shoes, tie and belt for a gig at Lamar-Airways shopping centre, Memphis, September 1954. (*Opal Walker*)

Naked fame – Elvis with fan Ardys Bell Clawson, who came to his aid at a concert in Jacksonville, Florida, May 1955, when crazed fans ripped off his clothes. (*Ardys Bell Clawson and Jacksonville Historical Society*)

All shook up – Elvis, in a green jacket, with tooled-leather, personalised guitar cover, Tampa, Florida, August 1956. (*commons.wikimedia.org*)

Tearing up the house – Elvis at the Cotton Bowl, Dallas, 11 October 1956. (*NGA National Gallery of Art, Washington (gift of Mary and Dan Solomon)*)

Mr DJ – Dewey Phillips and Elvis inside Lansky Bros. store on Beale St, Memphis, 1956. (*Lansky Bros. family archive*)

Key player – Elvis is presented with a guitar-shaped key to the city of Tupelo, September 1956. (*commons.wikimedia.org*)

He wore blue velvet – Elvis returns to Tupelo in his iconic midnight-blue shirt for Elvis Presley Day concerts at the Mississippi-Alabama Fair and Dairy Show, 26 September 1956. (*commons.wikimedia.org*)

Star and stripes – Elvis, *circa* 1958/9, with Hal Lansky, right (age 7), and siblings. (*Lansky Bros. family archive*)

Small screen idol – Elvis wears a bouclé jacket, statement abstract-print shirt and chunky rings for his first national TV appearance on the Dorsey Brothers' *Stage Show*, 1956. (*commons.wikimedia.org*)

New kid on the block – Elvis in the famous denim and cat-burglar top prison uniform for the cellblock dance scene in *Jailhouse Rock* (Metro-Goldwyn-Mayer), October 1957. (*commons.wikimedia.org*)

Oath of allegiance – Elvis, collar up, joins other young men to be sworn in to the US Army during an induction at Fort Chaffee, Arkansas, March 1958. (*commons.wikimedia.org*)

Soldier boy – Elvis dressed in USA Army uniform in Germany, 1958. (*commons.wikimedia.org*)

Hey, baby – Elvis, Priscilla and newborn daughter, Lisa Marie, leave Baptist Memorial Hospital, Memphis, 1 February 1968. (*commons.wikimedia.org*)

Sensational sixties – Elvis and Priscilla at the USS *Arizona* Memorial, Pearl Harbor, Hawaii, May 1968. (*Pearl Harbor National Memorial*)

When Elvis met Steve – on the set of NBC's *'68 Comeback Special*, New York, with Steve Binder. (*From* Elvis: '68 Comeback: The Story Behind the Special, *Steve Binder, Thunderbay Press, 2022*)

Black panther – Elvis in the famous leather suit created by Bill Belew for NBC's *'68 Comeback* show, 3 December 1968. (*commons.wikimedia.org*)

Carny and King – Elvis with Tom Parker on Universal Studios' *Change of Habit* set, Los Angeles, 1969. (*commons.wikimedia.org*)

Caped crusader – Elvis meets President Richard Nixon in the White House Oval Office to offer his services in the war against drugs, December 1970. (*US National Archives*)

Split-decision – Elvis and Priscilla leaving California's Santa Monica courtroom, arm in arm, after their divorce was finalised in 1973. (*commons.wikimedia.org*)

Phoenix rising – Elvis in Red Phoenix suit with matching belt and diamond Maltese cross medallion on the *Elvis in Concert* album cover. (*1977, CBS*)

Clothes encounter – Elvis browsing in Lansky Bros., in black shirt and trousers, striped metallic-effect waistcoat and two-tone brogues, 1956. (*Lansky Bros. family archive*)

Style council – Elvis with Bernard Lansky. (*Lansky Bros. family archive*)

Part II Tearing Up the House   77

were alone with Elvis, Ardys says, 'We were. He got away from 'em … he was just glad to get away from them girls.' And in an interview with *Jacksonville* magazine, she says, 'It looks like I was gaga over him, but I wasn't. I was smiling at him and thinking about what those girls had done to him.'

Amazingly, there's a second photo of Ardys and Elvis, this time on 23 February 1956 and thought to be backstage at the Gator Bowl. In this shot he is relaxed and fully dressed and has her in a tight embrace. Notably, she's in the same floral frock as before. When Trey Miller, wanting to ensure he's got the time frame right, comments that it's the same dress, Ardys's explanation is humbling: 'Let me tell you somethin' about that. Back then, we weren't rich. It was probably the only one I had.' Had Elvis known, he'd likely have bought her a dozen new ones. In the *Jacksonville* interview, she also says, 'He was more popular by then. But not so much that you couldn't get close to him.'

No kidding, Ardys!

In the later photo, Elvis is fashion central in tailored, high-waisted, pleated trousers with a whip-thin belt – buckle to the side – and, clearly not put off by the earlier mayhem, another lace shirt, which Ardys confirms was pink.

Elvis's belts could have a miniseries of their own, and more of that later, but an early style quirk I couldn't help but notice was how he often wore his belt buckle to the left-hand side. I needed to know why, so I consulted the oracle, Hal Lansky.

> This style was started by auto mechanics. When you took your car to the gas station and the auto attendant checked your oil with the dip-stick, his belt buckle was turned to the side so he would not scratch the paint on the fender with his buckle.

Then he adds, 'Musicians, including Elvis, did the same thing so they would not scratch the back of their guitars.'

Bingo!

Later, asked how he felt about having his clothes ripped off, no doubt to Gladys's horror, her precious son nonchalantly replied, 'My fans want my shirt, they can have my shirt. They put it on my back.' And when asked his opinion on his fans being labelled juvenile delinquents, unwashed adolescents and even idiots, Elvis, unruffled, replied with his trademark simplified wisdom:

> They're somebody's decent kids, probably that was raised in decent homes. … If they want to pay their money and come out and jump around, it's their business. They'll grow up some day and grow out of that. But while they're young, let them have their fun.

78   Elvis: The King of Fashion

Before Jacksonville, Elvis had toured for three weeks in association with Parker in Hank Snow's *Jamboree* show and had performed at other concerts afterwards. Around June, in need of a holiday and with Dixie Locke by then a sweet memory ('It was kind of a mutual thing,' she says on the DVD *Elvis Presley by Classic Albums*. 'His career was going in one direction and I didn't feel I could be part of it. His career kind of consumed him ... there wasn't much time for anything else'), he spotted June Juanico at a concert in Biloxi, Mississippi. Very attractive and in a white dress that showed off her suntan, Elvis flirted openly with her after the show and was so smitten that he spent as much of the summer as he could with her. He introduced her to Gladys and Vernon, who approved, and in 1956, they all holidayed and went sailing and fishing as a foursome.

In Juanico's book about what would be a fleeting romance, *Elvis: In the Twilight of Memory*, photos show them entwined together, as though 'playing house' as in the record, which, incidentally, despite the roars of disapproval, or possibly even because of them, made *Billboard*'s Top Ten. Juanico, however, in a 2021 interview with author Alanna Nash for fan site *elvis.com.au*, refutes any suggestion of a sexual relationship.

> For the one and a half years I dated him, our relationship remained chaste. He was just very tender and considerate. We spent so much time together, and we started talking about marriage.
>
> Mrs Presley liked me. She was always telling me that Elvis needed someone to take care of him.

And, there's the dilemma Gladys constantly faced. While she had supported Elvis on his trailblazing a path to stardom, she also dreamed of him getting married, settling down with a nice girl, like Dixie, or June, and having children. Her grandchildren.

But it was more a sweet and heady summer romance, where he discovered that he loved the smell of her perfume, Chanel No5, and she discovered that he wore mascara, because it ran in the pool. She cut her hair short and coloured it with the same black hair dye as his, so they matched, and had her photo taken with his brand new ivory '56 convertible Cadillac Eldorado.

Having swapped artist and writer Arthur Gunter's line 'You may get religion' in his song 'Baby, Let's Play House' with 'You may drive a pink Cadillac', Elvis later decided to have the car repainted pink by a neighbour who created a bespoke colour he coined 'Elvis Rose'. When it was finished, he gave it to Gladys – even though she never had a driver's licence. The famous, refurbished Rose Pink Cadillac is now on permanent display at Graceland.

By August, Elvis had signed a contract making Parker his manager, and in November, he secured the recording rights for a song called 'Heartbreak Hotel',

Part II Tearing Up the House   79

written by none other than his friend and tour publicist, Mae Axton. As Elvis infiltrated the national music scene, several record labels wanted to sign the hot new star and, come October, three major players had deals of up to $25,000 on the table. With Parker and Red West, he flew to New York to meet brothers Jean and Julian Aberbach of Hill & Range music, who sourced songs for artists.

Parker and Sam Phillips had met again and negotiated an astonishing deal with RCA Victor Records as Steve Sholes had managed to convince the powers that be to acquire Elvis's contract from Sun Records. It amounted to an unprecedented $40,000, of which $5,000 was a bonus for Elvis, honouring the back royalties owed to him by Sun Records. The historic deal was signed at the Peabody Hotel on 21 November and, since Elvis was just 20 and still officially a minor, Vernon signed the contract on his behalf. The signatures of Elvis and Vernon also both appear on a receipt, detailling the breakdown of Elvis's $5,000 bonus. It is typed on the official Peabody Hotel stationery of the then general manager, Frank Schutt – introducer of the famous ducks – and is retained for posterity in the hotel's memorabilia room.

I hope that Elvis got a massive buzz out of the life-affirming occasion, a direct result of his unique and blistering talent. Even more, I hope it dawned on him that he'd had the last laugh on those who ignored him in the Peabody's ballroom on the night of his senior prom.

Along with the RCA representatives, Bob Neal, Sam, Gladys and Vernon, Parker was there to oversee the fruits of his negotiations. A summing-up of Parker's character by the late Bob Pakes, who was an authority on Elvis and author of the *The EPE Catalog*, is startling:

As for Parker – good or bad for Elvis's career? Not just bad, but terrible. Before I started doing research for this book, I hated his character. By the time the book was finished, I totally despised the man.

Some people say that Parker was clever, or even a genius. I think he was a manipulative narcissist whose only mission in life was to help himself.

In response to the often-heard statement, 'Parker did a lot of good things for Elvis', I would say that even a pathological liar sometimes tells the truth.

Parker did Elvis way more bad than good, and I have zero respect for him as a human being.

With the RCA/Sun deal signed and the ink, as well as Gladys's congratulatory kiss on her son's cheek, barely dry, Parker altered his own original contract with Elvis and promoted himself to his overall manager and exclusive representative, with commission of 25 per cent of his total earnings. And expenses on top.

In every way, it was a sign of things to come …

Chapter 7

1956
The Year of Elvis
Look: Rockabilly Rebel

'A wild troubadour who wails rock 'n' roll tunes, flails erratically at a guitar and wriggles like a peep-show dancer.'

Look magazine

'The preachers cut up all over the place, jumping on the piano, moving every which way. The crowd responded to them. I guess I learned from them.'

Elvis

'In public, I like real conservative clothes, something that's not too flashy. But on stage, I like 'em as flashy as you can get 'em.'

Elvis

To say that 1956 was a big year for Elvis is like saying the Grand Canyon is a crack in the ground.

In a nutshell, and nationally speaking, it was when he went from nowhere to everywhere in a single bound. Between a dizzyingly intense touring schedule, where he racked up around 200 live performances, he appeared on national TV; became famous; had ten – that's *ten* – hit singles; released a million-selling album; got more famous; signed a Hollywood movie deal; bought a house and became a millionaire – all in a single year. At the age of 21.

To most of the world, Elvis suddenly appeared as if by magic. Even among friends and family, many hadn't even known he had ambitions to be a singer until the year before. Aside from in the South, where he was quickly becoming a major star, hardly anyone else knew who the hell Elvis Presley was. By the close of the year, the whole of America, and beyond, knew exactly who he was. Tom Parker, unmatched when it came to promoting, had certainly been as good as his word.

'Elvis was like a white-hot star,' says author William McKeen in Channel 5's documentary *The Man Who Shook Up the World*. 'If you think of it as an alien invasion, when he landed in 1956, that was earth-shattering.'

1956 The Year of Elvis   81

From that inauspicious launch pad – a shotgun shack on a dirt track in Tupelo, Mississippi – the countdown was over and it was time for the dream-powered lift-off. Nineteen fifty-six: the Year of Elvis, the year he took the world by storm.

It's impossible to ignore the paradox of how the shyest person in town became the most famous person in the world. However, although totally unprepared for the level of attention about to come his way, in true superhero fashion, Elvis had a secret weapon: a suit of armour that would protect him; namely, his fashion flair. Whatever life would throw at him, which turned out to be quite a lot, at least he was always perfectly dressed. This may sound trite, a tad *Zoolander* even, but the outfits Elvis chose to wear empowered him. He felt good in them (apart from one particular get-up that we'll look at presently) and, even in his early years, they lent him an air of confidence, of boldness, of not giving too much of a shit, which he often didn't really feel.

An instant radio sensation, Elvis's fame unquestionably stemmed from what he sounded like, but in a world of silky crooners and showy cowboys, it was his otherworldly looks that set him apart as much as his distinctive voice. And together, they made him peerless. Now he'd gone from free-form Sun recording sessions and swimming through seas of adoring girls, to being contracted to RCA, one of the country's major recording labels and – through the intrigues of Parker – being part of a partnership deal between the Hill & Range music agency and his newly founded Elvis Presley Music Inc. for the purpose of publishing his songs. He'd also released his first RCA single, the daringly dark and uniquely delivered 'Heartbreak Hotel'/'I Was the One' and a subsequent avalanche of other hits.

But it was the flurry of television shows, also arranged by Parker, that changed everything for Elvis. Incredibly, he made fewer than twenty major TV appearances in his lifetime, but, boy, did they count. A dozen were in 1956, with six in a row, including his national TV debut on *Stage Show*, a CBS series hosted by big band leaders Tommy and Jimmy Dorsey and broadcast from Studio 50 in New York.

For his 28 January debut, with Scotty, Bill and D.J. Fontana, Elvis let his dark, single-button, bouclé wool with pale specks sports jacket do the talking. His raw silk trousers and shoes were also dark; his wide tie, pale. I can find no record of the actual colours, but I'm feeling that the tie would have matched the pale plucks in the jacket. When he sang 'Flip, Flop And Fly', 'Shake Rattle 'n' Roll' and 'I Got A Woman', viewers were rendered speechless. The older ones from shock – as Elvis sang about being like a Mississippi bullfrog with so many women, he didn't know which way to jump (in 'Shake, Rattle 'n' Roll') – and the younger ones from, well, they didn't know from what.

It wasn't only the music that startled them. This guy Elvis moved differently, erratically, or was it erotically? He looked strange; in fact, he looked dangerous,

82   Elvis: The King of Fashion

especially to the older generation, with its entrenched beliefs, bias and social mores. This boy was crossing a line, the one that marked segregation, and they did not like it. This, they sensed, was music for awakenings, for puberty, for fertility and rebellion.

Initially, on *Stage Show*, the Dorsey brothers distanced themselves from him, getting another presenter to introduce him. However, when their ratings shot through the roof, especially after show three, when Elvis, described by one observer as a 'sex box' and by *Elvis* author Bobbie Ann Mason as a 'sex pistol', sang 'Heartbreak Hotel', they chummed up with him and began introducing him themselves.

Elvis received the vast – for him – sum of $1,250 for each of the shows, which ran on consecutive Saturday nights. By the time he'd finished the last *Stage Show* on 24 March, viewing figures were in the millions, and, funnily enough, he was invited to appear on an April episode of the hugely popular *Milton Berle Show*.

Between the TV appearances, a whole lot of shaking was going on elsewhere, including a screen test with Hollywood producer Hal Wallis. In his autobiography, *Starmaker*, Wallis describes seeing Elvis for the first time on his *Stage Show* debut:

[Elvis] wore a sport coat that was slightly too large for him and tight black pants. At first, he looked like any other teen-aged bopper, but when he started to sing, twisting his legs, bumping and grinding, shaking his shoulders, he was electrifying. I had never seen anything like him … I vowed nothing would stop me from signing this boy for films.

In the February, both songs on his single 'I Forgot To Remember To Forget'/'Mystery Train' reached No. 1 in *Billboard's* Country chart but it was 'Heartbreak Hotel' that floored everyone, entering the magazine's Top 100 *and* its Country & Western Best Sellers in Stores chart (where by March it was No. 1). RCA's own Top 25 Best Sellers list was peppered with six Elvis Presley records and they were overwhelmed when 362,000 advance orders flooded in for his, now iconic, eponymous first album, *Elvis Presley*.

Occasionally, something comes along that's so cool, people want to emulate it and, like Elvis himself, his first album cover has been imitated over the years, on the likes of The Clash's *London Calling* and k.d. lang's *Reintarnation*. At first glance, it can look unremarkable. The entire cover is a slightly grainy, monochrome photo of Elvis, with his name spelled out down the left-hand side and along the bottom. In design, though, the old adage 'the simpler, the better' is king and it's that minimalism, likely the result of RCA having to work a fast turnaround release to capture the zeitgeist, that makes it so unforgettable.

Imagine how the cover conversation might have gone.

1956 The Year of Elvis   83

Suit 1: 'You seen how fast this kid's records are selling?'
Suit 2: 'Uh-huh.'
Suit 1: 'We need to get an album out, and sharpish.'
Suit 2: 'Uh-huh.'
Suit 1: 'We need something for the cover.'
Suit 2: 'A photo? *This* photo?'
Suit 1: 'That'll do.'
Suit 2: 'Title?'
Suit 1: 'Elvis?'
Suit 2: 'He's not famous enough.'
Suit 1: 'Elvis Presley?'
Suit 2: 'That'll do.'
Suit 1: 'Make the font pink, he likes pink. And maybe some green …'

But it isn't just any old photo. It's rip-rollicking, snarling, 20-year-old, 1955 Elvis, frozen in time in all his untamed southern glory, eyes shut, mouth open in a roar and handling his new personalised, leather-covered Martin D-28 guitar as though he were about to wrangle it to the floor. Or perhaps he just had – since there's a string missing and he's lost one of the pegs.

His long jacket is a pale, lightweight cotton in a tiny baby pink-and-white check. It would have been perfect for the hot Tampa, Florida day in July 1955 on which the photo was taken (believed to be by William V. 'Red' Robertson) at Fort Homer Hesterly Armory. Around the waistband of his slightly darker and, in the original photo, sweat-drenched, pleated trousers is a thin, woven belt, its buckle typically to one side. Under the jacket, there's a black version of his favourite lace shirt with – unusually and obscured by his guitar – a white bolo tie with ornate metal slider hanging loose round the collar. Behind him is Bill on upright bass and some spectators on a gallery above looking down at him. But all you really see is Elvis. Vying for attention with the high energy of this shot of the boy who would be king, is the title – his name, 'ELVIS PRESLEY' – in bold, lipstick-pink and apple-green capital letters. Even that doesn't detract from the main image.

Released in March, with just twelve tracks, *Elvis Presley* made history as the first rock 'n' roll (finally, a label for his style) album to reach No. 1 in the *Billboard* Top Pop Albums chart and to stay there for ten weeks, and for being the first million-selling LP in the genre.

Around that time, Elvis put a $500 down payment on 1034 Audubon Drive, a ranch-style house in a well-heeled Memphis neighbourhood, populated by professional and business types. It had four bedrooms, two bathrooms and a carport, ready for his new Harley motorbike. Considering this was only three

84   Elvis: The King of Fashion

years after they'd vacated their last public housing property, it was a huge step up for the Presley family. With its pleasant location and manicured lawns, all it needed, as far as Elvis was concerned, was a swimming pool, which he duly commissioned.

While Gladys was proud of Elvis and the lovely house he'd bought them, she missed her old neighbours; and the sharecropper's daughter in her couldn't help but feel it emphasised how unlike their fancy new neighbours they were. Given that she grew her own vegetables and hung her washing out on the lawn, which Elvis's Harley and visiting fans had chewed up, and had endless family members coming and going and kept an array of noisy pets, including a couple of dogs and a monkey called Jeyhew, she may have had a point. If Gladys had her way, she'd have kept chickens, too.

By April, 'Heartbreak Hotel' was the Country & Western chart topper and broke all the rules by getting to No. 5 in the Rhythm & Blues chart.

Let's just pause for a breath here, shall we?

In less than half a year, this relatively unknown artist, who'd cut his first single before he'd really sung in public, was leap-frogging all over the national music genre charts because, highly unusually, people with differing tastes were buying the same records.

On 3 April's *Milton Berle Show*, broadcast from the USS *Hancock* aircraft carrier in San Diego, California, Berle announced:

> This is the first time that the *Hancock* is gonna rock and roll while still at anchor. Here's a young man who, in a few short months, has gained tremendous popularity in the music business.
>
> His records are really going like wildfire. He's an American singing sensation, our new RCA recording artist – here he is, Elvis Presley!

A roar went up from the live audience of sailors and their loved ones as the coolest-looking dude caused a commotion on the ocean simply by walking on stage. Berle's show was in black and white, so again, there are no colour cues, but it looks like Elvis is wearing black trousers, a black tailored shirt and a contrasting tie with matching socks and belt. Whatever the palette, it's a suitably dark and edgy look for the powerful and crowd-silencing rendition of 'Heartbreak Hotel' – with its implied theme of suicide – that he then delivered.

Despite being faced with a mass of burly, uniformed guys, there wasn't a hint of the inferiority that once plagued him. Watching the broadcast today, even the slightest, slowest move triggers screams from women suddenly oblivious to their other halves. When he breaks away from the mic, slings his guitar to the side and rips things up a bit, they go wild. By the end, even the men are whistling and whooping for more.

The Elvis Effect.

Prior to his next and last appearance on the following *Milton Berle Show*, which turned out to be memorable for all the wrong reasons, Elvis found out how much Hal Wallis liked his screen test when he signed him up to Paramount Pictures on a one-year movie contract with options on six more.

Elvis's life was becoming his dream, a dream he was terrified that he'd suddenly wake up from. For someone who was already a terrible sleeper, it was not ideal. He described his feelings about early fame with disarming honesty to a reporter at the time. '[It] feels pretty good. It all happened so fast and I don't know, I'm afraid to wake up and it'll all be a dream.'

Come June, he may well have wished that the consequences of his second Milton Berle appearance actually had been a dream. What began sedately enough, with a lighthearted skit featuring Berle, Elvis and a clutch of adoring girl fans, went on to spark a level of indignation and outrage that's now the stuff of legend.

Skit over, and on the studio stage with Scotty, Bill and D.J. Fontana behind, Elvis is guitarless; Berle had suggested he ditch it, saying, 'Let 'em see you, son.' Ever respectful to his elders, he did as advised, and what he 'let 'em see' blew the roof off. He was wearing black trousers, a sugared-almond pink plaid sports coat, a pink-and-black two-tone sports shirt, that came to be known, and still is, as the 'Milton Berle' shirt, and pink socks. His hair flopped across his forehead in a most noncompliant manner and his sideburns were sharper than shards of slate. Rings and chunky bracelets completed the look.

Watching the footage, you can see he's as nervous as hell, constantly fiddling with the mic stand before starting, making it impossible to miss the twinkling hand hardware. This in itself would have been enough to get the middle-class, middle-aged, middle-everythings tutting and adjusting their TV sets. So, when, without any ado, Elvis launched straight into roaring the 'Hound Dog' intro then completely letting himself go, cutting all the big down-South concert shapes while belting out the suggestive – some would say obscene – lyrics, they were completely outraged.

The way he looked, the way he moved, the stuff that he sang, joyfully embracing the type of music and actions associated with black artists, flew right in the face of their overt segregation complicity. It wasn't just how he presented *himself*, though, it was that he dared to endorse the 'enemy' culture. As far as the separation advocates were concerned, Elvis Presley was the devil in disguise. To the indolent white youths, he was the new messiah, leading them to a place where they didn't have to dress square or listen to the music their parents liked and, of course, to the awakening of their own potent sexuality.

And it wasn't over yet.

86   Elvis: The King of Fashion

As if to verify this perceived depravity, Elvis stared directly into the camera lens, therefore, into their very living rooms, pointed at the incredulous viewers while singing, 'Well, you ain't never caught a rabbit …' and then continued with a decelerated, pulsating version of the last few lines. All this while treating the mic stand in much the same way that a sex dancer would their pole.

Putting aside the furore caused by this performance, it really shows how much Elvis relied on Scotty, Bill and D.J. (who are behind him) to be a kind of reverse shield. He sidles up to them, like an uncertain toddler seeking protection when neither his armour – the cool outfit – nor his comforter, aka the mic, are cutting it.

Of the 40 million viewers who witnessed the full Elvis pelvis divested of its guitar, many were left scandalised. The youngsters, on the other hand, loved every minute, and that night, a superstar was born.

In the closing footage, the previously sceptical Berle is blindsided and enters stage right, whistling and shouting, 'Elvis Presley! … My boy! I love him!' He then spoofs Elvis's dancing, including an exaggerated take on his side-shoe drag technique. Yes, the crowd find it funny, but the joke is on Berle, who appears puerile while Elvis looks cool. He then joshes with Elvis, messing up his hair and embracing him. Elvis visibly twitches with yet further unleashed energy and looks awkward and dry of mouth – still, he politely laughs and smiles.

Having unwittingly unleashed a tsunami of protest and criticism, he was dubbed 'Elvis the Pelvis' by *Time*, one of many magazines featuring articles about music's enfant terrible. While being interviewed in a sweltering Florida dressing room by *TV Guide* magazine that September, where he's described as wearing 'black pants, white suede shoes and a baby-blue shirt. The silk of the shirt stuck flat to his shoulders and back,' he's asked if he likes the *Time* nickname. 'Naw, sir,' he says. 'I don't like them to call me Elvis the Pelvis. It's the most childish expression I ever heard from an adult.'

In between constantly protesting that he was only doing what came naturally, he went on to appear on *The Steve Allen Show*. Although no fan of Elvis and aware that the establishment believed him to be a danger to the very souls of America's youth, Allen had seen *Stage Show*'s viewing figures and wanted him on his own show anyway. The host, wanting to do 'a family show the whole family can watch', insisted that Elvis don a tuxedo and only move minimally – while singing 'Hound Dog' to a Basset Hound in a top hat. Parker convinced Elvis to agree to the preposterous idea, saying it would calm things down and then he could go straight back to doing his thing while he was touring – which was all the time.

Allen, who claimed he never intended to belittle his young guest, introduced the 'new Elvis' in white tie and tails. Looking serious, Elvis sang a short version of 'Hound Dog' to the baleful-looking hound. In his book *Hi-Ho Steverino!*,

Allen wrote: 'We certainly didn't inhibit Elvis's then-notorious pelvic gyrations, but I think the fact that he had on formal evening attire made him, purely on his own, slightly alter his presentation.'

The humiliation was real, though. Having worked so hard to rid himself and his family of those poor white trash and country bumpkins tags, Elvis felt he'd been made a laughing stock, especially since there was also a sketch in the show poking fun at hillbilly types. Watching it now, his discomfort is clear, yet, displaying the same mettle he had as a tormented kid, he met the commitment and he did it well. And he looks fantastic in the tux.

As was becoming the norm with Elvis in New York, the situation worked in his favour. For the first time, Allen's show beat *The Ed Sullivan Show* in the ratings. Subsequently, Sullivan, eating his words that he 'wouldn't touch Elvis with a 10-foot pole', booked him for three appearances, at a staggering $50,000.

And Allen lost out in the end. Elvis never forgot the experience and refused to appear on his show ever again.

It's claimed by many, including *Elvis* author Bobbie Ann Mason, that Parker later admitted to suggesting the dog and the penguin suit, in a bid, he said, to ensure that 'his boy' was seen as a good, clean family entertainer (but more importantly, that he got the well-paid gig and would be seen by as many people as possible). Learning this, and knowing the crafty carny's love of cheap gimmicks and tacky showmanship, the hound in the top hat certainly seems to have Parker's name all over it. As with his real identity and his citizenship status, he failed to enlighten Elvis.

Escaping the outcry in New York in August to play a typically frenetic Parker engagement of concerts, including six in two days at Jacksonville's Florida Theatre, Elvis found himself back at the scene of his unexpected strip show.

After the earlier concert riots (there were more than just the one at Wolfson Park), the local juvenile court judge, Marion Gooding, who had branded him a savage, was taking no chances. He called Elvis to a meeting, where he threatened to arrest him if he carried out any suggestive movements during the performances.

'They had me convinced that no teenage girl was safe around Elvis Presley,' the judge recalled later. 'They wanted to have him watched at the theatre and … his hotel room. They had him pictured as a real villain.'

As instructed, Elvis performed with little movement on opening night at the Florida Theatre. However, he couldn't resist goading the critics and Judge Gooding, who were all there – only to keep an eye on him, mind – by wiggling his little finger. Naturally, the crowd went mad. He also played the Municipal Auditorium in New Orleans, where he received no request to keep hips in order. Another riot ensued. The following day's review in the *Times-Picayune* read:

88   Elvis: The King of Fashion

Elvis Presley jerked his torturous way across the stage of the Municipal Auditorium twice Sunday, 'sang' eight or ten songs, thumped on a guitar, fell to the floor, knocked over microphones and set off a din of teenage squealing unparalleled since the heyday of Sinatra.

The finger wiggle incident clearly struck a chord with Elvis, since he recalled it during the band chat section in his NBC TV comeback show in 1968. It also inspired one of the most memorable scenes in Baz Luhrmann's *Elvis* movie. Using artistic licence, it's an amalgam of two important performances, the Florida Theatre finger wiggle concert and an earlier 4 July show at Russwood Park stadium in Memphis, where Elvis referenced the *Steve Allen Show* incident that had happened just days before.

In the movie, the concert venue set is Russwood, where Elvis performed to a packed house in aid of St Jude Children's Hospital charity (while wearing the exact outfit, a black suit, black shirt, red socks and a red tie with a white Nipper the RCA dog print, that Austin Butler, who plays Elvis, wears). In the riveting scene, Butler stands immobile on stage and tells the crowd, 'There's been a lot of talk about the new Elvis.' Now, that's the Steve Allen jibe. However, he then adds, 'And, of course … that other guy,' before lifting his little finger and wiggling it to reference the Judge Gooding moment – which, chronologically, hadn't yet happened!

The film is a clever meld of fact and fiction. Movie duration restrictions and a life as eventful as Elvis's meant it had to be. Baz Luhrmann needed to be smart and get pertinent points – not the entire story – across. It works well.

And when Butler utters the line (that Elvis did actually deliver – at Russwood) 'You know, those people in New York ain't gonna change me none. A'hm gonna show you what the real Elvis is like tonight,' it's hugely satisfying and feels as though the relevant boxes are ticked.

After addressing the crowd, Butler launches into 'Trouble', another example of artistic licence, since 'Trouble' wasn't released until July 1958.

The Russwood Park feel and the show-stopping black-and-red outfit were more cinematically exciting than the Florida Theatre, an indoor venue where Elvis wore a white shirt, greyish jacket and black trousers, would have been. As for 'Trouble', while chronologically out of sync, in the dramatised scenario it perfectly summed up the zeitgeist and Elvis's attitude during a period where he had to battle to be himself in an atmosphere of intense criticism and authoritarianism.

Now back in New York, contracted to appear three times on America's mightiest TV entertainment platform, *The Ed Sullivan Show*, Elvis, who'd also earned the nickname 'The Memphis Menace', was aware that the host had previously vowed never to have 'Elvis the Pelvis' on his show. However, he could

1956 The Year of Elvis   89

have taken great pleasure from Sullivan's public about-face and from the fact that when he did appear, he broke the viewing figures record to the tune of 60 million. Or maybe even from the eye-watering fee of $50,000 that he was paid for just three shows. Elvis wins again.

On the first appearance, his slicked-back hair and sideburns were more dirty blond than black. He was wearing a pink, bold-plaid tweed jacket, a zigzag patterned shirt that should have clashed terribly, but didn't, and black trousers. The ensemble was part of the wardrobe he'd bought from his friend in fashion, Bernard Lansky, after he visited his Beale Street store to tell him he was going to be on TV.

Elvis, with Scotty, Bill, drummer D.J. and his dream backing group, The Jordanaires, behind him, looked directly at the camera and announced to Sullivan (watching from a hospital bed having been in a car accident) and the audience, that being on the show was 'probably the greatest honor I have ever had in my life', followed by, 'Friends, as the great philosopher once said …' and then launched into a roaring 'Hound Dog'. The audience squeals at every move, every cheeky grin. The camera is aimed mainly above his waist, occasionally panning in tight to his face, or the backing band musicians; only towards the end does the operator dare to pan out and show the whole Elvis.

On show two in September, Elvis had already been filming his first film, *Love Me Tender*, in Hollywood for 20th Century Fox, on loan from Paramount. His hair appears darker. That time, the look was less maverick, but no less stylish – a rich, spotted velvet jacket, revere collar in a slightly darker shade, and a pale cotton brocade shirt with a plain satin, deep collar and classic satin tie with a geometric print. He sings his new song, 'Love Me Tender', from the upcoming film, and the crowd falls silent. At the end, they squeal more, cheer and rush home to order their copies of the record. A month later, Elvis receives his army draft questionnaire and *Time* magazine reports that RCA's advance orders for the new single have reached an all-time high of one million.

Controversy over Elvis's gyrations continued, to the distress of Gladys, and himself. As a God-fearing family, it was the condemnation by preachers of what they considered a God-given talent that hurt the most.

At a 1972 press conference ahead of his June concerts in Madison Square Garden, New York, a reporter says to Elvis, 'You used to be bitterly criticised so much for your long hair and gyrations and you seem so modest now.'

He laughs and replies, 'Man, I was tame compared to what they do now! Are you kidding? I didn't do anything but just jiggle, you know?'

As pressure mounted for Ed Sullivan not to allow Elvis on his show, Sullivan compromised and had his final appearance in January 1957 filmed from the waist up. Elvis performed the powerful and very respectful 'Peace in the Valley'.

90   Elvis: The King of Fashion

Despite the televisual neutering, Sullivan ended the show showering high praise on the lad from Tupelo:

> I wanted to say to Elvis Presley and the country that this is a real decent, fine boy ... Elvis, we want to say, we've never had a pleasanter experience on our show with a big name than we've had with you.
> You're thoroughly all right.

A happy ending, of sorts, and as far as Parker was concerned, even bad publicity gets the snow falling.

With Bob Neal's agreement to part manage Elvis now over, and having paid off Hank Snow, Parker had only one client – Elvis; just as he'd planned and just as agreed by Elvis, who saw him as the source of all his good fortune. As Elvis's exclusive manager, and he his exclusive artist, Parker spent every waking hour evolving and promoting Elvis the product, always including him and his parents in any plans and smiling benevolently, like an unnerving W.C. Fields, as the dollars rolled in – for all of them. It's hardly surprising, then, that Elvis, who hadn't a clue about, nor the slightest interest in, the commercial or administrative aspects of the industry he now found himself in, willingly agreed to Parker's suggestion that he should take care of the business side of things while Elvis took care of the music side, which he promised never to interfere with.

Parker's highly effective strategy of national exposure and, more to the point, Elvis's magnetism and that extraordinary succession of hit records, ensured that Parker's 'boy' returned to the South a huge star. To prove it, on 26 September, Elvis was invited to return to Tupelo and perform at the Mississippi-Alabama Fair & Dairy Show, where he last appeared as a daydreaming, bespectacled 10-year-old at the talent show where he came fifth singing 'Old Shep'.

It was to be quite the occasion, as it was to inaugurate Elvis Presley Day, with parades and a host of celebratory activities in honour of their most famous son. He and Gladys and Vernon were delighted to be asked and, in Elvis's new white Lincoln, it would have been a very different journey indeed to the one where they left for Memphis, under the cover of night, in their battered old car, stuffed with all their worldly goods, which didn't amount to much. As well as a life-affirming reminder of how far Elvis had come, both literally and metaphorically, from their humble roots, it would have been a very poignant occasion for all three of them. It was also when he wore a garment so distinctive, it has caused consternation, through a lack of confirmation of its origin, to many people, me included.

On the big day, despite it being gloriously sunny, with Elvis, style always came first. The conquering hero leapt on stage wearing a magnificent shirt of midnight blue velvet. It would have been stifling to wear, but it was a garment of pure theatre. Gleaming, gathered, billowy and blousy with long, exaggerated puff sleeves, a deep, stiff collar – a sign of things to come – and showy, silver, or perhaps pearlised buttons glinting like diamonds in the sunlight, it became a thing of legend. Theories abound on the shirt's origins but its actual provenance still eludes me.

In his 1998 ITV documentary *A Little Bit of Elvis*, English comedian Frank Skinner, having purchased at auction for £12,000 a blue velvet shirt described as having belonged to Elvis, was uncertain of its authenticity, so went to Memphis to find out whether it was real. Despite his best efforts, resulting in a highly entertaining show, Skinner never really found a satisfactory answer and, as far as I know, the jury is still out. Some say it came from Lansky Bros., others that it was made by Gladys. Or, that it was a gift from actress Natalie Wood – surely a case of mistaken identity, since Elvis first met her in November that year. When Elvis got to Hollywood, Wood did have two replica versions of the shirt made for him – one in the original deep blue, the other in scarlet, a shade that suited Elvis's dark looks, but which he wore only occasionally – so, perhaps that's why that notion exists.

Yet again, I consulted the oracle – Hal Lansky.

'No, this performance at the Tupelo County Fair, I think the shirt was hand-made by some relative.' Which relative, he's not sure, but he is certain that it was velvet and that it was hand-made. I'm rooting for Gladys.

So, did Elvis favour luxurious materials?

'When Elvis started out he did not ask for a certain fabric,' says Hal. 'What he was interested in was being different. Anything that didn't blend in with most of the traditional items in the marketplace, he liked.'

The minute Elvis took to the Tupelo stage with his band and The Jordanaires, the huge crowd cheered and Elvis gave them his all. He shook and shimmered through his opening song, 'Heartbreak Hotel', and performed superbly upbeat versions of the likes of 'Don't Be Cruel', 'Hound Dog' and 'Long Tall Sally'. At one point, he is presented with a certificate and a guitar-shaped key to the city by Mayor James L. Ballard.

Tupelo adored the maverick mic-hugger who they could barely believe was one of their own. They pressed against the stage in a state of frenzy and one overexcited girl charged the stage. She was quickly escorted away by security, but not before she got to touch her velvet-clad idol, who gave her his most dazzling smile.

Elvis's year of momentous happenings, all of which, individually, were astonishing, was rounded off with yet more.

'Love Me Tender', the single, hurtled to No. 1 in *Billboard*'s Top 100.

92   Elvis: The King of Fashion

In Vegas for a two-week engagement at the New Frontier Hotel, Tom Parker arranged for his friend, Mr Showman himself, Liberace, to pose for publicity shots with Elvis. The pair instantly clicked and even shared an impromptu fashion switch moment.

'We traded jackets,' Liberace told David Letterman during an interview on his *Late Night* show on 29 December 1983. 'He's wearing my jacket and I took his guitar and this picture went all over the world.'

Liberace put on Elvis's striped sports coat and Elvis took a seat at his piano and at one point fooled around with the candelabra.

> Elvis was impressed that I wore a sparkly jacket. He said could I wear a sparkly outfit in my next movie, would you mind?
>
> Ever since that picture ... we were very good friends. Every opening night he'd send me a guitar all made out of flowers and I would send, on his opening night, a piano all made out of flowers. He was a real nice guy.

The older Vegas crowd weren't impressed, though. Used to crooners and schmoozers, they were baffled by Elvis and their less-than-lukewarm reception rattled him. He vowed never to play there again.

It's always about the demographic, however, because around the same time, *Love Me Tender* the movie opened in 500 cinemas across America, giving many fans the first ever chance to see actual Elvis walking, talking, crying and – shockingly – dying. It was an instant smash, coming No. 2 in Variety's National Box Office survey.

In the December, 'Heartbreak Hotel' was declared the No. 1 single of 1956.

Finally, back at Audubon Drive for the holidays, Elvis must have felt that all his Christmases had come at once.

It really was the year that was ...

Chapter 8

Part I
My Best Girl

1957–60. Look: Screen Idol

'There was even a wild rumour that I shot my mother. Well, that's pretty silly. She's my best girlfriend, and I bought her and dad a home in Memphis where I hope they'll be for a long time.'

Elvis

I f your life resembles a movie, you may as well dress the part and get on with playing the leading role, which is more or less what Elvis did for the next decade.

After a year of national exposure, masterminded by Tom Parker, Elvis, the shy boy from Tupelo, was a bona fide movie star and the only homespun clothes he'd ever wear again were Hollywood wardrobe versions.

Being so young and inexperienced, it was quite the head spin for him to suddenly go from driving a truck for peanuts to earning mindboggling sums of money for doing what his heroes, Marlon Brando and James Dean (who by then had died in a car accident), did. Elvis often said that things happened so fast, there was no time to take it all in and he would disarm belligerent interviewers with his confession that he was afraid to sleep at night in case his good fortune was just a dream.

TV appearances in his flashy teenage-rebel outfits complete (tux and hound dog moment notwithstanding), he was back on a hectic touring schedule. Even so, since his debut film, *Love Me Tender*, was an instant hit, he had also stepped into his Hollywood dream, the one he harboured while watching actors on the big screen at Loew's cinema. As well as showcasing his acting skills, which, although in their infancy were considerable, Hollywood marked a new chapter in his fashion story, a tale of costumes, uniforms and a level of styling that elevated him to celluloid as well as music icon status.

Considering Elvis's instinctive, often predictive, fashion sense, the way he took off-the-peg or second-hand clothes and Elvised them with a twist here, a knot there, or a flash of colour somewhere, he was putty in the hands of the costume

94   Elvis: The King of Fashion

department staff. Of course, they loved him. He was a living mannequin; they could have put a bin liner on him and he'd have looked great, a useful commodity in such an appearance-fixated industry.

By then, kids on the street and performers were emulating his look. Photos of teenage guys, after 1956, ooze Elvis-inspired clothes and hair. Even wearing his 'everyday' stuff to record songs for *Love Me Tender*, he looked as though he'd walked off a movie set. Tailored black trousers, perfect ducktail and a pastel satin, side-buttoning, oriental-style top, which only Elvis could make look masculine. For the actual filming, he morphed into a farmer's son, all ticking-stripe shirts, dusty jeans and scuffed boots, without dropping a stitch of cool. Fans, starved of seeing him, swooned at his gorgeousness.

Among the endless wardrobe changes, as with the best films, Elvis's life was full of plot twists. The first came in January 1957, prior to filming and recording for Paramount's *Loving You*, when the army announced that he was classed 1-A for draft. Elvis and, of course, Gladys had dreaded this; he because he feared it could end his wonderful new career, she because she feared for his safety.

Almost in defiance of the news, Elvis instructed Gladys and Vernon to find a bigger, more secluded house, far from complaining neighbours and where the fans couldn't steal the washing off the line. They found it in Memphis's Whitehaven district, an attractive 1930s Colonial Revival style mansion, with Corinthian columns, perched on almost 14 acres. Once part of a larger farm, it was so upmarket, it even had a name – Graceland. Gladys and Vernon told Elvis he should come see it. He did, he loved it and he bought it that March for $102,000. So tight was his filming and touring schedule, it wasn't until the June that he spent his first night there.

Graceland. Tangible proof of how far Elvis, just 22, had come in so short a time. His glamorous new home was only a short car journey from their old Tupelo shotgun shack, scene of his dramatic entrance into the world, but it could have been on another planet. Lest they forgot those humble origins, they moved family members in, including Grandma Minnie Mae, Uncle Vester (Vernon's brother) and Uncle Travis (Gladys's brother), the latter two to help with the grounds and guard Elvis's new guitar-themed gates.

They increased their menagerie. Jeyhew the monkey came, but was eventually replaced by Scatter, a 40-pound chimpanzee with attitude and an eye for the women. There were donkeys and pigs and Elvis famously used his beautiful '54 Fleetwood limo to haul chickens, peacocks and an aggressive attack turkey they named Bow-Tie on account of the three black feathers at his throat, back to Graceland. Unsurprisingly, the birds shat everywhere and despite Herculean efforts by the Cadillac dealer to erase all evidence of the fouling fowls, the car never quite recovered. On the upside – Gladys got her chickens. They also

Part I My Best Girl   95

welcomed a stream of non-related humans, including staff, fans (make that girls, lots of girls), and the men who'd form the nucleus of Elvis's personal entourage, including Lamar Fike, Marty Lacker and Red West.

A magazine likened the Presleys' presence in the rarefied location to 'A jug of corn at a champagne party'. No matter; Graceland was Elvis's haven. A place to escape, in the company of folk like him, Southerners (mainly) from similar backgrounds who spoke like him, ate the same stuff and talked about the same things.

After New York, and to some extent, his first taste of Hollywood, Elvis was frankly tired of feeling inferior. He was never at ease with music industry suits, nor with movie types, and avoided celebrity parties like the plague; he had no interest in leaving Memphis, the place that made him. The family was also compared to the Beverly Hillbillies and later, to trashy lottery winners. I smell jealousy there and hope that they were blissfully unaware of being judged. They aspired to be decent people but were destined first to be dangerously poor before becoming richer than everyone they knew.

In Graceland, Elvis was in control. It was his lighthouse on a storm-tossed sea – and it was where he could be mothered. Still intensely close, friends and family would say they'd never known a relationship like Elvis and his mother's, complete with its own baby language. They'd also fight like cat and dog but still, she was his rock. And the house became a private club, a party pad, the local pool (by invitation) and zoo. Imagine the fun!

While away touring, and despite vowing it wouldn't happen again, Elvis fell prey once more to Parker's sartorial absurdity, the legendary gold lamé suit. Parker commissioned it from Nudie Cohn, Hollywood rodeo tailor to the famous. A stranger to subtlety whose motto was 'It's better to be looked over than overlooked', Nudie had already designed the red-and-white cowboy outfit Elvis wore while singing 'Teddy Bear' in *Loving You*. Elvis liked the stylised Western gear, but even to him, the gold number, seen in all its glory on the cover of his 1959 RCA album, *50,000,000 Fans Can't Be Wrong* (a cynical title courtesy of Parker), felt over the top. Made from metallic fabric, the baggy drape jacket and loose trousers were trimmed with rhinestones, as was the ruffled gold shirt and accessories, including a golden Western Kentucky style necktie, belt and tasselled brogues. A costume only Parker, Lord of Misrule, could have dreamed up. It cost 2,500 dollars, although the 'Snowman' christened it the '10,000-dollar suit'. The carny in him loved a gimmick, and what better for Elvis, sometimes called 'The Memphis Flash', than a suit that moved like lightning? Elvis disliked how it shed rhinestones and how the fabric shredded when he slid across the stage on his knees. However, he wore it for several concerts that

96   Elvis: The King of Fashion

year, including in St Louis and in Chicago, where he descended a staircase in front of 12,000 people, shimmering like the star he was.

The fans loved it, but Elvis did not; he felt it was clownish and soon swapped the trousers for stage-friendly ones. The jacket still made appearances, usually teamed with a black, open-neck shirt, dark trousers and, suddenly, a medallion.

In May and with 'All Shook Up' at No. 1 in the Top 100, Elvis was at MGM filming what would be a life-defining film. The one that made naysayers eat their words and which would come to be to be regarded as a work of cinematic joy. *Variety* described the main dance scene as 'arguably Elvis's greatest on-screen moment ever'.

I give you, *Jailhouse Rock*.

With outstanding Leiber and Stoller songs, exuberantly butch-camp choreography by Alex Romero, who channelled the power of Elvis's moves into the routines, and a teen-dream of a wardrobe, mainly by Lansky Bros. (apart from the bespoke denim jail outfit, which everyone remembers most), it is the late 1950s, preserved forever in celluloid.

Elvis, smouldering as Vince Everett, illuminated every scene, as did his outfits, which sashayed along with him, like New York catwalk models. The James Dean-esque cable-knit sweater (collar up, of course), pleat-front trousers, which alone could have earned him the 'Pelvis' moniker, and black-and-white loafers dominate the pool scene, where he absolutely nails 'Baby, I Don't Care'. The striped sports coats, dark with a Cuban-collar shirt for the calamitous 'meet-the-parents' scene and white with a bold stripe and raw-silk, geometric pattern shirt for dates, and the silk housecoat/cravat combo, that somehow works, and would have had Noel Coward green with envy, are all sublime. Cinemagoers of the time had never seen conservative silk, tweed and wool look so cool – and sexy.

As for Elvis's jeans outfit in the signature cellblock scene, since curtain up at the Memphis premiere on 17 October that year, it has been seared into the brains of humankind. As well as its original purpose of holding garments together, denim's contrasting stitching became a means of highlighting cut and design details. But Elvis's stitches are badass, super-sized slashes of white that define the shape of the hipster jacket, its Mandarin collar and double seams; on the jeans, it describes the lines of the pockets, waistband and crotch. Elvis's convict number, 6240, runs above his left jacket pocket and the black-and-white cat-burglar tee shirt pulls everything together.

His fellow inmates wore subdued versions of the outfit, so Elvis stood out like a fox in a henhouse, which was the intention. He's the neatest jailbird you ever did see, apart from his trademark rough boy leg-spread stance and his rebellious quiff that grooves along with a mind of its own.

Despite the success of the 1957 movies, they held sadness for Elvis. In *Loving You*, Gladys and Vernon played members of the audience in the scene where he sang 'Got A Lot O' Livin' To Do'. Making triple denim look like a good idea, Elvis leaps off the stage mid-song and starts shaking up the aisle. Gladys (in baby blue) and Vernon are about six rows back on his left. He rocks right up to them, gives full eye contact and then spins away. At the end, the fans roar their approval – two of them more than most …

After Gladys died, Elvis couldn't bear to watch the film. Around a month after filming wrapped on *Jailhouse Rock*, Elvis's beautiful and talented co-star Judy Tyler and her husband were killed in a head-on car collision. Elvis was devastated and didn't attend the October premiere.

So much was occurring in 1957, it almost eclipsed the previous year. 'Heartbreak Hotel' had charted in the UK in '56, but in the May, 'All Shook Up' made No. 1 there. The Brits went mad for this Elvis boy and a new swathe of fans was born. Singer songwriter Marty Wilde, dubbed Britain's answer to Elvis in the 1950s, was one of them. At 18, he was already performing but was inspired by the new sensation whose music and style was filtering in from the US. When I talk to Marty, now 84, he's admiring his cherished original 1956 pressing of the *Elvis Presley* album.

You can see there's a string missing from his Martin D-18 guitar and he's lost one of the pegs. That just shows how hard he played that thing.

That's why Elvis was so good. His music was massive, his sheer excitement came across and when that happens, people feel it. I never forget that when I do my own shows.

One of my band [The Wildcats] bought the album at the time but I wasn't sure, because his songs had that strange, echoing quality to them.

He's referring to Sam Phillip's innovative technique of running two recordings of the same song together, just out of sync, creating the reverberation that makes Elvis's Sun Recordings so exceptional. Marty continues:

It did sound strange, but I was hooked. I now love that original, raw sound. I played 'Jailhouse Rock' again and vocally, it's fantastic, a reminder of how Elvis's voice moved on.

He was the biggest influence in my early life. We'd never heard anything like it. It was liberating.

And the clothes! We were kids. The war hadn't been over for long and we relished the freedom. We'd been dressing like our dads, suddenly we wanted to be Elvis.

98   Elvis: The King of Fashion

Me, Billy Fury, Cliff Richard, we wanted to look like him, sing like him, dance like him and dress like him, collar turned up, sleeves rolled up, light jacket, black shirt, green trousers, two-tone shoes.

It took me a few years to admit to myself that I wasn't Elvis and that I should do my own thing.

Marty's own first hit single was 'Endless Sleep' in 1959, followed by 'Sea of Love' and 'Bad Boy', a copy of which he gave to Lamar Fike, who came to London from Germany during Elvis's army stint.

Lamar promised he'd get Elvis to play it. He even asked if I'd like to meet him. I answered 'What do you think!?'

The date coincided with my appearance on *Oh, Boy!* (Britain's first teenage music TV show), and my agent said I couldn't go – the TV show was too important.

Lamar later told me that Elvis loved 'Bad Boy' – that made me happy.

What still surprises me, is how no one realised he could sing. They dismissed him and, yet, he could sing the whole spectrum. His Sun Studio 'I'll Never Let You Go (Little Darlin')' – well!'

Marty wrote Lulu's 'I'm a Tiger', Status Quo's 'Ice in the Sun', and the hit '80s teen anthem, 'Kids In America', for his daughter, Kim Wilde.

He never did meet his hero.

Come July, 'Teddy Bear' was No. 1 in the Top 100, the R&B and the country charts; 'Loving You' was released to packed houses and Elvis took the train (he was afraid of flying) from Memphis for a five-day tour. At Spokane, Washington, 12,000 fans went crazy when he flew off the stage in his gold jacket and sang 'Hound Dog' kneeling in the dirt. Girls dug up pieces of the ground he'd knelt on.

An unexpected and unwelcome twist came when Scotty and Bill, but not drummer D.J. Fontana, said they were quitting, citing poor pay and scant credit for their work. They made a hundred dollars week, two if playing away, which compared to the dizzying sums rolling in, wasn't great and they were only paid *when* they worked.

Elvis, caught up in a whirlwind and with Parker managing all things monetary, may not have known this and he was shaken. He relied on Scotty and Bill. They *got* him. On stage, they anticipated his every move. Scotty once said they were 'the only band directed by an ass'. Elvis knew that they and Sam Phillips had been crucial in helping him find his true voice. It was they who accompanied him on long road trips with Bill's bass strapped to the car's roof and turned a blind eye to his philandering.

Beside himself, he called Parker.

'What am I gonna do?'

'You're going to get another band, that's what you're going to do,' was Parker's reply, empathy not being his strong point.

According to Lamar Fike, Parker then told Scotty and Bill ,'Fuck you. You're not going to get it. That's the way it is, boys. Cut-and-dried.'

Staying with the movie analogy, 1957's dénouement was a double plot twist. What felt like the happy ending, where news came in that *Jailhouse Rock* was in profit three weeks after its November release, was overshadowed by the closing scene where, just before Christmas, Elvis received his draft notice.

1958

Further chart-topping success heralded in the new year as Elvis headed to Paramount studios and then New Orleans to play misfit teenager Danny Fisher, in *King Creole*. It would be one of his most critically acclaimed roles.

Wanting to make the most of his two weeks in Memphis before going to Hollywood, he hooked up with his expanding 'gang', which, as well as Lamar, Marty and Red, featured his cousin Gene Smith, Cliff Gleaves, an itinerant quirky character, Alan Fortas, an outsider like Elvis from Humes High, DJ George Klein, and his latest girlfriend, Anita Wood (June Juanico, fed up with competing for Elvis's attention, finished with him, telling him that she was engaged). Anita, a petite blonde whom he nicknamed 'Little', helped him forget, as did a frenetic, pre-army fortnight of rough football, all-night skating, rollercoaster riding and watching movies – of his choice.

With the life of military looming, but *King Creole* already in production, Elvis had to request official permission to finish it, explaining that many jobs depended on its completion. The army consented. He finished filming and returned to Memphis fretting over how the other soldiers would treat him and feeling increasingly certain that his fans would forget him. Two years was a very long time in showbiz.

Parker, nothing if not the shrewdest of businessmen, got Elvis to record several songs prior to leaving, and drip-feed released them over Elvis's service phase. This was to keep him in everyone's mind until he got back, when they'd be desperate to see him.

Despite a chance to enlist in Special Services, the army's entertainment branch, Parker advised Elvis to serve as a regular soldier as it would look good back home and calm those still insisting that he was a dangerous, rebel-rousing disruptor who'd be better off in jail. More importantly, it would earn him the respect of his fellow soldiers.

100   Elvis: The King of Fashion

On a drizzly 24 March – the day his fans christened 'Black Monday' – Elvis, in a bold plaid jacket, open-neck striped shirt and dark navy trousers, reported to the local draft board for induction. He was accompanied by Vernon, a tearful Gladys, and other family and friends. As he was sworn in, distinctive among his fellow draftees as he just looked so, well, Elvisy, and assigned his service number of 53310761, a battalion of reporters and photographers, invited by Parker, scrutinised his every move. Elvis handled the intrusion with good grace and self-deprecating humour, while the Snowman doled out *King Creole* balloons to the fans who had gathered.

After fond farewells and a big hug and kiss for his 'best girl', Gladys, Elvis boarded the army bus bound for Fort Chaffee, Arkansas. Poor Gladys was already miserable about Elvis's absences from Graceland, so imagine how low she must have felt watching her beloved 'Boobie' disappear to God knows what. She'd also been unwell and experiencing tummy aches.

Fort Chaffee, too, was teeming with press, photographers and fans. Elvis was asked endless questions and every last snip of what became the world's most famous haircut was documented. Again, Elvis politely joshed as the military barber sheared off his DA, quiff and sideburns, yet he seemed forlorn. They may have been his trademarks, but they were no gimmick. They'd been his style choice since he started shaving and as well as a raft of trouble, equally had brought him a whole lot of love. Images of him in the barber's chair, staring at the hair trimmings in his hands, gives off Samson vibes; was he wondering whether his power, too, would disappear with the loss of his luxuriant locks? On top of the tumultuous change he knew was coming, this might have been a moment when he wished he actually was dreaming.

He needn't have worried. He was Elvis. He looked great with a crew cut. Add a well-fitted uniform and, to his legions of fans, their Hillbilly Cat was now their handsome soldier boy. The barber's is now a museum, the interior lovingly restored to exactly how it was during the 1958 follicular feeding-frenzy.

Next up for Elvis was Fort Hood for training. Parker reminded his greatest asset not to perform under any circumstances, explaining that maintaining an air of mystique meant retaining demand for his music and movies. Elvis got stuck in with the best of them and was an exemplary soldier, but he was way out of his comfort zone and utterly homesick. In May, however, Tom Parker learned that soldiers with dependents (usually wives and children), could live off-base so Elvis rented a house near the base and moved in Vernon, Gladys, Minnie Mae (aka 'Dodger' after she once ducked in time to avoid a ball Elvis threw at her), and Lamar Fike.

Home in Memphis for two weeks' leave in June, Elvis would sometimes wear his army uniform because he was proud of it; he also knew that, just as in

Part I My Best Girl   101

his school days, it made him stand out. It was a girl magnet, especially handy when surrounded by giddy fans at Graceland's gates who stood mesmerised as he explained his insignia to them. That fortnight, he somehow shoehorned in a recording session at RCA's Studio B in Nashville, laying down five singles, still in uniform. Steve Sholes produced and, as well as a group of new musicians, there were familiar faces in the shape of D.J. and The Jordanaires.

Come August, another plot twist arrived. Gladys's health deteriorated further. While she loved being with Elvis, she had been stressed about moving, which had put a strain on her existing health issues. She'd also been drinking more in Elvis's absence and those close to her have said that she took diet pills to combat weight gain. I sense the latter wasn't through vanity, but her attempt to look glamorous for her son; it wasn't easy being the mother of a Hollywood heartthrob.

Gladys was a beautiful woman; look at the genes she gifted to Elvis. However, years of hardship, the traumatic birth scenario, a poor diet, a cocktail of inherited genetic disorders and a propensity for fretting, had all taken their toll. Dark shadows under her eyes made her appear exhausted but were actually signalling illness. She was puffy and heavy in uncomfortable-looking clothes. Most of all, she looked sad. All of which would have been more bearable had she not been constantly photographed and filmed alongside her stunning son.

People seeing the photos drew comparisons, they still do, and Gladys knew that – because *she* did, too – and found herself wanting. In photos where she's smiling, which are rare, she is dazzling and leaves no doubt that she was indeed queen mother to the young king. Her anxiety was unfounded, everyone who knew her personally loved her, especially Elvis, but it's there in every photo.

There was some good news. *King Creole* was released to good reviews, so Elvis could relax, secure in the knowledge he was still relevant.

As the summer wore on, Gladys, always a fun and welcoming host, lost her zest for anything. Sensing something was wrong, she called her doctor, Charles Clarke, and on 8 August, she and Vernon returned to Memphis. The following day, she was hospitalised to be examined for what was described by Dr Clarke as a liver complication, 'not a typical hepatitis' but 'some sort of blood-clotting phenomenon'.

On Sunday, 10 August 1958, United Press International reported that 'Mrs. Vernon Presley, mother of rock and roll singer, Elvis Presley, entered Methodist hospital here Saturday … Elvis's parents were returning from Texas, where their son was living while taking advanced tank training at Fort Hood.' Vernon told a UPI writer that Gladys had been 'feeling badly' for some time and that while heading back to Memphis, she 'suddenly became worse'.

102   Elvis: The King of Fashion

That Monday, she was no better and the doctors were none the wiser. Elvis requested compassionate leave and he and Lamar flew into Memphis on the evening of Tuesday the 12th. He went straight to his mother's bedside.

'Oh, my son, my son,' Gladys cried on seeing him – she'd been terrified of him flying. She seemed better than Elvis had expected and he was told by staff that his visiting had perked her up somewhat. Vernon stayed by her bedside overnight and Elvis left, returning early Wednesday morning for a few hours and again late afternoon. He and Gladys talked at length and he left at midnight, telling her he'd be back the next morning to take the many flowers she'd received back to the house.

On 14 August, around 3.15 a.m., the main telephone rang in Graceland. Elvis knew something was wrong before his cousin Billy Smith answered the call.

'It was Vernon on the phone and he said, you need to tell Elvis … and that was as far as it got,' said Billy. 'By this time, I could hear him in the background and he was sobbin'.'

A nurse stepped in and told Billy that his aunt had taken a turn for the worse and that Elvis should get to the hospital right away. Although only 14 at the time, Billy sensed that Gladys was dying. He told Elvis she'd 'gotten a little sicker'. They ran to the car and raced to Memphis Methodist Hospital, left the Lincoln Mark II outside its doors with its engine still running and ran to the ward. On seeing his father's distress, Elvis knew. They were too late. His beloved mama, the most precious thing in his life, was dead. Vernon was with Gladys when she began struggling for breath around 3 a.m. He called for a doctor and tried to make her comfortable, but she was gone before they got to her.

Elvis went to her bed, dropped to his knees and wept. When Lamar Fike arrived shortly after, with Minnie Mae, they could hear Elvis and Vernon's wails when they stepped out of the lift.

The given cause was a heart attack with liver damage complications. She was 46.

Elvis and Vernon were overcome with grief. Their rock, the woman who'd protected Elvis, often on her own, and who'd worked when Vernon couldn't, had crumbled and been washed away on a tidal wave of illness.

'"She was all we lived for," Elvis sobbed at the hospital early Thursday morning after learning of his mother's death.' reported UPI.

An Associated Press story quoted him as saying, 'It broke my heart. She was always my best girl.' UPI also reported that Elvis had his mother's body moved to Graceland, and opened the doors 'to friends for a last look at his "best girl-friend"'.

To me, the saddest snippet of all is in an unnamed UPI writer's memorial note: 'The plump Mrs. Presley, who … followed her son from coast to coast, was

Part I My Best Girl   103

devoted to the youth who rocketed to fame as a rock 'n' roll entertainer in the space of a few years.' Why 'The plump'? At least poor Gladys would never see it.

Back at Graceland, Elvis was inconsolable, crying and clinging to Gladys's clothes. He lingered close to her coffin, talking to her as though she were still alive and gently rocked her and stroked her hands. Mid-morning, reporters arrived at Graceland to find Vernon and Elvis sitting, clinging to one another, on the front steps. Elvis was in a pale ruffled shirt with sleeves rolled up, khaki continental-style trousers and white leather shoes – possibly what he pulled on in the middle of the night to rush to his mother's side.

No quarter was asked for and none was given by the press who pushed for statements – nor by the snappers who photographed their desolation for the world to see. Elvis, sobbing throughout, told reporters that his mother's death had broken his heart. Indubitably, something fractured within him when his Satnin died, for, with hindsight, Elvis's life, in fact Elvis himself, altered forever that day.

He was left rudderless.

Of course, his daddy loved him, but in a dad-of-a-lad, cars-and-cook-outs sort of way. Vernon enjoyed the fun and the games, the parties and the pretty girls, all the trappings that money could bring. However, the emotion, the unconditional devotion, the moral compass and the sound guidance had mainly come from Gladys. Vernon hadn't her natural smarts, nor did he have her sense of humour or her engrained wisdom, born of a life of dark deprivation and childhood survival.

Although Elvis never realised it, he was liberated by her death, too. Liberated, that is, to play rougher; to play around more; and to play with fire, as in pills, which he'd already been using more regularly to stay awake or get to sleep and then to perk up again, especially during relentless touring schedules.

At Gladys's funeral, the Blackwood Brothers, one of her favourite groups, sang 'Precious Memories' and 'Rock of Ages'. Four years before, they had suffered a tragedy of their own when their brother, R.W., died in a plane crash.

Elvis and Vernon wept uncontrollably. Gladys was buried at Forest Hill Cemetery, but later moved to Graceland, where she remains in the Meditation Garden. She's not alone. Elvis, Vernon, Dodger, Jesse, Lisa Marie and Benjamin Storm, Gladys's great-grandson, lie with her.

That September, with army training completed and still overwhelmed with grief, Elvis was pushed further out of his comfort zone. For the first time in his life, he left America, boarding the USS *General Randall* in New York bound for Bremerhaven, Germany, and his next life-as-a-movie role: Private Elvis. He spent the rest of his two years' service living at 14 Goethestraße, a rented house in Bad Nauheim, close to his base. Bored and resigned, he stoically carried out

104   Elvis: The King of Fashion

his duties; those of being a good soldier and getting familiar with the local girls at evening soirées at his house, where there was no shortage of willing recruits to join him in his bedroom upstairs. Still, he was homesick in his new, khaki-coloured world, where the highlights were leasing a white convertible BMW, being promoted to private first class and being named the World's Outstanding Popular Singer.

Counting the days, Elvis was glad to see the year out, never having dreamed at the start that the two most momentous and commented upon scenes of 1958 would be the loss of his beloved mother and his beloved pompadour.

The following year began like an intermission.

'Those months were a strange hiatus,' says Bobbie Ann Mason in *Elvis*. 'Elvis was suspended between two worlds. He spent his days as a reluctant dogface, an ordinary GI. Then in the evenings he returned to the family's little Memphis-on-the-Rhine.' He was in limbo, yet even then, he dreaded what it might feel like to return to Graceland without Gladys there to greet him, mother him and holler at him when needed.

Visiting Graceland myself for the first time in March 2023, I was thrown by how it affected me. On the front steps, all I could think of was Elvis and Vernon trying to console one another after Gladys had died. In the hallway, a sweet photo of a smiling Lisa Marie around the age Elvis would have been when he wore his baby trilby hat in the famous sepia photo with young Gladys and Vernon, added to the feeling. Grown-up Lisa Marie had died just two months before, of cardiac arrest. Like Gladys. Like her father. Opposite, on the grand stairway, was a picture of a still-blond, angelic young Elvis. It was almost too much to take. Three instant reminders of three too-short lives.

Each room was suffused with the presence of Elvis, of the Presley family. It's not a shrine, more an homage, a museum of loving preservation, and it's utterly fascinating. Of course, there are glamorous touches and trimmings; the dining room is particularly sumptuous, the stained-glass living room and the music room are dazzling. However, the everyday ephemera are so emotive. The original kitchen, with its dingy but cocooning interior and gadgets and utensils frozen in time, evokes images of Elvis leaning on a counter, asking Alberta the maid, whom he nicknamed VO5 after Alberto VO5 shampoo, to incinerate some bacon and eggs for him. As for the Jungle Room, built as an extension and simply called 'the den', that really is something else. With its masculine, unrelentingly chunky dark, carved wood furniture and pound-shoplike tropical accessories, it's certainly quirky; the solitary teddy bear on a chair, waiting for eternity for Elvis to return, is slightly disturbing. It's not in keeping with Elvis's taste, but it's definitely tongue-in-cheek, which sort of scans. There are several takes on the inspiration behind it, including Elvis's trips to Hawaii. However,

Part I My Best Girl   105

I prefer the one where Vernon came home laughing one day about some God-awful furniture he'd seen in a nearby shop and, for a joke, Elvis went straight down there, bought a load of it and had the den kitted out by nightfall.

Steve Binder, producer and director (and hero for convincing Elvis to escape his movie mediocrity), told me, 'Elvis furnished the Jungle Room in an hour at one furniture store … he didn't want to hire a decorator or spend the time shopping.'

Moving on to Elvis's car collection and marvelling at the sea of gleaming, top-of-the-range, vintage vehicles on display in the Cadillac room, I remembered Regis Wilson's story about how Elvis spent most of his wages on hiring a nice blue Chevrolet (that matched his suit) to take her to the prom, since, in 1953 his usual car was his daddy's battered old jalopy. Suddenly, everything all makes sense.

In June 1959, the action kicked in again when Elvis had a two-week furlough that turned into a two-week binge. On a mission to have 'fun', he visited Munich and then Paris with Lamar and army pals, Rex Mansfield and Charlie Hodge, a musician Elvis knew from touring back home. It was an orgy of nightclubs and strip joints, including the Moulin Rouge, Café de Paris and the Lido. In photos from the time, Elvis is dressed to impress, Euro style. Dark, tailored suits, crisp white shirts, ties and pocket kerchiefs or beautifully cut New York-modern jackets and statement-stripe casual shirts. If the look had a name, it would be 'Cool Continental'.

His hair was its natural, lighter shade – the deep shadows under his eyes were not. Surrounded by champagne buckets and sexy showgirls wearing little more than clouds of Gitanes smoke, competing to show him some real French kissing, he has the glazed look of extreme overindulgence. Living the life nocturnal with debauched club parties and play fights with dancing girls – and an accidental dancing boy who was quickly bid 'adieu' – back at the grand Parisian hotel Prince de Galles – fun was definitely being had. Elvis and his friends' escapades were largely kept out of the press but are now legendary. Among the highlights, or lowlights, depending on how one looks at it, is where the Lido manager, whose Bluebird dancers spent all night at the Prince de Galles, called Elvis's suite in the morning to ask for his girls back.

Nineteen fifty-nine's closing scene began in deceptively innocuous fashion.

It was November and Elvis was in the nondescript living room of his German house, surrounded by pals and young women. Even so, he stood out a mile, not only because of his kinglike demeanour, leg slung over the arm of the chair, cigar in hand, but also because of his outfit. Tan continental-cut trousers, teamed with a simple, fine-knit red sweater and dark suede loafers was an unorthodox colour combo, but was pure Elvis at his most confident, or acting so.

Suddenly, one of his friends entered the room with a young girl wearing a navy blue-and-white sailor dress with white socks and shoes.

106   Elvis: The King of Fashion

Elvis says, 'Well. What have we here?'

The girl, dumbstruck, just stares at him.

'Elvis,' says the man who brought her, 'this is Priscilla Beaulieu. The girl I told you about.'

By early 1960, Elvis, now a sergeant, and Priscilla had fallen in love (or lust) at first sight. She said he looked even more handsome than in his photos; he was besotted by her delicate features and aura of innocence. He was shocked when the beautiful, doll-like daughter of an American Air Force officer told him she was 14. He soon got over it, though, and saw more of her, despite warnings from his father and Tom Parker about how the relationship could be perceived. Elvis promised them, and Priscilla's parents, who insisted on meeting him, that his intentions were pure – he just cherished having someone from 'home' to talk to. And he swore to Priscilla that he'd never do anything to harm her, saying, 'I'll treat you like a sister.' Which he did. For a while. Then they'd steal up to his room every night, separately to avoid attention (or so Priscilla thought). To this day, she's adamant that they didn't have sex until their wedding night in 1967 – seven years after meeting.

Many people find this hard to swallow, but I think that's what they conveniently believed. Priscilla has always been honest about how she begged Elvis for sex almost from the start and that it was he who insisted they wait. However, their definition of what *constituted* sex was open to interpretation. Their interpretation.

Elvis's stance fits with his fixation that his wife should be a virgin, a somewhat dated notion – that some women were for sex, others for marrying – for a voraciously sexually active man heading for the liberated '60s. Taking this further, Elvis also tended to avoid sex with consensual women, even those with no expectations of a relationship or marriage, if they'd already had children. This, in his mind at least, was honouring the sanctity of motherhood. Of Gladys. To him and the initially naïve Priscilla, whom history shows he was grooming to be his perfect wife, only actual penetration counted as real sex. Details revealed by Priscilla in a 1985 interview with journalist producer Barbara Walters alluded to them doing everything *but* the final act. And that their creativity in finding alternative means of satisfying their 'needs', some of which, in later years, involved recording intimate moments with a Polaroid camera, knew no bounds.

Come March, they'd been together constantly, in spite of Priscilla's parents' concerns and how the late nights that she was spending 'just talking' to Elvis were diversely affecting her schoolwork. Elvis had already been using pills to manage his sleep patterns and energy levels. In the army, it was no different. Amphetamines, or speed, were popular among soldiers for staying awake on nighttime patrols and for boosting stamina. That they were prescription drugs made them safe in Elvis's eyes, and since they also happened to lift his mood,

Part I My Best Girl   107

why not? He even suggested Dexedrine to Priscilla to help her stay awake for their late-night trysts and to cope with school.

For Elvis, March spelled freedom. At last, he could return home for good. *TV Radio Mirror* announced that he'd been voted the winner of a contest asking 'who should be the King of Rock 'n' Roll?'; he received a gold disc, marking more than *3 million* sales of his album; and *Photoplay's* cover featured a photo of him in fatigues and, inside, a letter from him to his fans, thanking them for buying his records and staying loyal. His departure meant leaving Priscilla behind, which he genuinely felt sad about since they'd grown close, too close, if Priscilla's later disclosures about their deeply passionate kisses and caresses, which had left her 'weak with desire', are anything to go by.

To Priscilla, it was the end of her world. How this relationship was allowed at all, let alone in an intensively conservative time, is baffling. Some, including Priscilla, say it was because she was very forceful and unusually mature for her age and that her parents, while usually strict, trusted Elvis after meeting him. Others think that the Beaulieus were interested in Elvis's status and his money, or at least in the benefits they could bring. Yet others cite an entrenched history and even at that time, a continuing prevalence of young girls in serious realtionships and child marriages in the rural South, making it somehow less notable. Opinions vary, but Priscilla, now 78, says that she was at her happiest and felt completely unpressured and safe in the company of Elvis.

Prior to leaving Germany, he assured her that he'd never forget her and that he'd work out a way to get her to Graceland. On 2 March, with his homecoming and photos of him looking very dashing in his uniform splashed over America's front pages, Priscilla had no choice but to join crowds of fans and bid him a tearful goodbye from Wiesbaden Airport. Elvis arrived the following day at McGuire air force base, Fort Dix, to a snowstorm of both the elemental and press variety. When questioned, he told the gathered press that he hoped to be a dramatic actor and to continue singing. He mentioned he'd be on Frank Sinatra's show. And said that there was no special lady in his life …

You can almost hear the young Priscilla's heart breaking on reading the reports.

Still wary of flying, Elvis boarded a private train with Tom Parker and some of his entourage for the twenty-four-hour journey to Memphis, arriving in snow at 8 a.m.

Before being packed off to Germany, the relatively innocent Elvis was being described by detractors in hyperbolic terms such as dangerous, feral, overtly sexual – now he looked the part. Watching footage of him on the train platform, the baby face has gone; he looks lean, his revealed bone structure lending him a chiselled look that emphasises the high cheekbones from his mother's believed Cherokee heritage. He appears worldly-wise, a little harder, a little darker.

108   Elvis: The King of Fashion

As though in a daze, he walks through the station; after shaking hands with dignitaries he heads straight to a waiting crowd of fenced-off fans who smile and call out and reach for him through the bars. It's riveting. Like watching people trying to touch some exotic, fabled creature – a unicorn, perhaps – to convince themselves it's real. As for Elvis, it's like seeing a man realising that he still matters and who longs to hug everyone for being there, but can't. He then seeks out Gary Pepper, his disabled friend who ran his Elvis fan club.

Unsurprisingly, his next port of call was Forest Hill Cemetery to visit Gladys's grave and see the stone angels headstone they'd had made.

After that, Sergeant Presley defaulted to big-kid mode, catching the *Holiday on Ice* show at Ellis Auditorium, playing rough war games at the skate rink and having all-night singalongs. From then on, he was basically nocturnal. Soon it was back to business and within a month Elvis and his entourage, and his old musicians Scotty Moore and D.J. Fontana but no Bill Black (who died later, in 1966, during brain surgery), went to Nashville for a recording session at RCA's Studio B. The musicians from his June 1958 Nashville session also joined them, as did The Jordanaires, Parker and RCA's chief studio engineer, Bill Porter.

The result, his album *Elvis Is Back* was released in April and charted for fifty-six weeks, three of those at No. 2, and his new single, 'It's Now or Never', reached No. 1, was single of the year and went on to sell over 25 million copies. 'Are You Lonesome Tonight?' followed, again soaring up multiple charts and staying at No. 1 in the UK charts for a month.

Elvis was well and truly back.

Early fashionista – baby Elvis (aged about 2–3) in tweed trilby and corduroy overalls, sits with his parents, Gladys and Vernon, in Tupelo, *circa* 1937. *Elvis Country* album cover, 1971. (*RCA Victor*)

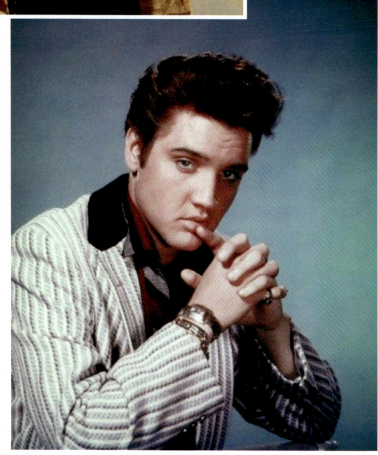

Hand candy – Elvis accessorises a striped, velvet-collared Lansky Bros. sports coat with chunky gold jewellery in promo shot for MGM's *Jailhouse Rock* movie, 1956–7.

Hollywood heartthrob – Elvis in yellow shirt with Greek keynote detail, on the set of *King Creole*. Production photo, June 1958, Paramount Pictures. (*wikipedia.org*)

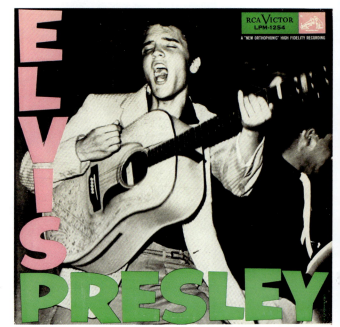

Record breaker – Elvis in white seersucker jacket, black shirt and whip-thin belt with buckle worn to the side, on the cover of his first recorded album, 1956. (*RCA Victor, wikipedia.org*)

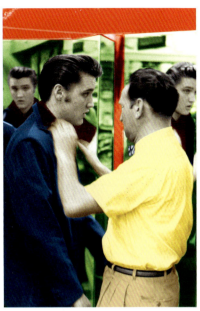

Mirror Man – clothier to The King, Bernard Lansky flips Elvis's collar, *circa* 1956. (*Lansky Bros. family archive*)

G.I. Blues – Elvis in Hollywood uniform for Paramount Pictures promo shot with co-star Juliet Prowse, 1960. (*wikipedia.org*)

Little red Corvette – Elvis chills in Western-inspired cream-and-black-stitched outfit on the set of *Clambake*. Promo shot for United Artists, 1967.

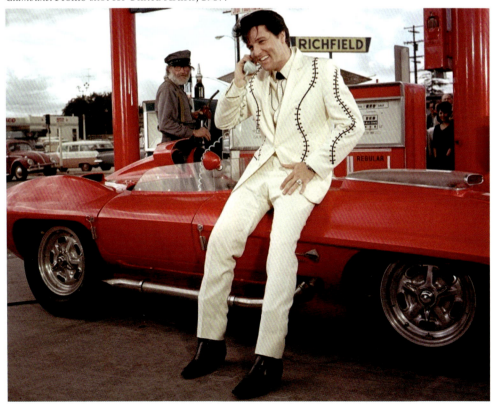

That's all white – Elvis wears a dazzlingly white suit with single crimson slash of silk scarf, by Bill Belew, to sing 'If I Can Dream' on the '68 Comeback Special. Detail from album *Elvis*, by RCA Victor. (*wikipedia.org*)

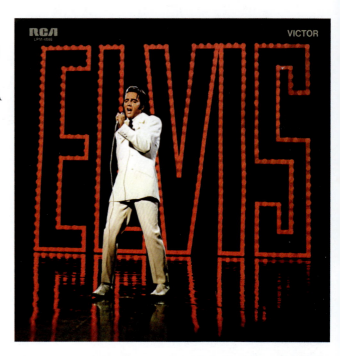

Hot chocolate – a shirtless Elvis in the author's favourite Bill Belew cutaway suit, with Mexican silver and turquoise belt, attends Barbara Streisand's 31 July 1969 show at the International Hotel, Las Vegas. (*Photographer Oscar Abolafia*)

Swinging the blues – Elvis jokes about his 'subtle' gold Hilton International belt during a press conference ahead of his Madison Square Garden concerts, New York, 9 June 1972. (*Hilton*)

High flyer – Elvis wears black abstract-print shirt and black suit, with burnt-orange trim detail, at Chicago Midway airport, 1972. (*Photographer Jack Baity*)

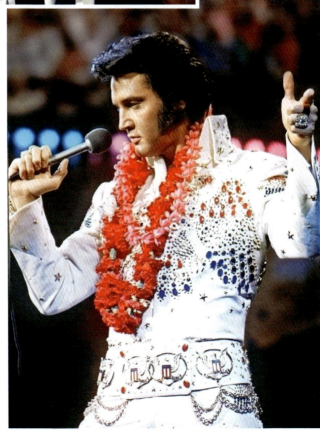

Aloha! – Elvis in the American Eagle suit by Bill Belew and Gene Doucette for the live satellite concert from Honolulu, Hawaii, 1973. (*Public domain*)

Ready to fly – Elvis in the bejewelled Pharaoh cape, Atlanta, 3 July 1973. (*From Keith Alverson's book,* Strictly Elvis; *image copyright, photographer, Keith Alverson, email eponstage@charter.net*)

Guitar man – Elvis in black leather suit by Bill Belew, *'68 Comeback Special*. (*commons.wikimedia.org*)

Life through a lens – a remarkably intimate photo of Elvis performing in his Chief suit at the Charleston Civic Centre, 1975. (*Courtesy of life-long fan, Teri Hammond-Kincaid*)

Sun god – The King in his legendary Mexican Sundial suit, taken during his next-to-last concert, in Cincinnati, 25 June 1977. (*Copyright photographer Keith Alverson, email eponstage@charter.net*)

Young pretender – actor Austin Butler in black leather *'68 Comeback* suit on a film poster for Baz Luhrmann's hit 2022 movie, *Elvis*, Warner Bros. (*wikipedia.org*)

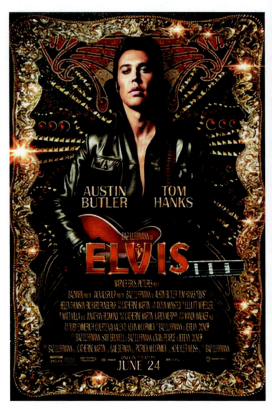

Legacy – collection of B&K Enterprises' Elvis-inspired jumpsuits. Left to right: Peacock, Totem Pole, Mad Tiger, Chicken Bone (Black Aztec), Chief, and Mexican Sundial. (*B&K Enterprises*)

Part II
Lights, Camera, Action!
1960–7. Look: Hot Hollywood

Before Elvis, there was nothing.

John Lennon

Knowing that his client's big ambition was to become an actor, Tom Parker had been busy. Having helped make Elvis the biggest singing star in the country, it was time to apply the same marketing genius to his movie career. Before you could say 'action', Parker tied him into a raft of profitable film deals with schedules that would keep him in work far into the future.

Elvis's new film role wasn't much of a stretch – he could even stay in uniform. Using the Beverly Wilshire Hotel as a base for himself and the guys, in May, Elvis joined director Norman Taurog to film *GI Blues*, a musical comedy, for Paramount. In keeping with life imitating art and vice versa, he played Tulsa McLean, a US Army tank crewman with a singing career and a penchant for German nightclub dancers ... In one scene, he even hears 'Blue Suede Shoes' playing on a bar's jukebox and notes that it's by some guy called 'Elvis Presley'.

It was as far from Brando or Dean as he could get without moving to the moon, but he was line perfect and picture perfect in his Hollywood uniform, even when rocking that most difficult to pull off of accessories, the cannonball tank helmet. And, of course, he steals the show. Soldiering, singing, kissing, babysitting, it matters not, because he's Elvis.

As became the norm in just about every film he did, he was romantically linked to his leading lady, in this case, Juliet Prowse, who played Lili, a club dancer, *naturellement*!

Between 1961, starting with *Blue Hawaii*, and ending in 1968 with *Speedway* and *Live a Little, Love a Little*, Taurog directed Elvis in eight films. Mid-filming, Elvis went to Miami to appear on *The Frank Sinatra Timex Show: Welcome Home Elvis* on ABCTV, with co-guests Nancy Sinatra, Sammy Davis Jr. and Peter Lawford. Despite being TV averse after Steve Allen's humiliating show and aware that Sinatra had previously said that rock 'n' roll music was 'sung,

110   Elvis: The King of Fashion

played and written for the most part by cretinous goons' and that 'Presley has no training at all. When he goes into something serious, a bigger kind of singing, we'll find out if he is a singer,' it went well. Perhaps because Sinatra's daughter adored Elvis and had befriended him. In footage, he's at ease with Sinatra; they josh and duet together, singing one another's songs. The 'cretinous' boy is cool and confident, even in what looks dangerously like a tux, and he nails his and Ol' Blue Eyes' notes with ease. Fans, however, accused Elvis of selling out, of being tamed, and of having lost his passion for music. Most damning, they said that he was just as conservative and middle class as their parents.

Worse, in the June, *Movie Mirror* announced, 'The King of Rock 'n' Roll is Dead!'

All the while, there was no Gladys for Elvis to consult and as for Vernon, he dismayed him by having a giddy affair with Dee Stanley, the wife of an army officer, just three months after Gladys died. Hurt and infuriated, Elvis saw it as too soon and disrespectful to his mother's memory. Vernon went on to marry Dee and take on her three sons, but while Elvis was polite to his stepmother and always kind to his new 'little brothers', he never accepted the marriage and didn't attend their wedding.

On a trip to Las Vegas, ahead of filming for 20th Century Fox, Elvis's entourage arrived in dark glasses and black mohair suits and it was then they were nicknamed the 'Memphis Mafia' – a name that has stuck to this day.

Shooting on director Don Siegel's *Flaming Star* started in the August and continued until October, and Elvis had a casual affair with wardrobe mistress Nancy Sharp. Women dressed women and men dressed men on movie sets at the time, so Nancy wouldn't actually have assisted Elvis in dressing, but she certainly wouldn't have missed him walking tall on set as Pacer Burton in his gorgeous rancher outfit. He was prairie-chic perfection – taupe Stetson; sand-coloured jeans; cropped grey suede jacket trimmed with rust-brown blanket stitching; open-neck linen shirt, all accessorised with tobacco-coloured suede cowboy boots and chocolate-brown leather gun and knife belts, slung low on his hips in a sign of jumpsuit belts to come. Ditch the hat and the hardware and Elvis could stroll down any high street in that outfit today and not look out of place. In his other scenes, stripped to the waist, ready to fight, Nancy would definitely have noticed him.

Attempting to be taken seriously, Elvis requested no songs in *Flaming Star*. Fox insisted on four. At least producer David Weisbart wanted to use them in relevant scenes. Even so, Elvis insisted that two songs be removed – and won. It would be the last say he'd have in song quotas until the release of *Charro!* in 1968, coincidentally another Western, with only a title track number.

By the end of the year, the Parker effect had really taken hold as *GI Blues* was named *Variety*'s No. 2 top-grossing movie and Elvis started filming *Wild in the Country*, another musical drama, again for Fox.

Whirlwind doesn't come close to describing the start of 1961. After filming *Wild in the Country* with Hope Lange as his leading lady (and seeing Nancy Sharp behind the scenes), Elvis was in California to film *Blue Hawaii*, for Paramount. His 'no songs' requests were ignored and the number stipulated increased exponentially with each film – as did the cheesiness of the plots. Howard Thompson of the *New York Times* called *Blue Hawaii* 'blandly uneventful', with a 'nonsensical and harmless' plot, adding, 'Presley delivers the songs and rhythmical spasms right on schedule. We counted fourteen tunes, about half of them replete with ukulele trimmings and exotic, weaving dancers.'

It may have been panned by the critics, but it was a hit with audiences and the soundtrack album was in *Billboard*'s Pop Albums chart for seventy-nine weeks, twenty at No. 1, and went on to sell 3 million copies. It defied detractors for one simple reason. Elvis was in it. His fans idolised him, still do, and there's no denying that Parker's ploy of keeping him in demand by keeping him under wraps really did leave them wanting more. Which is what they got as Elvis, tanned and toned and dressed in tropical-print Hawaiian shirts, or no shirt at all, shimmied in skin-tight white surfing shorts while serenading adoring starlets in conically upholstered swimsuits.

Keeping with the movie theme, in the middle of filming *Blue Hawaii* in Hollywood, Elvis flew to the actual island for a fundraising concert. A few months before, Tom Parker had read a newspaper appeal for help to boost funds for a memorial at the site of the sunken battleship USS *Arizona* in Pearl Harbor, to honour those killed in the Japanese attack in 1941. As his film would soon be released, and *Girls! Girls! Girls!*, another Paramount offering scheduled to start shooting on Hawaii the following year, it was a platinum publicity opportunity. Parker and Elvis agreed to a concert appearance and to donate the takings.

'Every penny … must go to the fund,' declared the Snowman at a press conference in Hawaii in early January to announce the concert, 'otherwise, we are not interested in doing the show.'

H. Tucker Gratz, the memorial fund commission's chairman, said, 'Not a living soul will get a free ticket to this show, and that includes the performers, and even Colonel Parker. Our sincere thanks to Colonel Parker. It's hard to believe this is real.'

Parker assured him it was and added:

You know, Elvis is twenty-six and that's about the average age of those boys entombed in the *Arizona*. I think it's appropriate that he should be

112   Elvis: The King of Fashion

doing this. There's no excuse for Elvis to leave this island without his raising $50,000.

Pearl Harbor's Bloch Arena was the venue, with 4,000 seats, including 300 premium 'ringside' ones that would cost $100 each. Other tickets ranged from a more fan-friendly $3 to $10.

Skilled as much in the art of perception as he was in deception, Parker announced widely and frequently that he and Elvis would personally pay all other performers out of their own pockets, and waive expenses.

There was a definite hint of snow in the warm Hawaiian air at noon on 25 March, the day of the concert. In fact, there was a snowman. Well, someone inside a full-size frosty costume at the bottom of the steps of the plane at Honolulu International Airport – no doubt a condescending ploy by Tom Parker to amuse the 3,000 fans gathered to welcome Elvis. Dressed in a dark suit with a black-buttoned, white ruffled shirt, a skinny tie and almost disappearing inside a collar of lei garlands, he moved along the wire fence, looking tired (small wonder), but smiling for his fans, some of whom, a reporter noted, 'looked as though they were ready to tear him limb for [*sic*] limb, and take home the pieces for souvenirs'.

The concert, which featured a line-up of other acts as well as Elvis, was a sell-out, with more than 4,000 attending. Elvis wore black trousers, the gold lamé jacket with the matching metallic ruffled shirt and a black crossover bowtie. It raised more than $54,000 towards the half-million memorial target and further donations flooded in on the back of it. The USS *Arizona* Memorial was dedicated on 30 May, Memorial Day, 1962.

As well as recording new records in Nashville, Elvis's summer was spent filming not one, but two further films for United Artists. In *Follow That Dream*, he played another life-as-art part, the jeans-wearing son of a family of vagabonds who pitch up in a pristine neighbourhood, much to the chagrin of the locals, and in boxing musical *Kid Galahad*, when he wasn't singing he was boxing in his pants. He also attended Red West and Patricia Boyd's wedding and saw the old year out happy in the news that *Blue Hawaii*, released in the November, had already grossed $4.7 million.

Critics, what critics?

In 1962, Elvis returned to Hawaii to film *Girls! Girls! Girls*; gleefully advertised as having '13 great songs!', it was yet another scenery-and-swoon fest for Paramount. Elvis was increasingly complaining about the vacuous quality of his film scripts and what he considered the endless bland songs he had to produce in a crushing, formulaic, corporate manner. His stunning talents were being suppressed. Being a natural perfectionist, the biggest kick Elvis got from recording was taking time over the songs, the arrangements and the feel of the

Part II Lights, Camera, Action!   113

final take. Sam Phillips was his benchmark and he knew what he was then doing was falling way short. He'd tell his guys that he was a laughing stock in Hollywood, which he liked to call Hollyweird, yet, when they urged him to stand up to Parker, he'd wriggle out of it. Elvis hated confrontation and the few times he did sound off, Parker would play the old 'you'll end up going back to being a truck driver' card.

Elvis was also spending money like water, so Parker frequently reminded him that it was his millions of dollars pay cheques that funded his lavish lifestyle. To underline his point that fame can be fleeting, the musical comedy film *Follow That Dream* was released in May to a rather tepid reception.

Remember Priscilla? Elvis did. Though not that often. Keeping his word, he didn't forget her but had only called her on rare occasions since leaving Germany two years prior. That he did so at all, though, is telling. It would have been very easy for him to let things fizzle out, so she must have made an impression. He would tell her he loved her and that he loved talking to her but if their relationship were a film plot, it would be deemed to be doomed.

After Elvis had left, Priscilla had taken to her room and refused to eat. Reporters and TV companies hounded her for Elvis titbits, but she said nothing. She was bereft and, at just 16, helpless to do anything about the situation. So she returned to school and waited in a cloud of gloom for weeks, often months on end to hear from him while feeling abandoned at every news report of Elvis's affairs. When he did call, he'd assure her that it was all made up to sell papers or for publicity.

In March, just as she began to give up hope of ever seeing him again, the phone rang. She nearly fainted when it was Elvis on the other end, telling her that he wanted her to visit him in America and that he would talk to her dad to arrange it, if it would help. After much wrangling with her parents and agreeing to very specific rules and itineraries, Elvis and Priscilla somehow convinced them to let her go and in the school summer holidays, young Priscilla Beaulieu, escorted by Memphis Mafia member Joe Esposito, arrived at Elvis's home in Las Vegas. The first thing she heard as she arrived with Joe was music and as they entered the den, there he was, in a crowd of people, dressed in smart dark trousers, the whitest shirt and caramel-blond hair under a sailor's cap, about to take his shot at the pool table.

Priscilla writes in *Elvis & Me*, "'There she is!" he shouted, throwing down his cue stick. "There's Priscilla!"'

He ran over to her, picked her up and kissed her and then joked, 'It's about time! Where have you been all my life?' One can almost hear the violins playing in Priscilla's spinning teenage head. For two weeks, they slept in the day and played at night. Among all-night sessions with Elvis's guys and their dates,

114   Elvis: The King of Fashion

visiting casinos, shopping for clothes that Elvis insisted she wear, having a baffling argument with him and generally being hyper, assisted by pills, suddenly it was time for Priscilla to return to Germany. By August, she was back at school, nursing a promise from Elvis that he would arrange for her to come to Graceland for Christmas. Elvis was now in Seattle, filming *It Happened at the World's Fair* for MGM, where he played a singing, crop-dusting pilot who inadvertently finds himself at the 1962 World Fair.

Ending the year at Graceland, Elvis got a doll for Christmas: the perfectly pliable, love-sick Priscilla. Dress her, do her make-up, style her hair, put her to sleep and keep her in your bedroom. Between experimental everything-but-actual-sex sessions, they plotted how to get her to live in Memphis and complete her schooling there.

By 1963, and ready to shoot *Fun in Acapulco*, Elvis was deep in the doldrums; he was embarrassed by his film career and felt that he'd sold himself out musically. Of course he hadn't; Tom Parker had. If only someone could have travelled back from the future to tell Elvis how loved and celebrated all those silly, technicoloured movies are today, and how the clothes that he wore still inspire fashion trends and how people still play all his songs, not just the cool Sun Studio recordings and gospel albums or the Memphis and Nashville stuff, but the cheesy ones that remind them of those movies and what they were doing when they saw them.

If time travel could have happened, perhaps he wouldn't have felt so bad or so compelled to medicate his mood to make it more bearable.

On the upside, their Christmas scheming bore fruit and Priscilla moved to Graceland with her parents' permission on the understanding that she would live with Vernon and Dee and finish her schooling. She was enrolled at the all-girl Catholic Immaculate Conception High School and fell right back into Elvis's upside-down time clock. Shattered in the mornings from little or no sleep, she still went to school and crammed for exams. She had stopped warning Elvis about the pills, as he'd simply point to his medical dictionary, with which he was deeply familiar. She began taking sleeping and diet pills herself. In the following March, by cribbing from another girl's exam paper, Priscilla, as promised to her parents, graduated.

In July, Elvis finally got a decent film. He returned to Hollywood to shoot *Viva Las Vegas* with the gorgeous Ann-Margret, a ballsy, funny, talented actress whom many regarded as a female Elvis. The world waited for them to fall for one another. They didn't wait long. Suddenly, there were wall-to-wall stories in the press about the sexual chemistry between them, about their passionate affair and even engagement, all of which, of course, Elvis dismissed as lies to an utterly distraught Priscilla.

Part II Lights, Camera, Action!   115

Movie romances, in Elvis's case at least, were short-lived, and come October, he was filming *Kissin' Cousins*, of which *Variety*, for so long his champion, damningly wrote, 'This new Elvis Presley concoction is a pretty dreary effort, one that certainly won't replenish the popularity of Sir Swivel [as in sir Swivel Hips, another nickname he loathed].' As if to rub salt in the wounds, *Love Me Tender*, Elvis's first film, made when he was shimmering with talent and ambition and rocking the hell out of every stage he slid across with his unique voice, was broadcast on TV at Christmas.

In 1964, *Movie Life* ran a provocative headline declaring that Elvis was marrying Ann-Margret – but on closer inspection, it came with an article about their characters' wedding in *Viva Las Vegas*.

The Beatles, huge Elvis fans, arrived in New York with their sparkly new songwriting skills and their ultra-contemporary looks and views, at a time when Elvis was reduced to tussling love interests onto haystacks or boats while singing retrograde songs. Recognising the impact that The Beatles had from appearing on *The Ed Sullivan Show*, Tom Parker, sensing a publicity opportunity, sent them a congratulatory telegram – from Elvis.

While filming *Kissin' Cousins* and *Roustabout*, he met hairdresser-cum-spiritual-guru Larry Geller, teaser of pompadours and catalyst for a transcendent journey that would significantly alter Elvis's outlook, demeanour, reasoning and life choices. Geller's encouraging him in his quest for a deeper understanding of why he was who he was, and why he'd been chosen for such great fame and fortune, took Elvis to a spiritual centre where he befriended its president, Sri Daya Mata, whom he affectionately referred to as 'mother' and consulted regularly over the years. A surrogate Gladys, at last.

From the mystical to the sensual, the fans clearly wanted to see the on-screen alchemy between Elvis and Ann-Margret for themselves, since *Viva Las Vegas* was a smash, grossing $4.5 million. In contrast, Parker had agreed to worse movies, with flimsier plots and faster turnarounds, sometimes as little as a few weeks, to meet ruthless contract criteria and, it's alleged, his own growing gambling debts. The titles *Girl Happy* and *Tickle Me* say it all.

By 1965, Elvis, who'd lived for his all-night sessions with his pals but now had Priscilla to manage while still trying to locate the meaning of life, celebrated his thirtieth birthday quietly at Graceland. By then he was churning out three films a year, yet, in a rare burst of optimism and with dreams of being Rudolph Valentino, Elvis was looking forward to filming the first, *Harum Scarum*, for MGM.

Panned on release, even a devoted fan later referred to it as 'The best movie Elvis ever made – in a turban'. Vincent Canby wrote in *The New York Times* that Elvis 'walked through the film with all the animation of a man under deep

116   Elvis: The King of Fashion

sedation – but then he had read the script'. *Variety* said the film 'suffers from a lack of imagination', and Margaret Harford of the *Los Angeles Times* said, 'Presley isn't Bob Hope, and Mary Ann Mobley, beauty winner though she is, won't pass for Dorothy Lamour. Put them together and you realize right off that *Harum Scarum* isn't going to be much fun.'

It was demoralising and frustrating for Elvis. He was always on time, always line perfect and the camera adored him and, judging by his earlier films and the opinions of professionals, he could, with the right scripts and guidance – not to mention a manager with more integrity than a cash-crazed carny – have been as great an actor as he was a singer. But we'll never know. That said, the fans loved anything he did and he would tell his guys that whatever the critics said, he was making millions of dollars a year. Parker had trained him well. In his heart, though, Elvis knew that he was trapped, like an exotic bird, in a gilded cage – by Parker, by responsibility for his now large and expensive-to-run entourage, by the cost of his houses, cars, jewellery and other obsessions of the moment. The nadir of Elvis's film career had arrived – and it was on steroids.

As filming began for *Frankie and Johnny* followed by *Paradise, Hawaiian Style* in the August, he was medicating more. Uncharacteristically, he failed to turn up on days three and four of the *Paradise* shoot with no explanation. Feeling low and deeply dissatisfied with the work he was doing, the last thing Elvis needed was to be reminded of it. So, Parker – perpetually tone-deaf to the emotions of others – arranged for him to meet The Beatles, who were flying high, doing groundbreaking stuff and taking the US by storm. Initially, Elvis refused – he didn't want a meeting with people he didn't know. After much cajoling by Parker, he reluctantly agreed to meet them at his home on Perugia Way in Bel Air, California. Unsurprisingly, it turned out to be a rather awkward encounter.

The band's arrival in America, marked by hordes of screaming and crying teenagers, coincided with the moment Elvis began to feel irrelevant, a bit old fashioned. He wasn't, of course, but it was the summer of '65 and he was pretty insecure, not helped by his latest album, *Elvis For Everyone*, with – at the behest of Parker – a cash register on the cover. He was feeling uncomfortable. As if to exacerbate things, here were these sharp kids, fresh and oh, so young, with their continental suits and 'mop-top' hairstyles that, while completely different, were as distinctive as Elvis's own famous quiff. It was like a quartet of young pretenders to the throne wearing crowns that threatened to overshadow The King's. Ironically, The Beatles were in awe of Elvis and credited him with inspiring them to become musicians. They loved his rock and roll music and respected him as a human being. John Lennon's quote at the top of this section was from the heart. Elvis really did change their lives (and the lives of so many

Part II Lights, Camera, Action! 117

young people) without realising it and The Beatles worshiped the ground his two-tone shoes walked on.

Elvis, however, didn't feel the same about them. It was nothing personal; they just made him anxious or, more to the point, made him realise where his career path was heading. He was impressed by their originality and admired their musicianship, and eventually, he would cover some of their songs. Nevertheless, unintentionally, they served to highlight how outmoded he was in danger of becoming. The fame trajectory of these young usurpers, with a huge following, progressive music and two highly acclaimed movies (*A Hard Day's Night* and *Help!*) was on the up, while his was moving downwards, highlighted by the cotton-candy title of his latest film, *Tickle Me*.

When the Fab Four arrived under tight security on 27 August at 10 p.m. to meet their hero, their hero wasn't quite what they'd expected. Priscilla and Parker were there, as were most of Elvis's latest entourage (including Joe Esposito, Marty Lacker, Billy Smith, Jerry Schilling and various wives, kids and girlfriends). All were excited about the encounter, apart from Elvis. It may have been an historic moment, but when John, Paul, George and Ringo arrived in the living room, Elvis was on the sofa watching TV with the sound down and listening to Charlie Rich's 'Mohair Sam' on the jukebox. They admit they were struck dumb in his presence and could only stare at him.

Elvis joked, 'Hey, if you guys aren't going to talk to me, I'm going up to my bedroom and calling it a night.' It broke the ice and they all got talking, but all of the Beatles said that, although he was friendly, he was also shy and definitely seemed far less excited about seeing them than they were about seeing him.

Things settled a little. It's said that John and Paul jammed with Elvis with guitars while George shared a joint by the pool, Ringo played pool and Parker gambled with Epstein at a home roulette table. And that was it. Two of the biggest – in fact, *the* two biggest – acts in the history of popular music were awkward and reserved in each other's company and then said 'goodnight'.

The end.

For Elvis, 1966 would close with an important engagement, but for the most part, it was a year of seeking self-enlightenment through endless books, drugs and religious tracts. There was much soul-searching and many group readings, much to the dismay of his largely unwilling congregation, aka the Memphis Mafia and the usual gaggle of pretty girls, with whom poor Priscilla had to jostle for prime 'pew' position in the living room 'church'.

Although Gladys's death had triggered a slight hardening in Elvis's demeanour, he had still been a naturally upbeat and humorous person. Now he was more about piety than parties, and although they could never say so, they were all

118   Elvis: The King of Fashion

really missing the King of Fun and the endless excitement and spontaneity that he once brought to the table.

Punctuated mainly by releasing and filming yet another trio of barrel-bottom films in the shape of *Spinout*, *Double Trouble* and *Easy Come, Easy Go* – the last one started filming in September and, shockingly, was wrapped by October. Imagine how Elvis must have felt reading reviews like 'a tired little clinker that must have been shot during lunch hour'.

His bittersweet Christmas present was learning that his exquisitely raw, pioneering, culture-changing 1956 album, *Elvis Presley*, had gone platinum.

Priscilla's festive gift was Elvis's marriage proposal.

And they all lived happily ever after …

Well, not quite.

By 1967, Elvis was living in his own ethereal, at times drug-enhanced bubble, and forgetting that everything had to be paid for, usually with his own blood, sweat and tears, Elvis bought a ranch. Not a few horses to add to Graceland's stables, but an all-singing, all-dancing 230-plus acres he named Circle G (kind of Graceland part two) in Walls, Mississippi, his old home county. Now he could be a real cowboy.

Increasingly farcical films being shot were *Live a Little, Love a Little*; *Clambake*, in which Elvis sings and drives cars, motorbikes and boats really fast, with girls around; *Speedway*, in which he sings and drives cars really fast, with girls around; and *Stay Away, Joe*, in which Elvis sings and rides Dominick, a gay bull … Here was the man who transformed America and then the world's musical narrative, was once deemed too hot and threatening to even be looked at and who as good as shook a generation of teenagers out of boredom, reduced to going through the motions to fund a lifestyle he didn't even particularly enjoy.

With *Clambake* there was a positive: at least fans would get to see him leaning on a gleaming Red '59 Stingray Racer Corvette, resplendent in a Cornish cream Western-style ensemble and matching shirt with black trim and arrow and eyelet stitching and accessorised by a black Stetson. It was dubbed the 'Millionaire Suit' and was designed by – you guessed it – Nudie Cohn.

Around this time, Elvis, having reportedly taken a cocktail of painkilling drugs, stumbled in the bathroom, hit his head on the edge of the bath and suffered a long-lasting concussion. It's unknown how long he was out for but he remained disorientated for some while afterwards, at one point even claiming that he'd seen Gladys. Although deemed fine, it was a head trauma; with hindsight, it is believed to have had ongoing repercussions and was likely one of the many contributing factors that accelerated Elvis's physical decline, which became more noticeable in the last ten years of his life.

There was, at least, time for rejoicing as, to the immense relief of Tom Parker and Mr and Mrs Beaulieu, Elvis finally married Priscilla, on 1 May at the Aladdin Hotel, Las Vegas, in a small, private ceremony. Parker controlled even this hurried and clandestine occasion and many friends were hurt and angered at being omitted from the celebrations, when others in Elvis's circle had key roles. To make amends, after honeymooning in Palm Springs and at the Circle G Ranch, Elvis and Priscilla held a second ceremony at Graceland for everyone.

The long-awaited consummation of the marriage was not discussed; however, it *was* confirmed nine months later when, on 1 February, baby Lisa Marie Presley, their little princess, was born.

Chapter 9

The '68 Comeback Special

It's Been a Long Time, Baby. Look: Caged Panther

'There is something magical about watching a man who has lost himself, find his way back home.'

Jon Landeau, music critic (1968)

Although the 1960s hadn't been kind to Elvis, 1968 more than made up for it. It would be a year that began joyfully with a birth and ended with an exultant rebirth.

With the end of the decade nearing, Elvis was thrilled about becoming a father for the first time when Lisa Marie was born. The proud parents, Elvis in a mid-blue, single-button cutaway suit and lighter blue turtleneck and Priscilla in a tight, Barbie-pink mini-dress, her hair teased into her husband's favourite towering beehive style, left the hospital beaming and cooing over their newborn in an electric storm of paparazzi flashbulbs.

On the career front, yet another trio of Elvis's movies were about to be unleashed. However, more importantly, there was finally light at the end of that particular tunnel, as shooting had also started on two of what would be the final three of his contractually obligated, golden-handcuff films. Like the new baby, though, the year was still young and its real defining moment was still to come.

Late the previous year, 'Colonel' Tom Parker, who, by then, on top of creaming off 50 per cent of Elvis's profits plus percentages from various bonuses and even charging film studios thousands of dollars for his own 'technical adviser' services, was seeking funding for Elvis's final film, *Change of Habit*, starring Mary Tyler Moore. Having bumped into Tom Sarnoff, vice president of NBC, Parker carved out a deal where NBC would fund Elvis's film, provided that he also did an hour-long TV show, a Christmas 'special', to be aired that December. The special was irrelevant to Parker, a throwaway sweetener to ensure the movie cash. In his mind, all it would entail was Elvis performing a string of festive songs, topped and tailed with him saying a quick 'Hello, and merry Christmas' and 'goodnight'.

The '68 Comeback Special   121

Citing the less enjoyable broadcast experiences of the 1950s and the fact that he hadn't been on TV since Frank Sinatra's 1960 show, Elvis refused. Ever the Snowman, Parker was relentless. He warned Elvis that if he didn't fulfil the request, there would be no money for the film, ergo, no cash in their depleted coffers. It had been a long time since Elvis shook up the world with his live music. His songs had become lightweight, mere movie fillers, recorded by rote and rushed straight to albums. His inspirational style statements were also as good as forgotten, relegated to the back of Hollywood's by then benign, technicoloured costume closets. He was in danger of being a cultural dinosaur, in need of a hit record and a serious career reboot after spending too much time in movie mediocrity and too much money on, well, everything. With even the 'Colonel' worried about how badly the films were performing, he had no choice but to capitulate.

Sponsored by the Singer sewing machine (although, in this case, knitting machine, on account of it being Christmas) company, the show would be part of a series of specials showcasing well-known artists! As Elvis had no idea that he'd end up in the talented hands of Steve Binder and Bob Finkel, a couple of progressive television producers whom he'd eventually thank, the prospect held little joy for him. Which is what makes the end result all the more astonishing. The show would become one of the most important events of his career … make that, his life.

On 3 December, almost half of America's TV viewing public watched riveted as Elvis Presley's face, at once beautiful and menacing, filled their screens and growled, 'If you're looking for trouble, you came to the right place.'

It was the extraordinary opening of *Singer Presents … Elvis*, no longer the pedestrian Christmas show dreamed up by Tom Parker, but a dazzlingly high-quality extravaganza that's now regarded as one of the twentieth century's most successful, perfectly timed and commented-upon broadcasts. The one where the real Elvis came back, not just to public performing, but to life, before their very eyes.

From that first, lingering close-up of a glowing, glowering Elvis – aquiline nose, penetrating glare and a perfect pout that was in danger of becoming a snarl – they were hooked. As he built to the raspy, feisty 'My daddy was a green-eyed lumberjack', his familiar, luxuriant hair actually trembled from the power of his voice. The camera tantalisingly pulled back a little and there he was, in darkness and dressed in black, giving almost Johnny Cash vibes, but for the splashes of blood-red accessories. Gripping the mic for dear life, but still looking moody, he ended on 'So, don't you mess around with me' … as the camera pulled all the way back for the full reveal.

122   Elvis: The King of Fashion

The mic had vanished, the backdrop changed to a black with hint-of-red *Jailhouse Rock*-style assimilation of a cell block. It was filled with real humans in silhouette, dancing like Elvis with guitars. They were lookalikes, just one of many genius ideas of Steve Binder, who had requested a hundred Elvis doubles but, due to lack of space, settled for eighty-nine. Elvis then went straight into a rollicking rendition of 'Guitar Man'. His straight trousers narrowed at the ankle to fit tightly over black boots, and the glossy satin shirt – open-neck, splayed collar, gathered sleeves, Western yoke – paid homage to the mysterious blue velvet one he wore for his Tupelo '56 concert.

Watching the show now, accessory-wise, he's as rock 'n' roll as you could get. A glossy redwood and black Hagstrom Viking II guitar, matching Ace woven strap (also the accessory of choice for Jimi Hendrix at Woodstock the following year and, in 2023, for Elvis's own granddaughter, Riley Keough, when playing the titular lead in Amazon's TV series *Daisy Jones and the Six*). A scarlet slash of scarf fastened at his throat by a metal ring and chunky, black-leather cuffs (one, a watch) buckled on to his wrists complete the look.

By then, the cell block's back lighting had actually morphed to a vibrant vermillion to match the red additions to Elvis's outfit. The ultimate in theatrical accessorising. And in case there was any doubt about who this singing Adonis was, the jail evaporates and everything goes black, apart from Elvis, who seems to be floating between the L and the V of a row of towering, red-lit letters spelling out his name. A big-impact TV moment that's been enthusiastically replicated ever since.

What had begun as a chore, turned out to be a blast and, ultimately, the solution to rescuing Elvis's reputation, all thanks to Steve Binder, the maverick televisual wizard who had the balls to tell Elvis that his career was 'in the toilet'.

Originally, NBC producer Bob Finkel was meant to make *Elvis* but was disconcerted by the star's reticence (make that shyness) and his insistence on calling him 'Mr Finkel' (an ingrained courtesy Elvis accorded all elders), instead of simply 'Bob.' Finkel decided that a director closer to Elvis in age might help. He called Binder, who was used to working with big-name stars and had just made a 'special' with Petula Clark that had proved successful, if controversial. While duetting with the black singer Harry Belafonte, Clark touched his arm. Actually, she didn't just touch it, she gently held on to it through the final part of their song – which included a line about people being equal, regardless of colour. The sponsor's ad manager complained and called for the scene to be redone, lest it offend people. Steve Binder, a principled pro, and Clark, who was cut from the same cloth, both refused.

'Even though I had shot multiple takes of the duet without either of the stars touching each other, I had refused to remove the take with "the touch",' wrote

Steve in his insightful book *ELVIS, '68 Comeback: The Story Behind the Special*, which was also the inspiration for his new 2023 documentary, *Reinventing Elvis*, made with Spencer Proffer, music and media producer of Meteor 17.

Petula aired, uncensored, on NBC in the April to great ratings and critical acclaim and marked the first time a man and woman of different races made physical contact on US television.

Steve declined Finkel's offer as he was genuinely busy. However, his partner, recording engineer Bones Howe, who'd previously worked on some of Elvis's albums, overheard the conversation and told him he'd be crazy to turn down a chance to work with him. He phoned Finkel back, asked for a meeting with Elvis, and said if they hit it off, he'd try to do it. Steve and Bones were summoned to Tom Parker's MGM studios lair.

For some reason, Finkel told them to take some Danish pastries for him. 'The meeting was early in the morning, so I figured we'd be joining the Colonel for breakfast,' said Steve. He handed them over and watched, bemused, as Parker 'squirreled them directly into his briefcase', never to be seen nor spoken of again. For half-an-hour, Parker talked at them, bragging about the one-page contracts he insisted on for Elvis's movies and how, once the magic million-dollar fee was agreed, Elvis would do anything the studio asked, within said contracts.

It was at that meeting that Parker boasted about his chicken-dancing carnival 'show', the sickening money-making trick, where he placed chickens on a hidden hotplate to make them leap up and down. 'I thought it was sadistic, barbaric,' said Steve when we talked about the so-called Colonel, 'and definitely not funny.'

I asked him whether he ever got any sense of Parker's alleged hypnotic abilities.

I think that he thought that he had these powers, but I thought he was a phony, he tried his damndest to hypnotise me – with zero success.

I believe that if you don't want to be hypnotised, you can't be. People who want to believe that they can, convince themselves and play along with con artists like the Colonel.

As they left, Parker handed Steve a festive-greetings box containing a publicity audio tape and script for the TV special, and a membership card for the Snowmen's League, signed the 'Colonel'. Parker cheerily told him that to be a member, 'you had to be a great bull-shitter'.

Despite the peculiarity of the encounter, Steve and Bones felt the ball was rolling and it might soon be time for a meeting of the mavericks. I ask Steve what surprised him most about Elvis when they first met that May and he says, 'Everything.'

He elaborates in his book.

124 Elvis: The King of Fashion

My first impression of Elvis was that he was physically perfect. His facial features were flawless, reminding me of the sculptured Statue of Liberty face.

Usually, most stars have a favourite side of their face that they insist the director favour. Not Elvis. He was perfect from any angle.

Finkel had been right, they got on; they conversed as equals and yes, Steve really did tell Elvis Presley that his career was in the toilet. Elvis didn't mind. 'He said to me, "Finally, somebody speaking the truth to me."'

He also told Elvis that he wanted him to return to his roots – to go back to what had made him a big star in the first place. And that the show wouldn't just be a list of songs, it would have a powerful and resonant narrative, it would be a nod to Elvis's own story, writ large on a backdrop of great music and dance. Yes, he admitted, it *could* tank, but at least he'd still be remembered as a rock 'n' roll star and actor who'd had a fantastic career. On the other hand, if it worked, he could take back his crown and re-establish himself as the King of Rock 'n' Roll.

Basically, it was make or break time.

'I love it,' said Elvis. 'Let's do it!'

'We liked each other from that first time that we met in person,' says Steve. '[We] had the same goals – to do the best work we possibly could without worrying about the politics behind the scenes.

'We also agreed to ignore whatever the Colonel said to us ...'

Gradually, Elvis and Steve became buddies, and discovered that as well as music, they had many other things in common, including their dry wit. They shared concerns about the direction in which society was heading and were affected by the recent assassination of civil rights leader Martin Luther King Jnr., who was shot on 4 April at the Lorraine Motel in Memphis, Elvis's hometown.

Shortly after their first meeting and while rehearsing for the show, US Senator Robert Kennedy, a supporter of human rights and social justice, was also shot dead by an assassin, on 6 June. Everyone in the Special's team was dismayed.

Steve says, 'Elvis asked, "What is happening to our country?"'

'That moment brought us closer ... gave us a better understanding of this compassionate man that we were beginning to know and love.'

Although a new dad, Elvis lived and breathed the rehearsals and decided to move into NBC's Studio 4's impressive king-size dressing room to be close to the team (and possibly the dancers). When Steve asked if he'd be moving Priscilla and Lisa Marie in too, Elvis said not when he was working, then added, 'And besides, with all these good-looking guys around ...'

It was a huge space, with a baby grand *and* another room with an upright piano. Elvis made it a mini Graceland, with room for the guys and his new

The '68 Comeback Special   125

show pals, and stocked with plenty of cola and cigars; he lived there until the show was done.

Every night after dinner, they'd all jam and josh and put the world to rights. It was in those late-night sessions that Steve witnessed the innocent Elvis step aside to make space for the raw, sexual, funny and, at times, mean 33-year-old man he'd become. He knew then that was the Elvis that he wanted people to see.

Of all the adjectives used to describe Elvis – talented, unique, iconic, powerful, stylish, generous, sensual – it's odd how 'funny' comes low on the list, if even on it at all. Yet, Elvis was naturally and exceptionally funny. Regardless of the relationship, most of his friends and family would say that he could crack you up, just like that. And, his jesting was often self-deprecating, which merely endorsed other glowing labels, such as charming, modest and humble. During the *'68 Special* press conference, a reporter asked Elvis, 'Has your audience changed much?'

Straight-faced, but nudging Steve's leg under the table, he answered, 'Well, they don't move as fast as they used to.'

In interviews, which are few and far between, Elvis's comic timing and off-the-cuff jokes, especially during his early army press calls, or later, when promoting the 1972 Madison Square Garden concert in New York, for example, are priceless.

Steve, now 90 and still full of the integrity, wit and cynicism that have made him so respected in his industry, says he knew exactly how the *'68* show should look. It would start with Elvis the 'Guitar Man', travelling a road unknown, then follow his journey with musical, improvised, and 'in the round' segments en route and ending with a big finale number – which the 'Colonel' had demanded would be a nice Christmas song but which Steve and Elvis decided would be anything but. At one point, when Parker uncharacteristically got involved and bulldozed Elvis into agreeing to a festive number in front of Steve, he and Elvis left his office in silence. Steve says:

No sooner had the door closed and we were out of earshot, than Elvis jabbed me in the ribs and said 'Fuck him!'

Remember that I never had to deal with his world but rather had Elvis join ours. Bob Finkel did a great job in keeping the Colonel away from us during the entire production that I never fully appreciated until years after.

Steve, as you may have guessed, is not a Parker fan.

Having conceived, produced and directed the *'68*, while Bones drove the music, Steve was responsible for its overall look.

'From the very beginning, I wanted to color-control the entire special with red, black and white. Color control was very important to me. I felt that

126   Elvis: The King of Fashion

the combination of dark red and black would grab the viewers' attention.' A simple enough statement, yet it gets right to the crux of his understanding that something bold and contemporary was needed to jumpstart Elvis's stalled career – and image. Steve continues:

> I might add that in 1968, NBC had a difficult time with the color red. It would usually start breaking up but I was happy when we made it work! CBS in those days had more of a pastel look. Much softer colors than NBC.

In my mind, I've a room full of Elvis's best outfits through the decades. There are a lot, since from his early days, even before he was performing, he instinctively, possibly subconsciously at times, wanted to stand out.

Baby Elvis rocking a mini-trilby with what I want to believe is a hint of coolness even at the age of 2 or 3.

Teenage Gunslinger Elvis, outside Lauderdale Courts, *circa* 1949, in a bomber jacket, rolled-up jeans and loafers.

Hillbilly Cat Elvis, mid-'50s, in his audacious black-and-pink gear, immortalised twice, once in monochrome on the Milton Berle Show, then with a little of Catherine Martin's costume designing magic, worn in glorious, gyrating colour by actor Austin Butler in the 2022 *Elvis* movie.

A big favourite is Rebooted Elvis, 1969, in the chocolate-brown 'cutaway' suit by his *'68 Comeback Special* outfits designer, Bill Belew, that he wore – shirtless, with a low-slung Mexican-style silver and turquoise belt – to see Barbra Streisand's show at the International Hotel, Las Vegas, shortly before his 31 July debut there. In photos of him strutting down the hotel corridor that night, he's in his prime, 34, bronzed, trim and as relaxed in his own skin as he is in the suit.

Perhaps I like that it's so stripped back compared to his later bejazzled stage wear? Then again, it did, and still does, look flamboyant and, with nothing under the jacket, a little bit 'fuck you'. So, it's because of how he looks in it. It's always about Elvis.

The list goes on, but the clothes he wore on the *'68* show are at the top of it. The era-defining ensembles designed by Bill and designed to make a statement. They left no one in any doubt that the old Elvis was back. In fact, you could argue that this new, more mature, Elvis looked even sexier, sassier and more dangerous than those outraged parents and do-gooders of the 1950s could ever have imagined.

Bill Belew had just designed the clothes for the Petula Clark special.

'Steve Binder called and said, "Bill, would you be interested in doing a special with Elvis Presley?"' Of course Bill did.

All the writers were there, Billy Goldenberg and Earl Brown, myself and Steve when Elvis came in and I … was totally taken aback, as most of us were.

He was sensational looking. The movies never did justice to him … he really was a handsome guy.

When asked what did he see Elvis wearing, Bill said he'd never seen him in all-black leather.

'I think it would be terrific and I think he could carry it off if we did an all-leather black outfit.'

Talking about the *Comeback* and Elvis's clothes with Steve, who was deeply involved in their design and creation – and who's still excited by them – is *fun*. I tell him that the black leather and the white 'If I Can Dream' suits are my particular favourites. He says his, too, is the black leather. I mean, whose isn't? Well, Elvis's actually. Yes, he loved the look (inspired by a photo he had of Brando as Johnny Strabler in *The Wild Ones*) and which Steve passed to Bill Belew who, in turn, reimagined it as Elvis's sleeker two-piece. However, Elvis said it was painfully hot to wear under the fierce studio lights.

For an insight into just how much Elvis's fans like his black leather *Comeback* look, I posted a single photo of him performing in the suit with the words 'Legend in black' on a Facebook fan page. In fairness, it was a global Elvis group called Elvis Presley Worldwide, but even so, within a few days, it had racked up 14,000 likes, 359 comments and 445 shares. Elvis fans – and innocent bystanders – male, female or anyone in between, frequently cite Elvis as being the most beautiful man who ever walked the earth and that wearing that suit was his best look. Now, I could use the old adage 'the clothes maketh the man' here. I probably should, since I'm writing about the crucial role his clothes played in his success and in creating his enduring legacy. However, this is Elvis we're talking about and I say to Steve, who had the final say in everything he wore in the show, that Elvis certainly carried clothes well, but, frankly, if you looked that good, you could wear anything. He says:

I agree with what you say, that he would look great in anything he wore. Almost everything on the *Special* was original and from Bill Belew's sketches and designs.

Bill didn't decide by himself what Elvis should wear. A lot of thought and time was spent by myself and my staff on Elvis's wardrobe and Bill needed me to sign off before he could actually proceed!

He did a tremendous job in delivering the look we wanted for Elvis in our creative think tank meetings.

128   Elvis: The King of Fashion

However, there is a line drawn in Steve's Elvis fashion sand. 'I remember rejecting Bill when he submitted his idea for the jumpsuit. I never liked Elvis wearing them after we parted ways.'

Considering the task in hand, Belew's role was crucial. Fortunately, there was an alchemy to his outfits. The exquisitely cut, subtle designs added an extra dimension; they gave Elvis a confidence that, being so anxious about how he'd be received, he did not really feel. They were an important asset to a man who was aware that some people felt he was past it. At times, even he did. They were modern-day suits of armour and you could see his confidence grow as he pulled them on.

When he arrived at the studio, he was already tanned and lean from a trip to Honolulu where he and Priscilla had visited the new USS *Arizona* memorial that his earlier 1961 concert appearance had helped fund. The young Mr and Mrs Presley had looked like the hottest '60s couple on the planet – he, in fitted flamenco-style trousers, an early version of the Napoleonic collar cupping his chiselled chin and a cravat-type scarf; she, in an ultra-bold, monochrome tropical-print dress with matching floppy hat, palest pink lipstick, tarantula lashes and industrial quantities of black eyeliner. So, in New York, Elvis was the perfect, leggy model and Belew's costumes simply added the magic that transformed him into the rock star he really was. The simplicity of Steve Binder's colour strategy created new, era-defining sets, forcing the monochrome-fixated '60s to dip red-varnished toes into the upcoming 1970s waters.

The first sighting of the famous leather suit almost never happened. In an almost repeat performance of the scene in 1954, when Elvis was too petrified with nerves to go on stage at the Overton Park Shell until he was coaxed on by Sam Phillips, Steve found Elvis in a state of blind panic just before the filming of the improvisation segment with a live audience. He'd gone blank on what to talk about. This was to be the nighttime jamming in the dressing room scene, where Steve saw Elvis come alive; it was to be the section that would show the true Elvis, the self-effacing, amusing, likable human. The audience waited and the crew prepared to roll, but Elvis's old stage fright had returned.

'I tried to hold my composure,' says Steve, in *Elvis '68 Comeback*. 'I found a piece of paper and scribbled down from memory what stories he had told and what songs he sang that I remembered.' In minutes, he'd filled a page. He gave it to Elvis. 'I looked him straight in the eye, and said calmly, "Elvis, do this for me."' And he did. It was the trust that Elvis put in Steve that made theirs such a historic collaboration.

The leather suit had its debut, albeit not in its entirety, as he was first seen sitting down in the small, intimate, red-and-white boxing ring set. Still, it is

The '68 Comeback Special   129

such a moment and it was the first official Napoleonic-collared garment Elvis ever wore. 'I designed it so as to frame his face,' said Bill Belew.

Elvis looked stunning, and although his hand was visibly shaking, his voice was perfection, wrapping its rich tones around a stripped-back, bluesy version of 'Lawdy Miss Clawdy' as sweat from the heat of the clothes and the lights poured down his face and chest. Seeing it now, it is as fresh as ever. Elvis is smiling and becomes lost in the music he loves. It's just him in black and Scotty Moore, Charlie Hodge, Alan Fortas and D.J. Fontana in red, all sitting playing (D.J., expertly, on a guitar case as his drums wouldn't fit in the space) on blue spindly chairs.

Even sitting, Elvis is unable to stop himself from moving every part of his body – head to feet – to the rhythm, just like in 1956, when people called him a primitive savage because of it. The audience is so close to the edge of the square, some are sitting on it – it's touching distance. His voice is real and raw. He's back to his roots. They launch into another glorious blues-fuelled number, 'Baby What You Want Me to Do?' And when the banter begins, turns out Elvis is a natural. He jokes that there's something wrong with his lip, does an exaggerated lip-curl and says to the laughing audience, 'I got news for you, baby, I did twenty-nine pictures like that!' The guys in the round crack up, as does the audience.

When he talks about the Jacksonville, Florida, concert and not being allowed to move, he does his famous finger wiggle and everyone's in hysterics again – so is Elvis. Suddenly, the camera switches to a bird's-eye view of the boxing ring stage. The lights are down and its white centre is lit up. Everything has gone, apart from a mic stand and a solitary Elvis – now standing – in the corner. Now the lens is back on him, the lights go up, and while everyone absorbs the full impact of the leather suit, he saunters over, picks up his guitar and, without a word, yells out a rasping and emotional 'Heartbreak Hotel' that suits its dark and painful subtext.

Barely catching breath, he resurrects his rock 'n' roll soul with a racier, frownier, more self-assured version of his original 'Hound Dog', dancing around the arena like his 19-year-old self, self-assurance fully restored as the mesmerised crowd looks on, totally gobsmacked. He falls to his knees with ease and the crowd loves it. On it went, song after powerfully delivered song, set after modernist set, until Elvis had taken everyone on a journey representing not only his life, but his rebirth.

Television was unprepared for what was unleashed, but it worked. Full of newfound energy and emotion, Elvis delivered his massive early hits and they sounded even better than the originals. Steve and Elvis had agreed that Scotty and D.J. be flown in to play and improvise in the round with him to recapture

130 Elvis: The King of Fashion

the essence of their halcyon days in Memphis and touring the South, and it was another stroke of genius. Elvis gave people new stuff, old stuff, different stuff and he gave them his true self; never had he looked or sounded better – the nation was in his hands.

There were tailored, mod-influenced jackets in dark claret red and obsidian black; there were scarves, lots of scarves; there were velvet, profusely buttoned, Napoleon-meets-riverboat gambler-meets-dandy coats, a version of which would later appear in the Whitehouse Oval Office – with Elvis inside it. He braved a triple denim ensemble, and it rocked, because of a gorgeous black leather and silver belt and, well, Elvis. There was even a contemporary, black-trimmed homage to the infamous Nudie gold jacket; but Lawdy, Miss Clawdy, it was the leather outfit that everyone was raving about as he moved around like, in the words of Bill Belew, 'a black panther stalking the stage'. And, like the animal, he seemed to be savouring the scent of the trembling, mini-skirted, bouffant-haired prey, gathered round the edge of the stage like hypnotised impala round a watering hole.

Steve wanted an unforgettable finale, not with a holidays ditty, but with a new song that would express who Elvis was right then. Despite Parker's protestations, the Christmas song was off the table and Steve asked Billy Goldenberg, the show's musical director, and songwriter Earl Brown to write a song for Elvis that would be both meaningful to him and relevant to the decade that he was finally catching up with.

In 1968, America was in a state of great upheaval. The civil rights movement was in full swing and societal and cultural mores were changing rapidly. Things were at boiling point, exacerbated by the Martin Luther King and Bobby Kennedy assassinations within months of each other. Steve said that he and Elvis would talk into the night about things that were unfolding in tandem with the show.

'We spent most of our personal time discussing Bobby Kennedy and what was happening to our country with the Vietnam War and all the political assassinations and college campus protests.'

Brown and Goldenberg quickly came back with a song they felt captured Elvis's character, along with the zeitgeist, and that they hoped he'd like. They sang it to Steve, who thought it would work. When Elvis arrived, they ushered him into the quiet piano room within his dressing room and sat him on the piano bench next to Goldenberg while Brown sang the song to him.

Elvis showed zero reaction.

He asked them to sing it again. And again, without a hint of what he was thinking.

Tom Parker, pacing around, said, 'This ain't an Elvis kind of song' and added that his client would perform it over his dead body.

The '68 Comeback Special   131

Elvis, appealed to him, saying, 'Let me give it a shot, man.'

This is likely the moment Baz Luhrmann used as inspiration for the scene in his *Elvis* film where an angry Parker, played by Tom Hanks, says to Elvis that the assassination incident 'has nothing to do with us' and an even angrier Austin Butler, as Elvis, looks at him in disbelief and shouts, 'This has everything to do with us!'

Elvis told his three allies around the piano, 'I'll do it. I'll sing the song in the show.'

Within seconds, Parker was demanding that Brown and Goldenberg sign their rights over to Elvis's music label; Goldenberg selflessly said that the songwriting credit should be Earl Brown's and after some ground given either way, the battle ended.

Written in haste and in a time of great division and turmoil in the country, the song is now carved into psyche of a vast swathe of humankind. It was, of course, 'If I Can Dream', the beautiful and powerful gospel-styled protest, inspired in part by Martin Luther King's 'I Have a Dream' address at the Lincoln Memorial, Washington, DC.

The rehearsals for the 'big finale' song were intense and powerful; according to Earl Brown, while Elvis recorded the song, tears rolled down the faces of some of his backing vocalists. But it was in an impromptu session to re-record vocals he'd already laid down that Elvis gave his most astonishing performance of it. The musicians and backing singers had left, he had the lights turned off and, on his own, gave himself more fully over to the backing music. After a few takes, he was on his knees on the concrete floor, losing himself in the song. He then went to the control room and got them to play the new take repeatedly, then gave it the thumbs up.

Finally, they had their finale.

It's a gut-wrenching performance to behold. Elvis is wearing a meticulously tailored suit so dazzlingly, ecclesiastically white, that it appears to be glowing, its intentional purity interrupted only by a crimson neck tie. He's alone on the set, aside from the gigantic red ELVIS letters from earlier. Otherwise, it's dark, stark; the pared-down simplicity of Steve Binder's black, red and white theme at its most compelling. As the brass intro washes in, Elvis stands perfectly still, head bowed, hands clasped, as if in prayer, but in reality holding a microphone – and likely praying, too.

He starts slowly.

As one of – or possibly *the* – most vocally dexterous and powerful musicians on the planet, Elvis could work songs like a magician, using anything from the lowest baritone to the highest tenor and, not only everything in between, but ranges in between those that most people don't even realise exist, and could

132 Elvis: The King of Fashion

combine them into an astonishing sound that left people spellbound. Even so, today, maybe more so, this particular performance is on another level.

I sense that the very visible and audible emotions in Elvis's scorching delivery – grief, sadness, frustration – stemmed not just from the seismic world events happening around him, but from years of repressed personal anguish over his childhood bullying, his mother's death, his fear of fading and his inability to escape a cycle of relentless responsibilities.

So it was his moment to let it all out, in a minute and half of fabulous fury, at times crouching as though in pain and utilising every tool in his voice box to express his outrage and show his super-power in the only way he had ever known. In song. If an angry angel were to sing, it would look and sound like Elvis did right at that moment. It left him, the studio audience, the crew and the viewers wrung out, speechless; many were in tears.

Watching the footage, it's inescapable to me that, yet again, his outfit, like his singing, did much of the talking. The unmistakable, possibly initially unintentional subtexts of peace, goodness and pain in the white double-breasted suit, where the buttons, even the three on each sleeve, are white, as are his shoes; and the position of the red of the silk neck scarf that clashes like an open wound, a bleeding heart, are hard to miss.

When Elvis sings 'We're lost in a cloud', he seems close to tears, yet his voice remains outstanding. Bear in mind, no one has ever heard this song before and he'd never performed it to an audience. It was a unique experience all round.

After the blistering closing crescendo, where he swings his arm back and forth and begs, 'Oh, please let my dream come true – right now' (with added flourishes), he stops, audibly breathless from his exertions, and leaves The Blossoms, his unseen backing singers' (Fanita James, Jean King and Darlene Love) beautiful voices to rise like the sound of rejoicing of seraphim and then fade. Then he simply says, 'Thank you. Goodnight.'

The King was well and truly back. Once witnessed, it's unforgettable, an impeccable televisual occurrence – both from a musical and a visual standpoint.

I ask Steve to name his favourite '68 moment (aside from overriding Parker!).

'Watching Elvis as he rediscovers himself,' he says.

For some reason, Elvis never performed the song on stage again. Imagine what a great closing number it would have made if he had. It remained a once-in-a-lifetime thing, like the show and the man himself.

The song was published by Gladys Music, Inc. (Parker's device for ensuring some degree of fiscal benefit came from any songs Elvis sang). Walter Earl Brown was – and still is – fully credited as the songwriter.

Elvis was so moved by 'If I Can Dream', and the whole experience, that he told Steve Binder, 'I'll never sing another song I don't believe in. I'm never going

The '68 Comeback Special   133

to make another movie I don't believe in.' And for the nine years that he never realised were all that he had left, he kept that promise.

*   *   *

Advertised as a Christmas TV special with the less-than-thrilling title of *Singer Presents … Elvis*, it was a triumph. The blend of big-budget production numbers, intimate improv segments, a socially aware message of peace and a hunk of raunchy, sweaty rock 'n' roll icon, made it a huge hit. For many, including Parker and even Elvis, the success was unexpected. It was the number one show of the season, giving NBC an early Christmas present – the biggest overall rating win of the year. Almost immediately, it became known as the *'68 Comeback Special*, or even just *The Comeback*. On 31 December, the show aired, advert-free, in the UK.

'It was the finest music of his life,' wrote Greil Marcus in his book *Mystery Train*. 'If ever there was music that bleeds, this was it.'

The *New York Times* declared that 'Elvis has found his way home' and fans rushed to buy his records again.

Chapter 10

The Caped Crusader

1969–72. Look: Star-Spangled Superstar

'I got tired of singing to turtles.'

Elvis, press conference ahead of his
opening show in Las Vegas, August 1969

'The image is one thing and the human being is another. It's very hard to
live up to an image, put it that way ...'

Elvis, Madison Square Garden press conference, 1972

Elvis ... make that ELVIS, was back in fashion.

In 1969, and buzzing from the roars of approval for the *'68 Special*, he wanted more. His wings had been clipped for far too long and he was ready to fly again. He told 'Colonel' Parker that he'd had enough of lightweight movies and wanted to return to live performing.

Parker, rumoured to be in debt, or at least fiscally troubled, and with his only client in a similar situation (Elvis was about to sell the Circle G ranch to cover his excessive – and wildly generous – spending), was more concerned about Elvis's ability to earn money, than about his career satisfaction. He had allowed the production priorities on Elvis's films (some approaching exploitation movie territory by focusing on his monetary rather than his acting value) to shift until they were being churned out with increasingly less regard for quality. The MO had gone from creating well-crafted pictures to ensuring maximum bums on seats for a minimum budget. Noting early on that dramatic films showcasing Elvis's acting skills and relying on fewer or no songs made less money, Parker had pushed for flimsy musicals-by-numbers. However, now even he realised that a new strategy was needed.

The *'68 Comeback* had been sensational, despite its refusal to pull on its festive jumper; Elvis, as always, had been right about the song and outfit choices. He was at his best doing what he loved, and they both knew it. Parker's main worry was that touring was expensive, with no guarantee that Elvis could draw the huge crowds he once did. To maintain momentum, what they needed was a

The Caped Crusader 135

second comeback. Something as lucrative as the NBC gig with the same, minimal outlay. Something equally big, or bigger.

Something as big as … Las Vegas.

Parker suggested to Elvis that they could do a version of his '68 show there and Elvis, who had always seen the glitzy and glamourous 'Sin City' as the pinnacle of showbiz success, agreed (despite, or because of, having bombed there years before), saying that they could tour afterwards. Before you could say 'Viva!', Parker had cut a deal. Elvis would perform at Las Vegas's fabulous new International Hotel, an engagement designed to ease him back gently into live performing and to give the hotel an exclusive show, hot off the back of his '68 *Comeback* triumph.

What it actually turned out to be was the start of the last and one of the most unforgettable, emotional and uniquely Elvis fashion-meets-performance chapters of his life story. He would play two shows every day for a month. That's seven days a week over four weeks with no day off. Elvis, so excited to be going back on stage, agreed, saying that he'd hate to sit twiddling his thumbs when he could be playing live. This kind of straight-run contract was unheard of in Vegas, as was Elvis's fee – an unprecedented $100,000 a week.

Regardless of the recent praise for Elvis's rebirth, the more cynical among the music culturati were skeptical. Was The King's throne built on anything other than sand? Did Presley's music have a place in a world that had passed him by?

Oblivious to his doubters and ahead of his big engagement, a revitalised and motivated Elvis, determined to steer his own career, entered the American Sound Studio, a small recording venue owned by producer Chips Moman at 827 Thomas Street in a run-down patch of Memphis, to make some new songs. Elvis was being pressed to provide RCA with more records for release after a stretch of receiving and dismissing unsuitable song options from Tom Parker and Hill & Range (the affiliated song agency with its stable of contracted writers), who were apparently only sending him demos from their own writers. So, it's said on advice from some of his inner circle, he decided to shake things up by finding new songs that he actually liked and record them in Memphis instead of RCA's usual studio in Nashville.

Elvis, as good as a recluse when not working – partly by choice, partly for security reasons – relied on receiving demos from any songwriters who hoped he would record their work (having Elvis use your song was considered a huge deal). However, Marty Lacker told him that when writers approached them (the entourage) with potential songs, all they could say was, 'Send it to the Colonel.'

It was a risky move on Marty's part. Elvis was no longer the meek, chipper boy of old. He was Hollywood hardened, rather indulged and increasingly reliant on medication. He did not take bad news well and had a short fuse, which once

136 Elvis: The King of Fashion

lit, quickly blew up, often in the face of the bearer. Although royally pissed off, Elvis remained calm and tasked the guys – some of whom, by then, had contacts or jobs in the entertainment business themselves – with sourcing decent song options. And he wanted *everybody*, he 'didn't give a fuck who they were' (read as, Parker), to know that he'd be picking his own music from then on. He'd listen to every song and if he liked it, regardless of getting rights or not, he'd record it.

George Klein called Neil Diamond and suddenly Elvis had 'And The Grass Won't Pay No Mind' to consider, Lamar Fike brought him Eddie Rabbitt and Dick Heard's 'Kentucky Rain', and yet more followed. Chips Moman and his in-house band specialised in creating a soul-based, uniquely Memphis sound, regardless of the artist. Elvis clicked with him and armed with superior songs, he hired the studio for around fifteen days over the January and February.

Although the American Sound was different, there were similarities to the '50s Sun Studio sessions: a meticulous and visionary producer; experienced musicians who weren't in awe of Elvis but rated his vocals and musical insight; a distinctive sound; a modest recording space; and an era-defining outcome. Buoyed by the high calibre of the new material, Elvis dived in and had his best recording experience in years; he completed more than thirty masters containing what would be regarded as some of his finest recordings. From the two sessions came a treasure trove of material, strong songs like 'In The Ghetto', 'Suspicious Minds' and 'Kentucky Rain'.

RCA would be happy for quite a while.

A subsequent album, *From Elvis in Memphis*, which melded rock 'n' roll, modern country and soul, drew universal approval and is still considered one of Elvis's greatest works.

Cue: sound of critics eating humble pie.

After the sessions, having completed filming on *The Trouble with Girls* and *Change of Habit*, marking the end of thirteen years of movie obligations. With a contemporary, Beatlesish hairstyle and Memphis University sweatshirt and jeans combo, he looked cool playing a ghetto physician. Who falls in love with a nun …

Imagine how he must have felt having made an astonishing thirty-one feature films and never getting to be the next Jimmy Dean or Marlon Brando. Parker's handling of Elvis's movie career had brought him riches beyond his wildest dreams, but it hadn't fulfilled his main one, to be celebrated for what his mama had called his God-given talent.

When *Change of Habit* wrapped, it was 'Goodbye, Hollywood', 'Hello, Hawaii' as Elvis, Priscilla, Lisa Marie and a bunch of the guys with their significant others went to the island for a chill-out holiday.

Back and looking forward to rehearsals for that July's Vegas run, 'In The Ghetto' went gold and *Charro!*, the first of his last three movies, came out, giving

The Caped Crusader 137

fans a chance to see him looking ruggedly handsome with a beard. Stubble aside, the film was notable in that Elvis sang no songs, other than the theme. Critics were ambivalent and fans bemoaned the lack of singing. Still, it made a profit.

Movies in the can, he could fully focus on being Vegas ready, starting with a diet and plenty of karate to get in shape. The exciting musicality of the television comeback had reignited his love and respect for great musicianship and he wanted that same big, full sound in his live shows. However, Elvis *was* the act. Yes, he had the Memphis Mafia, who catered to his every whim and protected, at times, overprotected him, but with no band mates to share musical experiences, to lend support, or to discuss plans with, he was on his own. Without realising it, he had gradually become very isolated.

And Parker was no use.

Despite the film commitments that became an albatross around Elvis's neck and regardless of his dodgy methods and motives, the 'Colonel' was probably the world's most effective (as in making his client a superstar worth a fortune) manager and merchandiser. However, he had scant appreciation or understanding of Elvis's creative and artistic ambitions. As always, the responsibility for Elvis the showman lay solely with Elvis the man, but this time he relished it, for at last, he would be calling the shots.

He became the Steve Binder of his own show, overseeing all aspects of it, instinctively building an innovative, record-breaking, mould-smashing spectacular, the likes of which had never been seen in Las Vegas and which became the blueprint for most of the gambling capital's future shows. Soundwise, he already had the International's resident orchestra, but he wanted more. For days, he auditioned and hired top musicians, forming what became his TCB (Taking Care of Business) band. In his interview for the MGM documentary film *Elvis on Tour*, he told Bob Abel, 'I wanted musicians who could play any kind of music. All of the musicians were hand-picked.'

On guitar was James Burton, whom Elvis knew from the *Louisiana Hayride* house band and who by then was one of LA's most sought-after session musicians. Burton was joined by equally lauded artists, John Wilkinson on rhythm guitar, bassist Jerry Scheff, Larry Muhoberac on keyboards, and drummer Ronnie Tutt, who said of Elvis, 'He had such charisma, you could understand truly why everybody was so attracted, so drawn to him. I mean, the guy had it.' They were the core of the main band that would feature a raft of awesome musicians over the years.

Foundations laid, Elvis, like a musical draftsman, added further layers to his wonder wall of sound with backing singers – white gospel group The Imperials and black soul group the Sweet Inspirations satisfied his hunger for spiritual

138   Elvis: The King of Fashion

inspiration. Finally, he added soprano Millie Kirkham – just to ensure the roof would be raised once in a while.

Rehearsals were during the two weeks leading up to the 31 July opening and Elvis encouraged them all to be experimental and spontaneous. Yes, he'd do his old stuff, but it had to be different, rearranged, fresh. With more than a hundred songs to play with, no show would be the same.

Parker was as good as resident in Las Vegas from 1969 and, although he'd always enjoyed betting, he became so addicted to casino gambling that he was known as a Vegas 'high roller' – a player consistently placing large wagers. Little did Elvis realise that he would later be a stake in Parker's game of roulette.

Now is a good time to pause for breath, and to assess whether there's a glimmer of light to bring balance to the shade of Tom Parker. Almost everyone that I have encountered in the course of writing this book, regardless of age, colour or creed, has either disliked, distrusted or downright loathed the secretive, peculiar enigma that was Andreas Cornelis van Kuijk, aka the 'Colonel', or 'the fat old man', as Elvis would call him. Would I have been kinder to him, indulged him more by using his self-styled title from the start of this story had I been unaware of the ending? Was Baz Luhrmann's pantomime-villain-esque version of Parker (played by Tom Hanks) accurate? Or fair?

Like all things in life, nothing's black and white.

We know the downsides.

Using stealth and coercion, he harvested money from Elvis's earnings and accepted him being humiliated and exploited in the name of contract fulfilment. He also used his insecurities against him like weapons in order to control him. In spite of promising not to interfere in Elvis's private life or creative decisions, provided that he, in turn, stayed out of the business side things, Parker continued to dictate many aspects of his life, including his marriage, his choice of films and which records he made. Parker would agree contracts for grueling concert and film schedules and then, apart from overseeing merchandising sales opportunities, would step away, leaving Elvis overstretched and, no doubt, exacerbating his growing compulsion to take drugs in order to meet his commitments.

According to Larry Geller, spiritual and follicular guru and entourage member, when Elvis was in Louisville, Kentucky, six months before he died, Parker – very unusually – turned up before a show, barged into Elvis's room and finding him barely awake with his doctor, George Constantine Nichopoulos, aka Dr Nick, 'dunking his head into a bucket with iced water', stormed up to Geller and said, 'The only thing that's important right now is that that man is on the stage tonight.'

Baz Luhrmann included this event in *Elvis*, but places Austin Butler, as Elvis, in a theatre corridor, rather than in a hotel room. Butler is in a purple velvet

The Caped Crusader 139

suit and satin shirt and gold Nautic sunglasses. The other accessories are a wide black leather belt with gold studs, chains and panels, a la the Hilton champion belt (more of which later), four knuckle-duster jewelled rings and several gold pendants around his neck. Always in favour of opulence, instead of a bucket, Butler's head is plunged into a gold champagne bucket. It's an emotive, some might say manipulative, scene that caused almost everyone I spoke to (who didn't already) to despise Tom Parker; and Vernon's suggested complicity in drugging Elvis in the same scene also elicited fury.

Geller says that he had hoped that Parker seeing Elvis in such an awful state in Louisville would help make him see the reality of how badly Elvis was doing, but no. Parker, he says, 'walked out. And my heart dropped.'

Worst of all, though, Parker destroyed Elvis's dream of touring the world to meet his loyal fans who couldn't get to America, and give them an opportunity to see him live.

So far, so shady.

The upsides.

Alanna Nash, author of *Elvis Aaron Presley: Revelations from the Memphis Mafia* and particularly insightful on Elvis's life, says that, at times, she was chilled by Parker. However, she still believes that he could be deemed the father of American popular culture on account of his blisteringly effective marketing of Elvis, the star.

Parker did get a relatively unknown and, at the time, controversial Elvis on national TV, which unquestionably made him a countrywide celebrity overnight. And he worked endlessly to ensure that his boy remained on the fans' radars throughout his army service absence. He also negotiated one of Hollywood's first $1 million-a-movie deals for him and secured the record-breaking Vegas contract. As well as carving out the deal for the 1968 NBC movie/TV special deal that, albeit inadvertently, resurrected Elvis's career, he conceived and staged the world's first live, global satellite-television broadcast, *Elvis: Aloha from Hawaii*, beaming his star straight onto the retinas of more viewers than had watched the moon landings. And by moving quickly to protect the Presley estate when Elvis died in 1977, he protected certain rights for Elvis (and other dead celebrities). But then, that suited his own interests, too.

Was Baz Luhrmann right to portray Parker in *Elvis* as the devil in a Christmas cardigan?

The majority of fans say 'yes.'

Did he have any redeeming characteristics?

Apart from being a very efficient salesman, it's hard to think of one. I could be wrong, since everyone has their own take, truth or opinion, and even with rigorous research, facts get mired in fiction and vice versa.

140   Elvis: The King of Fashion

Did Parker have a softer, empathetic side?

A lone example cited occurred in Las Vegas on 31 July 1969. When Elvis returned backstage to the sound of a screaming, sobbing standing ovation after his blistering opening show, Parker had tears in his eyes. Of pride, or love – or of joy at how much money they would make from the next engagement? We'll never know.

But let's head back to Vegas 1969 now. With his idea of music heaven in place, it was time for Elvis to bring out the big guns, costume-wise. He called Bill Belew.

Aware that the town was in the thrall of the ostentatiously camp style of Liberace, Bill wanted something different for Elvis as he felt he wanted protect his image. Talking to Butch Polston, owner of B&K Enterprises, who create impressively accurate reproductions of Elvis's stage outfits (on *Bill Belew's Early Days*, Dumas Entertainment), Bill says, 'That's why I stayed away from any rhinestones and anything like that, I wanted the clothes to be easy and seductive. And I never wanted anything to compromise his masculinity.' A sweet consideration which led to some of his best designs, but he would soon learn that the only question over Elvis's masculinity would be 'how come he gets the lion's share?'

In shades of his preference for baggy trousers in the 1950s, Elvis asked Bill for something that he could easily move around in. His priorities hadn't changed. The result was a highly original, two-piece outfit, inspired by Elvis's karate gis and that he looked fantastic in. In essence, it looked like a martial arts suit that had been crafted by a top fashion designer – because it was. Bill used one single colour and made versions in dark inky-blue, jet black and pure white so that Elvis could alternate them. Even the trim panels and belt, embroidered to mimic the edging of a karate jacket, toned perfectly. The simple, perfectly cut tunic top had bell sleeves, a deeply slashed V-neck and a sash belt that, when not resting on his thigh, swung around to Elvis's playfully sensual version of his frenetic '50s gyrations. Slender, kick-flare trousers (the mega-bell-bottoms were yet to come) and a draped, tonal silk scarf finished the look. The tailoring, the statement colours and the figure-hugging shape were as flattering as candlelight on an ageing starlet.

For his shows, Elvis ditched Vegas's customary booming announcement of 'Ladies and gentlemen …' and simply walked, smiling (to pretend he wasn't petrified), onto the stage. Lean and glowing, with razor cheekbones, he had been refashioned into something more exalted than merely on-trend. He was a style supernova. George Klein put it beautifully when he said, 'Elvis wasn't just a superstar, he was the whole damn Galaxy.'

The Caped Crusader   141

Picking up his guitar, he tore into 'Blue Suede Shoes' and, even with weeks of unprecedented levels of excitement in Vegas about Elvis appearing, it was right then that he knew the audience was his. The ultimate performer was back in the house and, sensing their excitement, played them like his favourite guitar. He talked to them, sharing self-deprecating jokes and anecdotes, like how the New Yorkers said of him, 'Hot damn, he's just got out of the trees.'

Elvis had poked fun at himself in this way throughout his career. I believe he was subconsciously playing down his talent and his looks to protect himself from being seen as conceited or, in earlier days, from being bullied. Regardless, forget the Memphis butterfly, this second metamorphosis was of phoenix-from-the-ashes proportions. One can just imagine the men in the audience, some really big stars, making mental notes to up their fashion game and the women, many, also celebrities, imagining all sorts of things.

Bill Belew went to Vegas to see his muse – and his clothes – in action with Cathy McEvoy, whose husband, Jim, designed Elvis's set. He recalled her reaction: 'Elvis came out. Cathy leaned over to me and she said, "Bill, that's got to be the sexiest man alive … you can feel the sexual heat coming from him."' Bill could.

Priscilla was there for the opening night, and, although she and Elvis had known each other for ten years by then, she had never seen him perform on stage, other than during the filming of the *'68 Special*. She was blown away. In *Elvis and Me* she wrote: 'Elvis exuded a maleness about him, a proudness you'd only see in an animal … and you look and you say, "My God, is this the person that I – ?"'

All hail the showman!

Prior to reviewing the invitation-only first show for *The New Yorker*, sharp-penned and thoroughly progressive reporter Ellen Willis expected little more than a harkening back to old times with a side serving of mawkish balladeering; she hoped that Elvis would surprise her and at least be crude, or surly – or both.

Surprise her he did, but not in the way she expected.

Then Presley came on, and immediately shook up all my expectations and preconceived categories. There was a new man out there. A grown man in black bell-bottoms, tunic, and neckerchief, devoid of pout and baby fat, skinny, sexy, totally alert, nervous but smiling easily. …

He still moved around a lot, but in a much different spirit. What was once deadly serious frenzy had been infused with humour and a certain detachment. … Though the show was … an affirmation of Presley's sustaining love for rhythm and blues – we knew it all the time, Elvis – it was not burdened by an oppressive reverence for the past.

142 Elvis: The King of Fashion

For me, Willis's killer line was, 'He knew better than to try to be nineteen again. He had quite enough to offer at thirty-three.'

With another success on his hands, Elvis attended a post-show press conference the next day. He wore my favourite Bill Belew 'cut-away' suit in blue-black with a draped red-and-black silk scarf. He looked on top of the world – he *was* on top of the world.

Asked, somewhat pointedly, if he decided to perform after so long because of the success of Tom Jones and Engelbert Humperdinck, Elvis ignored the bait and told the gathered press:

> My decision to return was made in 1965, and it was hard to wait … I don't think I could have waited any longer. … We had to finish up the movie commitments … before I could start on this. …
>
> I missed the live contact with an audience. It was getting harder and harder to sing to a camera all day.

On what Priscilla felt about her husband being a sex symbol, he replied: 'I don't know … you would have to ask her.' And when asked, 'How do you manage to stay so young?' With a complete lack of egotism, he answered that he'd just been lucky, adding, ominously, with hindsight, 'One of these days I'll probably fall apart.'

He also confirmed that he dyed his hair and explained that he chose songs for the show by just picking those that were his favourites to sing and that he hoped to tour the world ….

To the disquieting sign-of-the-times question 'Why did you chose a Negro back-up group?' Elvis said, 'They help get a feeling in my soul.'

Throughout the questioning, he was open, patient and humorous, as always. To another loaded enquiry, 'Why have you led such a secluded life all these years?' Elvis joked, 'It's not secluded, Honey. I'm just sneaky.'

The inquisition roared and whooped and did so again when he was asked, 'Elvis, is there anybody else you'd rather be?' and he replied, 'Are you kidding!'

Over his four-week engagement, Elvis created and perfected a unique, one-man extravaganza on a scale and with a level of entertainment the Nevada desert had never seen before. He gave them what they wanted, on Elvis level 10.

He rocked the hell out of the likes of 'Jailhouse Rock', put his heart into 'I Can't Stop Loving You' and 'Can't Help Falling In Love', and he told them stories, grass-roots, musical ones, as he introduced audience members from around the world to the story behind 'Polk Salad Annie', with which he paid respect to his own lowly beginnings – and to Gladys, who no doubt picked him a mess of the stuff now and then. The Shake Rag kid was finally singing his own blues.

The Caped Crusader   143

ELVIS – spelled out in gargantuan letters on the front of the hotel, something the other hotels soon copied – was the most successful show in Las Vegas history, pulling in $1.5 million in a single month, with hundreds of people having to be turned away.

That night, Parker outlined a further contract on a tablecloth in the hotel's coffee shop. Elvis was signed up for a further series of whole-month runs twice a year, inaugurating his reign as the undisputed King of Sin City, a sovereignty that would last until he died and would become a confinement bound to an unremitting schedule of hundreds of performances. His vision and matchless appeal brought a seismic change to how Vegas regarded and entertained the public and paved the way for future performers by highlighting the importance of big star residencies later enjoyed by the likes of Bette Midler, Cher, Jennifer Lopez, Elton John, Britney Spears and Celine Dion.

In August 1969, the Hilton Hotel group, owners of the International, presented Elvis with a large, ornate, gold belt styled like a boxing champion's as a reward for attracting record-breaking attendances. Also read as: to thank him for making them piles of money. Big and showy, made from silver, faced with melted gold, it weighed a ton. Elvis didn't wear it much at first as his early 1970s shows outfits were only just shifting towards the trademark jumpsuits. Later, however, he grew to love it.

'At first he hates it,' said Lamar Fike, 'then you couldn't get the damn thing off him.'

In December, *From Memphis To Vegas/Vegas To Memphis*, a collection of the songs from Moman's studio and live performances from Vegas, went gold, making for a happy Christmas ahead of his second International engagement the following January.

In the four-week stint that ran from the end of January through February 1970, belying his growing dependency on prescription drugs and increasingly erratic behaviour, Elvis was still as bouncy as Tigger on a trampoline; he was on top form musically, physically and stylishly, as a new costume phase was unveiled.

Bill Belew said, 'It wasn't until we were so advanced into the wardrobe that the fans begun to demand more.

'That's when I knew we were OK [he's referring to his protecting Elvis's image and that it was by then clear to all that Elvis was straight], and it just went from there.'

He approached Elvis suggesting a new wardrobe and, in view of the triumph of his previous designs, Elvis was in. And so, the jumpsuit era was born. 'I loved working with Elvis. He was great to dress,' said Bill.

To ensure that his star shone brightly in the hotel's Showroom Internationale's dark firmament, Bill suggested Elvis should mainly wear white. Made not, as

144 Elvis: The King of Fashion

some people think, of a synthetic fabric but from finest wool gaberdine from Milan (making them, actually off-white, or pale cream, but always referred to as 'white'), they perfectly met Elvis's mobility criteria, they had pointed cuffs, high collars and bell-bottom trousers, the latest thing and usually with kick-pleat inserts for extra flair – or even flare – power.

He was literally ready to kick off!

During that month and the following one-month's run of increasingly spectacular, sell-out concerts, which set the schedule for all Elvis's Vegas shows right up to his last on 12 December 1976, the jumpsuits were still fairly restrained, adorned mainly with metal eyelets, fringes, studs, beads and hipster belts. Each was outstanding; however, I have to namecheck two.

The White Cossack – a slim-fitting, beauty of a suit where a little decoration goes a very long way. With a slashed V front and tied with an understated macramé belt, its only other embellishment is a circular yoke of white pearls and white and gold woven threads that fray into a shimmering waterfall of cords that flow down Elvis's bare chest. It's simple but regal, exquisitely crafted and so effective.

The Fringe, debuted in the August 1970 opening show, is another example of simplicity over excess. Again, it's plain white and perfectly cut. Stylewise, the drama lies in rows of long fringes, sparingly threaded with coloured beads, inspired by Elvis's native American heritage. In backstage footage of him striding towards the wings with his musicians and backing singers, he's all you see. His deep tan makes the suit appear to be lit by ultra-violet. Even with the fringes barely moving, the effect with the beads is striking. And when Elvis does move into action on stage – it's electrifying. I can't think of another human who could have carried this off.

A later version, the Wing suit, which Elvis wore during November and early 1971, had fabric 'wings' (revealed when he raised his arms) and far longer but less adorned fringes. It wasn't as sleek as its predecessor and, while it looks dramatic in photos, Elvis had trouble with the fringes getting tangled around the wire of the mic and, at times, around himself!

Like the 1969 shows, both the 1970 runs were record-breakers and were only part of a series of further live concert tours as Elvis went on the road for the first time in years. Over three consecutive days from 27 February, he played six concerts (matinee and evening) in Texas at the Houston Astrodome's livestock and rodeo show. Beforehand, he hosted a press conference wearing a red, extravagantly puffed-sleeved shirt (a nod to his favourite Tupelo blue velvet one) under a sleeveless white tunic tied, karate style, with a red-and-black fabric belt. A matching geometric-print scarf completed the '68 Comeback-influenced colour palette.

The Caped Crusader   145

In footage, Elvis looks striking but his eyes look heavy and tired and he's sweating; he seems edgy and coughs frequently. Excusing the cough, he jokes that it's because the air's too clean as he's more used to being around dumpster bins in Vegas. Asked if he's nervous, he says, 'Yes', and admits that he's worried about whether enough people will come as it's such a big arena (the performances would also be his first in public outside of Vegas in almost a decade).

He needn't have worried. An astounding 207,000-plus people came to see him. He arrived for the first show waving from a jeep that circled the arena and, over the three days, smashed all previous attendance records. This was becoming a habit.

At a second press conference, just days after Houston, Elvis looks like a different person. Talking easily, laughing, fresh-faced and in a fantastic outfit. A white, Napoleon-collared shirt, with an almost granny-patterned silk scarf that perfectly tones with deep-plum trousers and a rebooted bolero jacket, both trimmed with beige leather punched through with metal rivets. It's part hussar, part matador. Until you see the Stetson and the belt, a marvel of patchwork leather with a huge exploding starburst buckle (definitely a sign of things to come) and suddenly he's Rodeo Elvis. Yee-ha!

Was it anxiety, exhaustion, medication or a mix of all three that caused Elvis's uneasy manner in the earlier press call? Who knows? One thing is certain, though; whatever elements brought about the change in him for the second press meeting, where he was presented with five – that's five – gold discs (for 'In The Ghetto', 'Suspicious Minds', and 'Don't Cry, Daddy' and the Memphis/Vegas albums), the main one must surely have been relief that he still had it.

For the three days' work, where the new jumpsuits, including the White Cossack and the Thin Green Leaf, with its ecclesiastical robes vibe, were put through their paces, Elvis earned more than a million dollars.

Apart from returning to Memphis ahead of his next Vegas run, where he checked into the hospital and discovered he had glaucoma, other dramas included dealing with a paternity suit (later disproven) and a threat to kidnap him during an August Vegas show, which turned out to be a hoax, but left Elvis rattled.

After the year's final Vegas show in September, he performed at the Veteran Memorial Coliseum in Phoenix, Arizona, and in sell-out shows in St Louis, Detroit, Miami Beach, Tampa and Mobile.

Still unsettled by the perceived kidnap threat, Elvis became fixated – as was his wont – with firearms and law enforcement, and, after becoming a special deputy in Memphis that October, could legally carry a gun.

That same month, also more obsessed with jewellery than ever and by then designing his own pieces to be crafted by his favourite jeweller, Lowell Hays, who was often beckoned to travel throughout the US to deliver items, Elvis

146   Elvis: The King of Fashion

gifted all the Memphis Mafia gold pendants in the shape of the letters TCB (Taking Care of Business) with a lightning flash running through them.

As the shows grew bigger and more dynamic, so did the jumpsuits, becoming a major part of the audience experience and, in the ensuing years, growing in extravagance in correlation to Elvis's growing popularity and, depending on the year, his stature.

Behind the scenes, things were getting stressful between Elvis and Priscilla, who, left behind for long periods of time and expected to play house, was becoming increasingly upset about his blatant infidelity and his unpredictable, partly drug- partly illness-induced behaviour. In November, after telling the press that his marriage 'had difficulties', he toured Portland, Oakland, Seattle, San Francisco, LA, San Diego, Oklahoma and Denver, followed by a three-day shopping spree in December, when he splurged $20,000 on guns.

By this time, Elvis's offstage outfits were getting more flamboyant in line with his onstage ones. He regularly wore chunky metal-framed Nautic prescription sunglasses, by German company Neostyle, who would customise them with the initials EP in the frame above the nose or with 14-carat gold, diamond-encrusted TCB along the arms. They were to help with the glaucoma rather than to make him look cool, but they did both. In May 2021, an authenticated pair that Elvis had given to his friend Kathie Spehar during a party in his suite at the International in 1974 were sold at auction in Las Vegas for $126,000.

Elvis was also favouring richly coloured, sumptuous, tactile fabrics (a security blanket, if you will; think Satnin) and wore velvet and corduroy suits with high Napoleonic collars and heavy satin or silk shirts, adorned with ruffles and frills. Larry Gellar once claimed that Elvis wore the high collars to imitate the spiritual masters in David Anrias's book *Through the Eyes of the Masters*; Priscilla, on the other hand, said it was because he thought his neck was too long.

In this new fashion epoch, the previously ignored Hilton gold belt became a wardrobe staple, his superhero artefact, his talisman. And, speaking of protectors of the universe, capes – yes, capes – also entered The Kings' wardrobe of wonders. Elvis in a purple-caped Edwardian gentleman's frock coat, glossy shirt, velvet flares, grandiose pendants, jewel-encrusted watches, bracelets, vast rings and jewelled cane on a normal day was not an uncommon sight.

Police uniforms would come into play, too, as his determination to become a law enforcer showed no signs of abating and took him into contact with police forces around the country, who presented him with outfits, badges and titles, while Elvis bestowed cars and other gifts on some particularly welcoming police employees.

Cop, Caped Crusader or Emperor, he looked wonderful in everything.

The Caped Crusader   147

But he was at his most majestic when he embarked on his next big, and most bizarre, life adventure – Elvis Runs Away to Washington.

If it weren't so well recorded, this event would sound too far-fetched to be believable, but it actually happened. It occurred at the end of the year, after a series of circumstances that led to a frazzled Elvis reaching peak boiling point. While performing live, Elvis was invincible, singing and moving freely in shimmering, bejewelled suits, the unconditional love from his audience like a protective barrier. In the real world, things were rather different. He now had a family, a wife and a young child, but as he'd hinted earlier to a reporter, things were strained.

Priscilla loved him and he loved her, so she'd suffered his womanising for years, while hanging on to the promise of becoming his wife and living happily ever after. When the marriage did finally happen, the icing on the (wedding) cake was the birth of Lisa Marie a year later. Their bond was sealed. Or so Priscilla thought. Elvis had other ideas (don't forget his attitude that motherhood and sex were incompatible bed fellows) and continued with his bachelor's lifestyle, leaving them somewhat estranged – she, creating a routine for herself and Lisa Marie at home, and he, partying all night in Vegas with pals and an endless stream of women.

Sadly, Elvis was harbouring a growing array of underlying medical issues, some undiagnosed, later, largely attributed to genetics and his famously unhealthy lifestyle. These led to an exponential rise in his already well-documented drug use, initially for pain relief, to help him sleep, then to wake and to manage his moods, but which had become dangerously addictive. In *Elvis By The Presleys*, Priscilla wrote about how touring was so demanding that its logistics overwhelmed his life and that Elvis was so swept up in it that his struggle to sleep, 'a lifelong dilemma, was gravely exacerbated. His dependence on pills – to chase away the blues or just to give him the energy to make it through the day – became more extreme.'

Along with enlightenment and religious books, his constant bedside companion was his copy of the *Physician's Desk Reference*, an index book of pharmaceutical drugs and their specific properties and uses.

Pills were prescribed or sourced not just from Dr Nick, but from myriad suppliers around the country, all happy to take Elvis's money. Using his in-depth, but far from professionally based knowledge of medicines, combined with a misguided belief that, being prescriptible, the drugs were 'safe', he often had a mixture of them. In his mind, his drugs of choice were not those of the addict, the junkie, but just those of a guy trying to get by.

148   Elvis: The King of Fashion

Along with a large staff to manage – and pay – he was also paranoid about being kidnapped or assassinated after the Vegas hoax and his debts were mounting daily.

It was a perfect storm of woes that left Elvis in a perpetual state of flux and an unspecified sense of urgency and anxiety. The storm swept in on 19 December 1970, when, after a blazing row with Vernon and Priscilla over his volatile behaviour and how his compulsive, reckless spending was building up to another Circle G Ranch scenario, or worse, Elvis ran away from home.

This was big. Elvis hadn't gone out on his own without saying where he was going since he'd become famous in the 1950s. Priscilla and Vernon were frantic. Normally, he was encircled by his entourage; however, unwell and over-medicated, he just stormed out, drove to Memphis airport and bought a plane ticket to Washington, DC, apparently using an emergency credit card he had in his wallet but had never even used.

His original mission had been to hook up with sometime girlfriend Joyce Bova, who worked on Capitol Hill. Unable to track her down, he then flew to Los Angeles, where erstwhile Memphis Mafia member Jerry Schilling lived, and asked him to help him find her. Jerry, shocked at Elvis's puffy appearance and odd behaviour, but determined to keep his friend safe, agreed. They flew back to Washington and en route, Elvis asked a Californian senator how he could get a federal narcotics badge. The senator suggested he go straight to the president, so Elvis began to compose a letter, mid-air, to President Nixon on American Airlines stationery.

On 21 December, he made an impromptu visit to White House security and delivered the hand-scrawled letter outlining how he could help Nixon and the American government restore pride in the flag and tackle the youth's drug problem. The security guard at the Northwest Gate couldn't believe his eyes but forwarded the missive, which made its way to White House staff. In it, Elvis had also stated that he wanted to give the president a gift and that he'd like federal agent credentials in order to participate in the war on drugs.

Incredibly, Nixon agreed to see him.

Throughout the meeting, Elvis, resplendent in a Bill Belew-designed navy blue Edwardian-style suit, complete with caped jacket and flared trousers, teamed with giant gold belt and gold-buckled boots, kept his Nautic gold shades on. Like a kid at show-and-tell, he showed Nixon his police badges and other cop paraphernalia he'd been obsessively acquiring. He also gave him some family photos, mercifully not the Priscilla Polaroids, but including one of Lisa Marie. And he discussed how he could appeal to 'youngsters, hippies and the Black Panthers' since he wasn't establishment, before rummaging through Nixon's proffered box of badges and such in search of prize collectibles.

The Caped Crusader   149

To Elvis's joy, the official credentials were granted, with Nixon telling Egil Krogh, his top enforcement advisor, 'See that he gets it.'

Beyond excited, Elvis hugged the bemused POTUS and clearly emboldened, during a quick photo session with him, asked if his buddies – Jerry Schilling and Sonny West (who'd raced to Washington to find them) – who were waiting outside the Oval Office, could also get a photo.

Again, request granted and in they came.

Before leaving, Elvis surprised Nixon with another gift – a beautiful vintage Second World War Colt revolver that he'd carried through the White House!

An historic moment and happy Christmas, Elvis.

The year 1971 opened with the news that Elvis had been voted one of the Ten Outstanding Young Men of the Nation by the United States Junior Chamber of Commerce, also known as the 'The Jaycees' (JCs), and on 16 January, he did something that terrified him – he made a public speech.

He was to accept the award – an honour previously bestowed on powerhouses like John F. Kennedy, Robert Kennedy (which would have resonated after the 1968 assassination), Orson Welles, Howard Hughes and Henry Kissinger – in front of an audience in Memphis.

In true Elvis fashion, he went the whole hog, arranging a glamorous cocktail party at Graceland for after the awards, where guests would be given grand tours by members of his entourage, followed by a Chateubriand dinner at a local restaurant. And instead of staying at Graceland, he took a suite at the Holiday Inn to ensure he was on time for the next day's proceedings. Even so, having stayed up all night writing the speech, with help from Priscilla, he was late for the Jaycee prayer breakfast – due to losing a cufflink. Only Elvis.

In the newsreel footage, he has never looked so Kingly. The trademark collar is stark white and taller than ever before – as though proud of its own achievement. Encircled by an almost clownishly large, but very on-trend, black bow-tie, it also acts as a capstan around which Elvis's award medal, attached to a two-tone dark- and baby-blue satin ribbon, is suspended.

Pre-fame, Elvis was a fan of Roy Hamilton, a black singer with a sublime voice who he said inspired his own style. They met and became friends and even spent time together in the American Sound Studio in '69. Elvis loved Hamilton's 'Without A Song', so he decided to make his speech a blend of some of the song's lyrics and his own words.

As he stands at the podium, facing the audience of lofty sorts, including George W. Bush, pre-presidency, who'd just spoken before him, he's clearly as nervous as hell. However, the applause is thunderous and he's not said a thing. After a hesitant start, Elvis starts to look more assured and begins his speech. The place falls silent. It's absolutely riveting. It starts slowly, then speeds up (he

150   Elvis: The King of Fashion

just wants it to be over) but due to the sheer simplicity, humanity and humility of it, it's an absolute killer.

> When I was a child, ladies and gentlemen, I was a dreamer. I read comic books, and I was the hero of the comic book. I saw movies, and I was the hero in the movie. So every dream I ever dreamed has come true a hundred times.
>
> These gentlemen over here [he gestures to his fellow award recipients] these are people who care, they're dedicated. You realize it's not impossible that they might be building the kingdom of heaven … it's not too far-fetched.
>
> I can say that, uh, I learned very early in life that without a song, the day would never end; without a song, a man ain't got a friend; without a song, the road would never bend … without a song.
>
> So I keep singing a song. Goodnight. Thank you.

The room exploded.

The rest of Elvis's year was mostly concerts. A twenty-eight-day run at the Sahara Tahoe hotel in Stateline, Nevada, in July and a road tour in November that took in Minneapolis, Cleveland, Louisville, Philadelphia, Baltimore, Boston, Cincinnati, Houston, Dallas, Tuscaloosa, Kansas City and Salt Lake City filled the gaps before and between his two fifty-seven-concert stints in Vegas in January to February and August to September.

The damp squib finale was when Priscilla, left alone too long and having finally discovered the world outside Graceland, left him. She cited his out-of-control behaviour, his insistence that she could only go to the openings and closings of his Vegas engagements and his leaving her for weeks on end.

Worse was to come. After his fifty-seven January through February Vegas shows in 1972, Priscilla told Elvis that she'd been having an affair with martial arts expert Mike Stone – whom Elvis had recommended she should train with.

A schedule juggernaut of back-to-back concerts in April and June of 1972 would certainly have helped take Elvis's mind off his real life for a while. In April, his first stop was Buffalo in New York. Bob Abel, interviewing him for the *Elvis on Tour* documentary, asks him about the intense two weeks of concerts involved in his tours. Elvis just shrugs and says it's because they all love doing it.

'In Vegas, we'll do two shows and we'll go upstairs and we'll sing till daylight. Gospel songs.'

Abel asks, 'How do you do that?'

Elvis jokes, 'Not too often.'

Out of frame, one of the guys (maybe Red West) points out that the upcoming April road tour is 'all one-night stands, too'.

The Caped Crusader   151

Elvis nods, smiling, and says, 'Yep. But that's fine. It's excitement.'

He genuinely could not wait to get to Buffalo and then onwards to hit the stages of Detroit, Dayton, Knoxville, Hampton Roads, Richmond, Roanoke, Indianapolis, Charlotte, Greensboro, Macon, Jacksonville, Little Rock, San Antonio and Albuquerque, where he stunned audiences with his powerful sound and his latest red, white and blue collection of breathtaking jumpsuits. Names like the Pinwheel, Fireworks or Nail described the designs of spinning, whirling, sparkling studs and pinheads that decorated them. Many had matching capes that he'd open out with his arms stretched wide at the end of the show, giving him the look of a religious deity. Several of these concerts were filmed for the documentary.

Still going strong, on 9 June, ahead of another immense run of concerts, Elvis attended a press conference in the New York Hilton to launch the first stage – four concerts in a row at Madison Square Garden. Filmed and photographed extensively, it is the stuff of rock 'n' roll folklore, not just because it would be his last press call or because he was funny and nervous, charming and humble, but because in his sensational outfit he was just so exquisitely and unapologetically high-octane Elvis. In a room packed with hard-nosed journos and snappers, all dressed in various shades of work-friendly neutrals and with some poised to prove that he was just a joke in a jumpsuit, his blissfully showy cornflower blue and black – maybe navy – trimmed outfit, with cape, of course, meant that he stood out like a nudist in a nunnery.

Watching it now, it's not just the suit, with its exaggerated jacket revers and trademark collar. Nor is it the black-and-cream, gender ambiguous floral shirt, or the boulder-sized jewellery pieces, including a diamond ring with a black sapphire the size of a Greek Kalamata olive. It's the whole package. At 37, with his easy smile, concert-toned figure and deeply, almost ridiculously, tanned face accentuating his Arctic-sky eyes, he's reached peak Elvisness. No one in that room can look at anything other than the astounding man on the stage.

Throughout his life, Elvis had to use his charm and his talent to win over people who'd misjudged or dismissed him, and this was no exception. He answers both friendly and barbed questions with equal frankness, honesty and wit, revealing what they hadn't expected – that he's a normal guy underneath the flamboyant facade. Which he clarifies when a male reporter asks, with a hint of sarcasm, 'Are you satisfied with the image you've established?'

Elvis smiles indulgently and turns the other cheek. 'Well, the image is one thing and the human being is another, you know, so …' then he looks him right in the eye.

The questioner persists, 'How close does it come? How close does the image come to the man?'

152   Elvis: The King of Fashion

Elvis's straight-faced reply, 'It's very hard to live up to an image, I'll put it that way,' is so open and authentic that the guy gives up goading him.

'I hear that you really are a shy, humble, wonderful human being. Would you agree with that?' asks one sarcy woman.

Elvis batted back beautifully with, 'Oh I don't know what makes them think that. I got, you know, this gold belt and …' he stands up, unbuttons his jacket and, laughing, shows off his golden power belt.

The room falls apart and when a photographer jumps up to take several pictures, he fakes alarm and cries, 'What are you doing, woman?'

She says, 'I'm reminded of the Ed Sullivan show …'

Elvis replies, 'So am I, that's why I'm sitting down, man!'

The four Madison Square Garden shows were huge hits, as was the rest of the tour that took in Fort Wayne and Evansville, Milwaukee, Chicago, Fort Worth, Wichita and Tulsa. One of my favourite photos of Elvis, wearing one of his best outfits ever, was taken by Jack Baity, a rhythm guitarist friend of Elvis's guitarist, John Wilkinson, as Elvis was leaving Chicago Midway Airport on 18 June after three concerts. Wearing a geometric-printed black and white shirt and an all-black, tailored suit with bold, burnt-orange trim, buttons and lining, he shines like a lighthouse in the sea of neutral-coloured, tense aids and musicians who surround him.

The suit fits like a glove. The high collar is there, but it's understated, the jewellery is subtle, apart from the rings, and he's holding his EP-monogrammed shades. This is his 'daywear' and it's a truly unforgettable look. Still, Elvis outshines it completely as he looks so amazing; a small, beatific smile hovers and he looks contented and much younger than in many photos of the time.

Elvis showcased more jumpsuits, including the Wheat, Adonis and Eyelet as well as a fantastic white suit with black-trimmed pockets worn with a beautiful paisley swirl-patterned silk shirt in classic '70s brown and orange – with the gold Hilton champ belt, again.

I bet everyone went clothes shopping after witnessing that style sensation.

In July, Elvis and Priscilla legally separated and Elvis met and fell for Linda Thompson, a young, former beauty queen; she moved into Graceland within a few months.

But August was the big month, with Elvis's first show of his sixty-three-concert run in Las Vegas and, on a personally painful level, he filed for divorce from Priscilla.

In the wake of the last run of '72's Las Vegas concerts, the release of the 1972 documentary film *Elvis on Tour* grossed nearly half a million dollars in a single week.

The Caped Crusader   153

In November, Elvis played Lubbock, Tucson, El Paso, Oakland, San Bernardino, Long Beach and Honolulu.

Elvis's Christmas present that year was a Grammy for the Best Inspirational Performance for his LP *He Touched Me*, and the documentary was voted Best Documentary of 1972 by the Hollywood Foreign Press Association and was nominated for a Golden Globe award.

Just trying to comprehend the intensity of Elvis's early 1970s touring schedule – so far – is exhausting. Imagine how he must have felt.

Surely, it was time for a rest?

Chapter 11

Elvis Leaves the Building

1973–7

'Elvis was always stunning. He loved clothes. He loved fine fabrics. Even at home, even on casual days, he'd wear a beautiful silk shirt and tailored trousers.'

Priscilla Presley

'Only Elvis could have saved Elvis.'

Jerry Schilling

In January 1973, Elvis finally got to tour the world. Well, sort of.

They say that necessity is the mother of invention and never was there a finer example than the feat that 'Colonel' Tom Parker pulled off in order to avoid being exposed as an illegal immigrant. While Elvis talked optimistically, often publicly, about his hopes to perform abroad, Parker sweated in the background like a prizefighter after ten rounds – since he knew that to leave America would require a passport.

For Elvis, that wasn't a problem, but for Parker, aka Andreas Cornelis van Kuijk, it wasn't an option. It explains why, despite swathes of lucrative offers flooding in from around the world for Elvis to perform, Parker, to whom cash was normally king, turned down every one. He had a library of excuses, but knowing how paranoid Elvis was after the kidnapping hoax, he'd regularly cite (fabricated) higher security risks abroad as a reason for not touring outside the US. He got away with it by ensuring that Elvis did go out on the road, that he did tour, but only within America.

Elvis could have gone global without him; by that time his team knew how to run a fantastic show and most of his musicians would have loved to perform abroad with him. That, however, would leave Parker too far away from, and therefore not in enough control of, his greatest asset. The situation got tricky, but being the biggest trickster of them all, Parker devised a cunning plan. Elvis *would* perform around the world – by satellite.

Having shrewdly recognised the global marketing possibilities of a new space technology that could broadcast simultaneously to different locations on Earth,

Elvis Leaves the Building   155

he devised a world-spanning entertainment event in association with old pal, NBC. Elvis would perform a live concert from Hawaii (no passports required), that would end up being seen by an unprecedented 1.5 billion people worldwide and go down in history as the first broadcast of its kind. As the location for three of Elvis's films, his USS *Arizona* charity concert and one of his favourite holiday destinations, it seems fitting that Hawaii should have been the stage for what many believe to be his swansong performance, *Elvis: Aloha from Hawaii – The Ultimate Experience.*

Of course, Elvis performed in countless other unforgettable shows after that, but somehow, watching *Aloha* today feels like witnessing Elvis reach the peak of his career mountain. And when he reached that summit, he was wearing the American flag – in the shape of a red, white and blue bald eagle – emblazoned across his white jumpsuit.

Although he trusted Bill Belew to design perfect suits for him by then, on this occasion, Elvis made a special request. Since his concert was going around the world, he told Bill, 'I just want the suit to say "America".' First, Bill suggested a design based on the outline of the US map. Then one based on the flag, before finally opting for the bald eagle. A powerful and patriotic symbol, it was a 'Yes' from Elvis.

By then, less was never more for Showtime Elvis. The iconic white suit was studded with golden stars and emblazoned with lavishly jewelled eagle decals in red, blue and gold gemstones, on both the chest and back. Although weighing in at a hefty 75lb, Elvis loved the American Eagle jumpsuit and it became one of his staples. Bill also created what should have been the ultimate matching accessory, a stunning, 4-inch deep, white leather belt with five oval panels depicting the Great Seal of the United States. But there was more to come. A matching cloak. The superhero cometh. Initially a floor-length garment, the plan was for Elvis to arrive on stage wrapped in the cloak to his trademark music, *Also sprach Zarathustra* (theme to *2001: A Space Odyssey*), thus keeping his magnificent Americana jumpsuit under wraps until the big reveal.

At least that was the plan. During rehearsals Elvis found it too heavy (it weighed 12lb) and unwieldy and ditched it. Unphased, Bill returned to the drawing board and designed a calf-length version which a crack team of tailors and embroiders, who worked miracles behind the scenes, brought to life just in time for the show. While Bill did the sketches, Ciro Romano was the expert tailor who precision-cut and fitted Elvis's garments, including those in the *'68 Special*.

Fittings were mainly in person; Elvis would either fly Romano to Graceland or visit him in LA, and regularly tipped him $500 – a handsome sum in the 1960s and '70s.

156   Elvis: The King of Fashion

And the creative process didn't end there. Kim Polston of B&K Enterprises, who make accurate reproductions of Elvis's stage wear (including the jumpsuits worn by Austin Butler as Elvis in Baz Luhrmann's *Elvis* movie), explains:

Ciro made the cloth jumpsuits, but the real artwork happened when Gene Doucette put the designs on them. He would put the studding on Elvis's suits.

Once they realised how talented Gene was, they were turned over to him to do the designing as well. From the *Aloha* suit on, he did about 90 per cent of the designing on Elvis's suits.

Describing the American eagle suit, Gene says:

Well, it was done for that famous Telstar [satellite] *Aloha* thing. The eagle was entirely made out of nail head combinations, punch-on jewels and settings to create the eagle and, for it to be very American, very patriotic, red, white and blue.

Later, he evolved the eagle suits, interweaving elaborate stitching in red, white and blue among the nail heads and jewels to add depth of colour.

And I added extra rhinestones for shimmer. This gave it more punch under the lights.

There was eventually going to be a third version where I wanted the eagle to be very realistic, to have shape and form, and actually have action. I wanted it to be almost three-dimensional.

The beautiful sketch for the suit that was destined never to fly shows a sleek, sleeveless catsuit rather than a jumpsuit, with a huge fluid eagle and a flamboyant puff-sleeve shirt worn underneath. It would have looked sensational.

'Unfortunately, this was further down the line … it never did come about,' says Gene.

Due to the enormous amount of embroidery and jewels – 6,500 gemstones were required – for the shorter replacement cape, it took an entire team of staff to manufacture it. It even had its own seat on the plane out to Hawaii and when the air hostess spotted it, she asked its courier (Bill's friend), 'Is that Elvis's cape?'

When he confirmed that it was, she asked if she could touch it; he said, 'Yes', so she did. The next thing he knew, she went flying down the aisles of the plane yelling, 'I just touched Elvis's cape!'

Mid-rehearsals, as though trying to test Bill Belew's patience, Elvis, in typically generous fashion, gave the one-off American belt to actor Jack Lord's wife, Marie, as a gift. Marie was thrilled, but entourage member and logistics whiz Joe Esposito alerted Bill, who was all out of rubies and almost had to go to Europe for more before luckily finding some locally. Again the team worked flat-out to produce a replacement belt, which Bill flew with to Hawaii himself and stayed for the show. He and his associates designed Elvis's stage wear as well as his amazing personal wardrobe, up to his last performance.

'You could be daring as a designer and put anything on Elvis and he could make it work,' Bill said at the launch of a 2007 Elvis stage wear exhibition at Graceland. 'The simplest outfits that didn't seem particularly remarkable on the rack transformed into something spectacular when Elvis put them on. He was that beautiful and powerful a presence.'

On 14 January 1973, Elvis won the world as the concert travelled live via satellite to audiences across Asia and Oceania, and with a delay, to Europe. In the United States, to avoid a programming clash with Super Bowl VII and *Elvis on Tour*, which was playing in cinemas at the time, NBC aired a ninety-minute television special of the concert on 4 April.

When Elvis appeared on stage, the crowd went crazy. He smiled and started steady, almost subdued; he performed classics like 'Blue Suede Shoes', 'Hound Dog' and, while singing 'Love Me', beat the mic on his chest to show how fast his heart was beating – possibly not a joke. As he got into his stride, he relaxed.

Sparkling like sunlight on rippling water, with his big diamond rings, his star-spangled jumpsuit slashed to the navel and with smaller, appliqué eagles shimmering on the sleeves and thighs, he delivered emotive ballads, like the audience-delighting 'You Gave Me a Mountain', 'My Way' and the always rousing 'An American Trilogy', after which, once the applause and the screaming had died down, he said, 'Thank you. Thank you, you are fantastic,' then casually undid the precious second belt and, laughing, threw it into the audience.

As he introduced the final song, Charlie Hodge draped the shorter American Eagle cape over Elvis's shoulders and he launched into a cracking rendition of 'Can't Help Falling In Love'. Sweat poured off him and the adoring audience was left wrung out but elated from being in a constant state of excitement. After the big finish, Elvis spread the cape dramatically wide, took the knee before his congregation of fans, made the Shaka sign and then stood up. Next, clearly in mischievous mood, he then removed his cape, which had cost thousands of dollars, and gleefully tossed that into the crowd, too.

Thankfully, it wasn't the full-length version – the weight of which could have knocked someone out!

158   Elvis: The King of Fashion

Partially disrobed, though still in his $65,000 American Eagle suit and holding a golden crown handed to him by an audience member, the triumphant King left the building.

When 22-year-old Lonnie Fuqua settled into seat 10, row N, section 27 of the upper level of the Honolulu International Centre Arena on 14 January 1973 for the *Aloha* concert, he didn't expect a life-transforming experience.

> I wasn't an Elvis fan, I didn't buy his records. In the mid-sixties I was 15, I liked Motown, R&B and Rock 'n' Roll. Elvis movies were a turn-off, except *Blue Hawaii*, but when I saw he was doing a concert I thought my brother Gary and I should go, because it was ELVIS.

Originally from Nashville and now living in Asheville, North Carolina, the 73-year-old added:

> The show started at 1 a.m., but we were told to be in our seats at midnight. Gary and I walked from Waikiki to the arena and when we arrived there was a red carpet from the street to the doors, both sides lined with flowers and plants containing wishes of good luck for a successful performance.

The *Aloha* concert was in aid of a charity founded in honour of Hawaiian songwriter Kui Lee, who died from cancer at 34. People, Elvis and Tom Parker included, donated money for tickets and it's said that some fans got to see Elvis play live for a few cents. Still, it raised $75,000.

Lonnie said:

> I knew very little about what the show was for, the donation was whatever you could afford and we were poor, I donated two dollars. It was for the Kui Lee Cancer Fund. He wrote the song 'I'll Remember You' and watching Elvis perform it for Hawaii was interesting, the audience reacted very loudly when he started to sing it, and there's a look that he gives during it that says he did the song just right. Remember Elvis was very popular in Hawaii. They loved him. He kicked tourism into full swing with *Blue Hawaii*.
>
> The highlight was when he got his cape in place and dedicated the song 'I can't Help Falling in Love' to all the people in the audience there in Honolulu to close off the show with. How appropriate, it still brings tears to my eyes fifty years later. And when he threw the cape it was fast and it was exciting.
>
> At this point in my life I'd seen a few shows – the Temptations, Jethro Tull, the Monkees, the Rolling Stones, Alice Cooper, Janis Joplin and many

Elvis Leaves the Building   159

more, but when Elvis came out, it was overwhelming, unreal. Fan, or not, you still had knowledge of his history and you knew it was an honour to see him. I now consider it to be one of my all-time greatest life moments – when I saw a star come on the stage. I save all my concert tickets, but I mailed my Elvis ticket to my mother in Nashville – I still have it now. The next day, I called my Mom to tell her I saw Elvis and that he was so amazing, he could have just come on, waved to the crowd and talked to them for a bit – that's all he had to do.

As we know, that wasn't all Elvis did.
Lonnie continues:

Though I started out not really a fan, I know that what I saw and experienced was something more, much more than just a concert … it was a life event. It was truly remarkable. His stage presence is no joking matter and years later, when I got the DVD, it just blew me away.

Via the live satellite transmissions and subsequent broadcasts of the video recording of *Aloha from Hawaii*, an estimated 1.5 billion viewers have seen it and it remains the most watched entertainment show featuring only one performer.

The following day, Elvis and the 'Colonel' thanked Hawaii in full-page newspaper ads.

Less than two weeks after Hawaii, 1973 was concert central as Elvis fell back into his usual and increasingly debilitating schedule of two Las Vegas seasons and the life nocturnal, where he'd sleep all day, play a dinner show, followed by a midnight show, finishing around two in the morning, and would then host parties or gospel singalongs, often till dawn.

During the first season of fifty-four performances, he presented his friend and fellow legend, the heavyweight boxer Muhammad Ali with an Elvis-style, jewel-encrusted robe. He had requested the words 'People's Champion' across the gown's back, but when Ali opened it in front of him, it read, 'People's Choice'. Someone had cocked up and Elvis was not happy. Ali, being the sweetest as well as The Greatest, loved it and wore it anyway, telling everyone Elvis gave it to him.

Also during that run, Elvis unusually missed several shows due to 'illness' – in reality, adverse effects from the combination of drugs, including uppers and downers, that he was taking.

At his 18 February midnight show, a group of four men crashed the stage as he was doing some karate moves. Apparently, they were just exuberant fans who simply wanted his autograph, but Jerry Schilling and Red and Sonny

160   Elvis: The King of Fashion

West stepped in to remove them. One man was left on stage and Elvis, after the death threats and thinking he was there to kill him, sent him flying back into the audience.

Things were getting weird.

Within these already hugely demanding schedules ran a series of road tours. First up was in April, taking in Phoenix, Anaheim, Fresno, San Diego, Portland, Spokane, Seattle and Denver. The Orange Sunburst, Fire, Aztec Star and American Eagle were among the now dazzling array of jumpsuits Elvis wore for audiences to marvel over. Next came a twenty-five-concert engagement at the Sahara, Tahoe, in May. Once again, several concerts were cancelled as Elvis became incapacitated. Various medical conditions, some caused, others exacerbated by the side effects of years of overusing prescribed drugs to sleep or to keep up, in more ways than one, were finally catching up. Sadly, Elvis was already too invested to fully realise.

Despite being exhausted and feeling unwell, he went back on the road in June, this time delighting crowds in Mobile, Atlanta, Uniondale, Pittsburgh, Cincinnati, St Louis, Nashville and Oklahoma City. Seeing the reactions of the fans to Elvis's onstage costumes, he and Bill conceived ever more elaborate designs. During his next fifty-nine Vegas shows, Vegas Elvis dazzled in a parade of suits, including the world culture-inspired Pharaoh, with its dramatic Ra god-style motifs and the black-and-white Spanish Flower suits, opulently decorated with golden tendrils and jewel 'petals'. Natural elements also came into play with the Lava, Blue (and Multicoloured) Rain, Fire and Snowflake.

Again, Elvis missed concerts due to illness.

Las Vegas commitments over, it was time to join Priscilla in Santa Monica, California, to finalise their divorce. Since both were with new partners, it was a good-natured meeting that 9 October as they walked arm in arm through the courtroom. Priscilla, while concerned about Elvis's fatigued and puffy appearance, still described it as an amazing day, mainly because when they signed the final decree, they held hands and smiled like a happily married couple rather than soon-to-be divorcees. Radiant with the glow of a woman who was getting undivided attention from her new man, devoid of the heavy make-up and hair of old and wearing a cool, bang-on-trend outfit, Priscilla looked stunning. Her high-necked, antique lace Victorian-governess blouse was in direct contrast to her ragged-edged, rough-stitched coat made from scraps of chamois leather in shades of coffee, cream and cocoa brown and fastened with shell buttons. It was a bit desert-scape meets Raquel Welch's deerskin bikini in the movie *One Million Years BC* – in a good way. Liquid leather beige flares, high, caramel, peep-toe mules and a slouchy, leather and fur blanket-stitched bag iced that particular peak early seventies fashion cake.

Elvis Leaves the Building   161

In contrast, Elvis looked a bit mid-season transitional – in both fashion and demeanour. He was tanned but slightly swollen and wore his tinted EP-monogrammed shades through the proceedings. His uncharacteristically plain and shapeless dark two-piece leisure suit – default wardrobe choice of the 'can't be arsed' – came perilously close to making him look a bit, well, ordinary.

Yet, despite the clashing white showtime-collared shirt, the waist-length gold tassel pendant, slim gold choker chain, ruby, diamond and sapphire-encrusted American flag brooch and Gucci loafers, he pulled it off. Because he was Elvis – never knowingly outshone. Again, uncharacteristically, he wore no rings, somewhat explained by Priscilla, who wrote in *Elvis by the Presleys* that Elvis's hands, usually 'always smooth', were 'puffy, swollen. I knew something was different … I could feel it in his hands.' She sensed that something was wrong as she saw it in his eyes, too.

Still, the deed was done; they parted amicably and would stay friends, enjoying their shared responsibilities and love for Lisa Marie. Inside, however, Elvis felt down, not just because it was a big and very public blow to his ego, but because he had allowed his little family to become fractured.

Luckily, he had Linda, for shortly afterwards, on suffering breathing difficulties in California, he chartered a plane home; mid-flight, Linda noticed it was getting worse and called Dr Nick on arrival, who was shocked at what he found. Elvis was semi-comatose and barely recognisable from severe swelling that gave him an alarming 'cushioned appearance'.

Unable to alleviate or improve his condition at home, the doctor had him admitted to hospital where his condition was described as 'grave'. They managed to stabilise him and, ruling out congestive heart failure, settled on a severe reaction to drugs. On coming round, Dr Nick questioned Elvis on what drugs he'd taken – his answer threw up nothing to explain the extreme swelling. Another doctor questioned Elvis on the black and blue marks all over his body, which he said were from acupuncture treatments he'd been having for months. Questioned about the needles, he said the treatment was administered by syringe and when asked by Dr Nick what was in said syringe, he replied that he didn't know. Linda stayed by Elvis's side until he was eventually discharged, presumably after some rehab treatment, after two weeks.

By December, terrified over Elvis's near-death drama, Dr Nick was in constant attendance, treating him for hypertension, and bowel and colon issues associated with an enlarged intestine. A relieved Vernon was regularly, often just silently, by his side, and Linda, a naturally caring soul, looked after him, monitored his routines and, importantly, made him laugh.

Elvis felt recovered enough and keen enough to get back to recording new material, since back in March, he and Tom Parker sold his back catalogue

162   Elvis: The King of Fashion

(including its future royalties) to RCA for a lump sum of almost $5.5 million, which they split 50/50. In essence, Elvis would get no further royalties on records made pre-March 1973, but *would* get royalties on sales from records after that date. Elvis was living and performing in the moment, with no inkling of how valuable and treasured his astonishing body of work would become. He was even embarrassed by some of his early material. RCA were taking a leap of faith, based on industry instinct, since there was no guarantee of robust, if any, future sales. Parker felt he'd done a great deal. The words crystal and ball spring to mind.

Loving the music that was coming out of Memphis's sanctified Stax soul recording studio and having already recorded there in the summer, Elvis returned. Named from an abbreviation of the surnames of brother and sister team Jim Stewart and Estelle Axton, who founded the label with artists such as Isaac Hayes, Booker T. & the MGs, Otis Redding and Rufus Thomas, the studio normally only recorded Stax artists. However, they made an exception for Elvis, and his friend, the mighty Hayes, whose *Shaft* movie soundtrack was still taking the planet by storm, rescheduled his own sessions to accommodate him. Stax being only a short drive from Graceland meant that Elvis got to see Lisa Marie, too.

Before he could draw breath, he was back in Las Vegas for his 1974 winter season, starting 26 January and with the schedule pared down to twenty-nine concerts. Gold Vine and Nail Mirrored were among the show-stopping suits and in February, the American Eagle soared again.

Amid speculation that he was about to marry Linda, Elvis embarked on yet another road tour. The gruelling (knowing now how unwell he was becoming) series of March concerts took in Tulsa, Houston, Monroe, Auburn, Alabama, Montgomery, Charlotte, Roanoke, Hampton Roads, Richmond, Greensboro, Murfreesboro, Knoxville, and ended back in Memphis, where Elvis thrilled fans over a series of shows at the Midsouth Coliseum.

In the city that he still called home, the place that facilitated his first, formative steps to shaking up the world with his matchless voice, it had been more than a decade since Elvis had stood on a stage there. He was nervous. He looked older, a little heavier (but not much, since he was straight from doing Vegas and the other tour concerts) and there was a little less shakin' going on, yet, he looked outstanding. His inimitable features had settled into a more mature but still as mesmerising kind of handsome and, as throughout his life, his exclusively Elvis outfits, including the Flame, the Blue Starburst and, his real-life superhero suit, the American Eagle among them, immediately lent him full icon, almost godlike status before he even sang a note.

Elvis Leaves the Building 163

Listening to the opening of the live recording of the 16 March show is very evocative. It's not the thumping, tympanic intro of Richard Strauss's unfailingly dramatic *Also sprach Zarathustra* opening music, it's the blanket silence of more than 12,000 breaths being held in an almost distraught level of anticipation at the prospect of seeing The King. When he appears, leaving only enough time for them to exhale, he jumps straight into his usual opener, 'See See Rider'. Once the well-behaved cheering and squealing from his now older fans, some there with their own children, dies down, Elvis's first words are, his trademark 'Thank you very much', in a surprisingly light, young-sounding voice. This, however, is followed by a deeper, sexier 'Hello, Memphis' that gets the women screaming before he goes into a cool, free-form blues and acoustic guitar moment.

They start to loosen up together.

Then it's full Elvis mode, with a cracking mix of gospel, complete with halleluiah amens, blues, country and modern, and demos of how low he can go – vocally speaking.

Elvis told them, 'It's a pleasure to be home again for the first time in a long time.'

A woman calls something out to him and he laughs and says, 'OK, ah'll turn around honey,' and then perfectly sings a honky-tonk, gospel and blues-infused version of the sublime 'Love Me'. Other attempts to talk get drowned out, so he as good as gives up, and introducing it as 'the third song I did for Sun Records', rocks out a hot r 'n' b version of 'Tryin' to Get to You'. After a rousing, vocally athletic 'Cant' Help Falling in Love', channelling his inner butterfly, he spread his wings and was gone.

At some point, between this tour, and his next twenty-two-concert engagement at the Sahara Tahoe hotel in May, where audience reaction was described as 'tepid' and Dr Nick was brought on board full-time, apparently to monitor and attempt to minimalise Elvis's drug usage, he played San Bernardino, Los Angeles and Fresno.

In June, audiences at twenty-one concerts – taking in Fort Worth, Baton Rouge, Amarillo, Des Moines, Cleveland, Providence, Philadelphia, Niagara Falls, Columbus, Louisville, Bloomington, Milwaukee, Kansas City, Omaha and Salt Lake City – got to see Elvis in all his flared, crystal-encrusted, hipster-belted, cat-suited glory in, among others, the aptly named Peacock, the Blue Swirl and the by then ubiquitous American Eagle.

August was Vegas season, again with a reduced and revamped twenty-nine-concert schedule where he had dropped the *Also sprach* (*2001*) opening and swapped his tried-and-tested concert favourites for more bluesy back catalogue numbers. While the press was keen, audiences were unconvinced and by the following night, the show was back to its old formula.

164   Elvis: The King of Fashion

Being a sensitive soul, Elvis would have realised that he was now doing what was expected of him, rather than what excited him and what touched his soul. Still, he could always add a few karate moves, since he was then obsessed with the sport. Parker disapproved – he wanted music, not martial arts – and he cringed at Elvis's now regular bouts of talking, sometimes rambling, instead of singing, where he let loose on the press, about paternity suits, about his family and relationships and his failed marriage – once while Priscilla and Lisa Marie were in the audience.

Priscilla, shocked, said that Elvis had never shared his personal feelings on stage like that and in such an aggressive manner; his usual way of releasing his feelings had always been through song. In Peter Guralnick's *Careless Love: The Unmaking of Elvis Presley*, Priscilla says, 'This was out of character, for someone who had so much pride ... everything that he was against, he was displaying. It was like watching a different person.'

Soon after this, like a kid who'd just got his pocket money, Elvis embarked on a wild spending spree, buying more than a dozen vehicles for pals, family and staff; he even bought a car for a stranger who was just browsing in the showroom and gave her a job as a maid. He bought his cook a house and her brother a car, bought Charlie Hodge a boat and gave his cousin Billy a double-width trailer so he could live in it with his family at Graceland.

Despite the reduced programme of performances, Elvis cancelled two. Unsurprisingly, this was becoming a pattern which, despite the obvious reasons – nearing 40 with lower energy and stamina levels – should still have sounded alarm bells. Or at least elicited more empathy and concern from those around him. Perhaps a little less TCB and a little more TLC?

Which clearly didn't happen, since by autumn, often heavily medicated in order to sustain the rigorous schedules – before one concert, he accidentally fell to his knees while leaving the limo before going on stage – he was on tour again, this time performing in College Park and Detroit followed by a string of concerts coming into October that took in South Bend, Saint Paul, Minnesota, Dayton, Indianapolis, Wichita, San Antonio and Abilene, followed by eight concerts at the Sahara Tahoe, Nevada.

Elvis was now using cocaine. According to entourage member Dave Hebler, when Red West arrived in Detroit, having not seen Elvis for a few weeks, he was so upset at the state of him that he teared up. When Red aggressively confronted, injured and threatened the supplier with further consequences, Elvis found out and was livid, telling him, 'I don't like these bully tactics. I need it [the coke].'

Red replied, 'Man, if you need it, I'm not going to say any more about it. You can have it.'

Elvis Leaves the Building   165

Everyone around him at the time said that there was no reasoning with the increasingly antagonistic and deluded Elvis. No one could tell him what to do. He did what he liked and if they didn't like what he liked, his usual advice was 'there's the fucking door'. Reviewers berated him, though, calling him 'bored to death' in St Paul, 'hostile' and 'disappointing' in Indianapolis. Ending the tour in Tahoe, on the last night, bass player Duke Bardwell said, 'Elvis was just standing there not really knowing what else to do, cause he just pretty much run out of gas.'

Having then been examined and diagnosed with an ulcerous stomach by a Las Vegas doctor and given a special diet and sleep regime, Elvis retreated, delirious with exhaustion and devoid of motivation after a relentless, pitiless and wellness-free performance programme, to Graceland from November to recuperate.

Conciliatory news that month came in the form of a *Rolling Stone* magazine report declaring that he was 'still a superstar' and being told that he'd won a Grammy Award (incredibly, only his first) for Best International Performance for 'How Great Thou Art'. However, a headline in the *National Enquirer* – 'Elvis at 40: Paunchy, Depressed and Living In Fear' – soon took the shine off that and set off a skewed view of Elvis that stuck to him for the rest of his days.

Come December, like many people, famous ones in particular, who are often judged by their youth and their beauty as much as their talent, Elvis, then staring 40 in the face, was deeply depressed and would shut himself away in his darkened bedroom. A despondency not helped by another article in *Celebrity*, tagged on the cover as 'Elvis: the myth and the malady', that commented on the reasons for his declining health. It turned out be prophetic.

As difficult as it is to accept or to dwell upon, an increasingly self-destructive bent to Elvis's behaviour, rigorously concealed from fans behind a near impenetrable screen of collusion, self-interests and misguided over-protection by insiders, Tom Parker, his father and even Elvis himself, was getting noticed by the media.

One can only imagine how his deteriorating health, weight gain, rumoured drug and even alcohol (which was rarely his chosen poison) addictions would have been treated by today's pontificating, judgemental, Achilles-heel-seeking, social-media dominated era. Even so, 1975 opened with a further cruel article headlined, 'Elvis – Forty and Fat', which seemed intentionally published on 8 January, his dreaded fortieth birthday. A truly callous 'surprise' to spring on a famously kind, immensely talented man who'd brought so much pleasure to the world and who, in an era when mental illness was often swept under carpets and addictions cloaked in secrecy and shame, was by then overwhelmed and could find little pleasure himself.

166 Elvis: The King of Fashion

Elvis, life and soul of every party, spent his 'special' day alone. By choice.

Perhaps as consolation, on 20 January, he bought a jet – a Boeing 707 – but that excitement over, a pall fell over Graceland and before the month was out, Elvis's lifestyle caught up with him. Linda woke to find him in pain and again, struggling for breath. Instead of heading for Las Vegas, Elvis was rushed to Memphis's Baptist Memorial Hospital with the added complication of extreme abdominal pain. Officially described as a liver problem, it instigated an admission and another attempt to get his drug use under control.

In an odd twist of fate, on 5 February, while Elvis was still there, Vernon had a heart attack and was put in the room next door to him.

After a couple of weeks, Elvis was discharged under the care of Dr Nick and a nurse who, between them, would maintain a new regime – one or other of them would deliver prescribed doses of medicine to Elvis on a daily basis.

By March, he'd made it to Las Vegas for the delayed early season with a reduced twenty-nine shows; on opening night, the press commented that he looked and sounded back on form. He was relatively svelte, perhaps explaining the absence of capes in his new wardrobe of cool, understated but still glamorous two-piece white suits with shimmering embellishments running mainly just across the shoulders and down the arms and legs.

While there, Barbra Streisand talked to Elvis about the possibility of him co-starring with her in the movie *A Star is Born*. He was interested, but wary, as he'd be playing a faded rock star with an addiction problem. He needn't have worried. Tom Parker scuppered the idea by insisting that his client got twice the offered fee, top billing, five times the offered percentages and the soundtrack rights. No further offers were forthcoming.

So, Elvis bought another plane. Renovations included the addition of gold bathroom fixtures, a full audio system, a queen-sized bed and blue-and-white livery with its name, *Lisa Marie*, and a TCB logo added. The final tab was three-quarters of a million dollars.

He also bought a home near Graceland for Linda Thompson.

Someone had to pay for all that – and that someone, of course, was Elvis, so he really needed to embrace his April through July mega tour that took in Macon, Jacksonville, Tampa, Lakeland, Murfreesboro, Atlanta, Monroe, Lake Charles in Louisiana, Huntsville, Mobile, Tuscaloosa, Houston, Dallas, Shreveport, Jackson, Memphis, Oklahoma City, Terre Haute, Richfield, Cleveland, Charleston, Niagara Falls, Springfield, New Haven, Uniondale, Norfolk, Greensboro and Asheville.

Critics said Elvis was looking good, with more two-piece outfits, including the Armadillo with contrasting 'scaled' shoulder panels, and fabulously decorated jumpsuits, including the Chief and the Phoenix (which came in red, black and

Elvis Leaves the Building   167

silver variations). He even felt good enough to joke about his weight, at one point saying, 'You should have seen me a month ago, I looked like Mama Cass.'

On 5 May, he played a benefit concert at the State Fair Coliseum in Jackson, Mississippi, raising $108,000 for hurricane survivors in McComb, and then had cosmetic surgery on his eyes to appear younger. Billy Smith said that he felt that it ruined Elvis's eyes. 'He always had these sleepy, sexy eyes. And they took the droop out. The droop was part of his mystique.'

On 12 July, little Teri Hammond attended the 8.30 show at the Charleston Civic Centre and saw nothing but wonder in Elvis.

My first live concert ever was forty-eight years ago when our man, Elvis, came to my hometown of Charleston, West Virginia. My grandmother, mother and aunt took me and my sister to see him.

We were near the front, but on the side of the stage. We were only a few rows up from the floor. My grandmother decided to take me up the middle to get me to the stage so I could see him better but a security guard sent us back to our seats – we were almost there.

Excitement was everywhere! I was only six years old but I can still remember it like it was yesterday. He was electrifying and beautiful. I've been a fan for as long as I can remember because my family are fans and Elvis's music has been a part of my life always.

What I noticed most was his outfit. It was an Indian [Native American] print [the Chief] and it was beautiful. I have Indian heritage, as does Elvis and it's stuck with me.

Later on in life, I have found out that he and I are eighth cousins. Seeing him for the first time it was amazing. I was lucky enough to see him again the next year at the same venue. July 24, 1976 at 2:30 pm.

Teri has three fantastic photos of Elvis from the 1975 show, including one stunning close-up showing his Chief suit in great detail and in which Elvis, looking directly into the camera lens, looks neither jaded nor sick, but strikingly other-worldly, almost angelic – and breathtakingly young.

My mom's friend, who was a photographer there, made copies for us. I still have the original photos. They are one of the most prized pieces of Elvis memorabilia that I own.

I can remember leaving after the show, wanting a t-shirt, and the smallest they had was an adult small, which was way too big, but my grandmother told my mother to go back and get two so we could have a shirt.

168   Elvis: The King of Fashion

I also have the Elvis button that my grandma wore to the concert too. It's in my curio cabinet.

Elvis's performances were coming into question as they got more erratic and his onstage behaviour and humour grew more bizarre – even aggressive – as he berated band members and singers, sometimes cruelly, and even told the audience off occasionally. In Asheville, after berating the crowd, he gave a fan his $6,500 ring to make up for it.

In Memphis, Elvis's trousers split when he bent over to kiss someone and the press went into frenzied lampooning mode, with the *Memphis Commercial Appeal* calling him a 'fat, sensuous clown'. Word spread and the burst pants story went global.

But the fans didn't care – they loved Elvis, regardless of reviews. They thought his banter was just him joking and they laughed at his rants and cutting observations; they felt he was talking to them, sharing his personality, and it made them feel special. To Elvis, they were special. They compelled him to perform, to keep going.

His actions became more surreal. Clearly addled, ferociously fighting with his team and insulting his musicians, some of whom walked off the stage (including the Sweet Inspirations and soprano Kathy Westmoreland, with whom he was annoyed for dating a band member after they'd had a brief romance) after some particularly rough treatment.

Away from the limelight, he was waving guns about and changing plans without informing anyone. At one point he left everyone who was supposed to be flying with him stranded on the runway as punishment for arriving a few minutes late. He was also compulsively spending. He bought and then gave away more than a dozen Cadillacs and feeling bad about marooning his crew, which included Dr Nick and his jeweller Lowell Hays, who now toured with him toting cases of jewellery Elvis might wish to buy or gift, sent the plane back to get them. When Hays arrived at Asheville, location of Elvis falling out of the limo, he summoned him and bought every piece of jewellery he had. Then sent him back on the plane to Memphis for more.

'Elvis bought what I would call practically a whole jewellery store,' said Hays. 'He gave something to everybody in the group. He gave each of the Sweet Inspirations a five-thousand-dollar ring.'

For the rest of that summer, Elvis was sick and, apart from a handful of shows where he wore his unusually colourful and elaborate new purple-and-white Totem Pole suits, most of his August Las Vegas concerts were cancelled. In late August, and in dismal health, he was again admitted to hospital for testing, resting and rehab.

Elvis Leaves the Building   169

Linda left – only to return a few months later to support him briefly in Las Vegas during his delayed seasonal commitment of seventeen concerts, ending mid-December.

And if there were any question over Elvis's pulling power, receipts for a New Year's Eve concert in Pontiac, Michigan, broke all records.

Clearly, Elvis had not made giving up reckless spending his New Year's resolution as, in the January of 1976, he bought another five cars and then gave them away.

Frustrated by his disinclination to get into the recording studio and make some records, RCA reluctantly agreed to install a mobile recording studio in Elvis's den (later the Jungle Room) at Graceland. It didn't go well. The temporary studio set-up had limitations and sessions would just fizzle out. Elvis was too shattered, distracted, sombre and, frankly, out of it, to emulate his studio recordings of days gone by. However, of the cuts that Elvis did make before everyone finally gave up and left, one in particular made the entire, days-long exercise worthwhile. Described by Greil Marcus, author of *Mystery Train*, as an 'apocalyptic attack' on Roy Hamilton's (he of the Jaycee speech lines) soul classic, 'Hurt', it was extraordinary and moment defining.

Having reached his life's nadir, the beautiful song of anguish and aching perfectly summed-up Elvis at the time, both physically and emotionally. Unexpectedly, it woke him from his torpor, offering him a way to vent at the world by hollering out his repressed emotions in the words. Seizing the chance, he let rip.

It is startling to listen to, beginning with a high bellow of unquestionably genuine pain. He continues with a voice raw with emotion. At times, he sounds as though he is singing through sobs and underneath is that voice, an emotion-powered engine neglected for too long, it is let loose in all its fury and by the closing lines, Elvis sounds utterly expended but in a relieved, delirious way that says, 'Yes! I've still got it.'

Alanna Nash wrote of it: 'If he felt the way he sounded, the wonder isn't that he had only a year left to live but that he managed to survive that long.'

With no early year Las Vegas season booked, Elvis embarked on yet another gruelling series of touring commitments. By this time, it feels as though everyone who'd been part of team Elvis, those who'd had his back, or who'd tried to help him had given up, accepting his deterioration as unavoidable. In fact, it had become the norm. Instead of glorying in the company, the irrepressible exuberance, the emotional rollercoaster and the talent of Elvis, The King, regarded by some as an actual god, they'd resigned themselves to simply managing him, like some dangerously injured beast, Graceland's very own minotaur, and hoping for the best.

170   Elvis: The King of Fashion

Adding to his woes, Elvis now also had worsening money problems. Having earned nothing in the first part of the year, he was faced with mounting bills for hundreds of thousands of pounds worth of obsessions – jewellery, guns, planes, women (mainly just to talk to), the list was endless. He had borrowed money against Graceland, which needed to be paid, then there were the law suits from people alleged to have been roughed up by Red and Sonny West, plus the everyday cost of running his friends, staff and family had been rising alarmingly.

It was time to hit the road again. A quick tour of Charlotte, Cincinnati, St Louis and three shows in Johnson was booked, the result of which had even Tom Parker worried that perhaps Elvis should avoid the limelight for a while.

The first show was unrehearsed, with Elvis telling the surprised musicians to just go with him. He looked pale, tired and his suits, including the Phoenix, the spectacular black Chicken Bone and V-Neck were snugger than he'd have liked. At times he appeared confused, or forgot his lines and in St Louis, he was so overmedicated that Dr Nick had trouble getting him on stage. This seems to be the incident that Larry Geller referred to (in Chapter 10) when poor Elvis had his head plunged into a bucket of iced water to ensure that, as reportedly ordered by Parker, he would get 'on that stage tonight'.

Between April and June 1976, Elvis played a further eight concerts in Kansas City, Omaha, Denver, San Diego, Long Beach, Seattle and Spokane, followed by a further fourteen straight at the Sahara Tahoe hotel where, according to drummer Ronnie Tutt, he looked so tired and down that there were nights that he felt he had to hit his drums 'much, much harder' to help get him going. Tragically, Elvis was increasingly forgetting the words of even his most frequently performed songs – not helped by that fact the he liked to purposely play around with the words when he was bored.

In Long Beach, a local reviewer wrote, 'An eerie silence filled the concert hall when he sang 'And now, the end is near …'.

Peter Guralnick, citing Charles C. Thompson II and James P. Cole from *The Death of Elvis: What Really Happened*, says that when John O'Grady, the private investigator who'd been involved with Elvis's paternity suit, went to see him during his Tahoe run, he was appalled. 'I felt so strongly for him, I cried,' said O'Grady. 'He was fat. He had … attacks where he couldn't' walk. He forgot the words to his songs … I really thought he was going to die.'

He decided he had to do something and knowing he could rely on total confidentiality from Priscilla, he contacted her, told her the score and suggested a clinic that could help Elvis. She agreed and spoke to Elvis about it, but nothing further came of it.

Elvis Leaves the Building   171

And yet, the concerts continued throughout June, moving on to Bloomington, Ames, Oklahoma City, Odessa, Lubbock, Tucson, El Paso, Fort Worth, Atlanta, Buffalo, Providence, Largo, Philadelphia, Richmond and Greensboro.

Tired? Think how Elvis must have felt.

It was relentless.

In Landover, Largo, on 27 June, Elvis bumped into Jerry Schilling, who had left his employ in the January and was then working as road manager for Billy Joel. Despite some initial awkwardness due to the parting of ways, Elvis had always liked Jerry, who is now 81, and who comes out of the entire Elvis story as one of the most trustworthy, loyal and genuine of all of his friends. He gave Jerry a hug and took time to catch up with him, causing Elton John – a massive Elvis fan – and his mother (who bought him his first Elvis record) to wait their turn to see him.

Elton, then with a string of hit singles including 'Candle In The Wind', 'Rocket Man' and 'Saturday Night's Alright For Fighting' and as no stranger to drug-induced chaos himself, was shocked and saddened when he did meet Elvis. He said the conversation was awkward and that he got the 'impression of immense loneliness'. 'He had dozens of people around him, supposedly looking after him,' he says, 'but he already looked like a corpse.' Recalling the show itself for *Far Out* magazine in 2022, he said: 'It was someone who was in a complete drug haze giving nylon scarves away to these fans. And yet it was still, in a way, magical.'

June became July and after Shreveport, Baton Rouge, Fort Worth, Tulsa and a closing show in Memphis, Elvis, apparently in a vile mood, went straight home to Graceland. Ignoring guests, gathered there for his traditional, fourth-of-July fireworks show, he went directly to his room and stayed there.

The next day, he and Linda (who was back again) flew to Palm Springs – somewhat conveniently, since a few days later, with Elvis's knowledge, Vernon, never a fan of the West cousins and looking for ways to save money, sacked both Sonny and Red along with relatively recent fellow entourage member Dave Hebler, saying things hadn't been going too well and giving each of them one week's severance pay. Outraged, especially with Elvis, who they felt hadn't had the guts to tell them himself, they subsequently began planning a book – an exposé – about the real Elvis.

Unaware, but still frantic to clear his debts, Elvis returned from Palm Springs for the 23 July tour – his fifth that year and in more of the same, nearby friendly locations, now too many to list.

Almost universally, reviews referred to his alarming appearance and demeanour, and alluded to perfunctory, going-through-the-motions type performances. Rumours were rife that Elvis was a 'junkie.' Even his friends in the police had

172   Elvis: The King of Fashion

noticed and some even warned him, off the record, that he was treading on thin ice – that something would have to give. Parker was frantic. He urged Elvis to pull himself together and to put more effort into his shows so that people would feel they were getting their money's worth – completely missing the irony that it was he who had created, then exploited, the near-dead horse that he was now attempting to flog.

Although feeling paranoid, Elvis was still on a mission to acquire 'medicines', since Dr Nick had been administering some placebos, which, knowing so much about prescriptive drugs and their effects, Elvis sussed immediately and sacked him during a late-night rant. A different doctor was hired, and Larry Geller was welcomed back – by Parker, who'd previously ousted him for using 'mind control' techniques.

At the Summit concert in Houston, some of the troupe complained that Elvis was so 'loaded' he could barely walk – let alone sing. The performance was agonising and some felt they should no longer go on. What worried Tom Parker the most was that the Houston police were openly discussing Elvis's condition; he felt that at any minute, someone could decide to expose him.

They were able to rush Elvis out of town, but couldn't stop the *Houston Post*'s review by critic and ardent Elvis fan Bob Claypool: 'Elvis Presley has been breaking hearts for more than 20 years now, and Saturday afternoon in the Summit – in a completely new and unexpected way – he broke mine.'

Both Parker and Elvis asked Dr Nick to come back and help. By reducing Elvis's access to drugs, he did achieve a degree of balanced medication, mixed with placebos and designed to address his many and very real health issues. However, those around Elvis would say, if he wanted something, drugs or otherwise, he always knew how to get it.

With that tour finally over, rumours started circling again about Red, Sonny and Dave Hebler's book. Within weeks, it was sounding like a reality and, despite an offer of $50,000 to each of them to desist and a personal call to Red from Elvis, they refused.

Incredibly, more tours followed throughout the autumn right up to 31 December and including what would be his last ever engagement in Las Vegas.

And, relieving him of any hope that his disgruntled, sacked bodyguards might decide not to betray him after all, an October issue of *The Star* ran a story about how he had been pleading with them not to write the book. It contained much of the personal conversation he'd had with Red on the phone, suggesting that the call had been recorded.

Elvis was devastated and could think of nothing else.

Until November, when, with Linda gone for a while and finding little comfort in the various women George Klein brought to the house to 'cheer him up', he

Elvis Leaves the Building   173

met former beauty queen, Ginger Alden. She became his new obsession and he asked her to join him during his November concerts in Nevada, Oregon and California, at which point Linda, having made allowances for Elvis's other dalliances, left for good.

When Las Vegas time came around, Elvis – not realising it was his last hurrah – started off well but within days seemed to lose steam and was then alternating twixt exhausted and shambolic. Described as looking 'sad and tired', he cursed at stage equipment, at one point holding his mic aloft and yelling, 'Does anyone want this tinny sonofabitch?' He told one audience: 'I hate Las Vegas.'

The run ended with a review that questioned whether fans were just going to his concerts as they thought they might be his last – how little did they know of the loyalty of Elvis fans – and an uncommonly thunder-faced Tom Parker failing to deny rumours that he'd lost a million dollars at the roulette tables and openly admitting, 'My artist is out of control.' *My artist.* A phrase that says it all.

In 1977, the prospect of Red and Sonny West and Dave Hebler's dreaded warts-and-all book being published truly blighted Elvis's life and no doubt overshadowed his forty-second birthday celebrations with Ginger and her sister, Rosemary, in Palm Springs. Perhaps feeling his age or thinking that he could make a go of marriage again, and in spite of those around him suggesting that, unlike Linda, Ginger cared less for him than he did for her, he suddenly proposed with a freshly minted Lowell Hays ring set with the huge, 11½-carat central diamond from his own TCB ring. This was because, in typically Elvis style, the proposal was done on impulse and Hays, called in the middle of the night to produce a ring with a giant diamond the same size as his, had no time to source a matching gem that big.

Ginger appeared to prove them right to an extent by putting her friends before Elvis – in her defence, she was only 20, after all – and finding excuses to miss or just plain refusing to go to his concerts. Elvis would argue with her and even pretend to be ill to get her attention, but she was strong-willed and did her own thing. He discovered that having her family around made her more willing to join him at his concerts, so in March he took them all on a two-week holiday to Hawaii.

Before they went, Elvis (sensing his end?) made out his will after years of Vernon badgering him to do so. It was straightforward. Vernon was the executor and trustee with the 'health, education, comfortable maintenance and welfare of Lisa Marie, Vernon and grandma Minnie Mae', all specifically mandated and Vernon authorised to 'expand funds for such other relatives of mine living at the time of my death, who, in the absolute discretion of my trustee are in need of emergency assistance for any of the above-mentioned purposes ...' On Vernon's death, such assistance would cease, and upon Minnie Mae's death, all funds

174   Elvis: The King of Fashion

would reside in a trust for Lisa Marie until she reached the age of 25. Notably, there were no individual requests nor specific mentions of any other people.

Peter Guralnick sums the omissions up in a moving section from *Careless Love*:

> in the end it seems scarcely surprising that he should have returned to the same small, tightknit, and set-apart group that first nurtured him when he and his mother and father occupied a lonely strip of safety in a hostile world.

With Elvis due to go on tour in March, Billy Smith was concerned about his cousin's condition and, after years of refusing to join him again, decided to do so. When the time came, Billy expressed doubt that Elvis would even make it onto the plane. In this real-life scenario, Tish, the nurse, took one look at Elvis and said to Billy, 'If he was my son, I'd have him in hospital.'

According to Billy, 'Uncle Vernon said, "Well, do what you can." And Dr Nick put all these IVs in him.' This moment was portrayed with artistic licence in Baz Luhrmann's 2022 *Elvis* movie, not in Graceland but back in the hotel lobby in a riveting scene just after Elvis's face is plunged into an ice bucket.

Elvis did make it onto the plane, taking the only two suits that still fitted him – the 1974 Arabian, resplendent with sky-blue panels and swirling, golden filigree threads – and the Mexican Sundial suit, also known as the Aztec and, jokingly, the Pizza. Decorated with Gene Doucette's blazing artistry, it remains one of the most revered of his extraordinary designs and also the most mythical of all Elvis's outfits. It was based on the Mayan calendar, with two giant suns, one to cover his chest and another, his back, like plates of armour.

Elvis loved the glamour and mysticism of the Sundial – a couture extravaganza of precision-stitched gold, bronze and silver threads and studding, brought alive with light-reflecting red, and clear gemstones – so much that he wore it for more than forty performances. It's first outing was during his month-long residency at the Sahara Hotel, Lake Tahoe, in 1974; its last, in Indianapolis at his final performance on 26 June 1977. Most notably, though, was its appearance on 21 June 1977 at Rapid City, South Dakota, where Elvis blew everyone away with an historic performance of 'Unchained Melody'. The front sundial has sixteen points that are divided by the front opening into two lots of eight and since Elvis died on 16 August, the eighth month, some people believe it predicted when he would die.

Which he almost did during the tour. Still ill and on a mix of medication, Elvis almost choked to death as he feel asleep while eating. He was also found wandering a hotel corridor saying that he'd seen a white light and the face of God.

His security team made plans for smuggling him out of venues should he overdose.

Elvis Leaves the Building   175

Due to go on stage in Baton Rouge, with dignitaries and police ready and waiting, he collapsed. As the announcement was made that the concert was cancelled and Elvis's panicking entourage prepared to fly him back to Memphis Memorial Hospital – again – there were disappointed howls and calls of 'rip-off' before everyone was dispersed.

As impossible as it may be to comprehend, almost as if to tempt fate after the will-making session, despite Elvis's obvious need for medical care and complete rest, not one, but three concert tours were still scheduled and went ahead between April and June. Despite his clearly grave condition, not a single person considered, or better still insisted on, contesting this. Totalling around forty concerts, over several states with little more than a couple of weeks' planned respite, he hit the road again, more or less wearing the Mexican Sundial suit for every show.

Feeling at his lowest ebb and more alone than he'd ever felt, a hugely diminished, but almost persistently puffy Elvis confided in Billy and Larry Geller about being worried about his appearance, about his thinning hair and about news leaking that the 'Colonel' was hawking his contract around to raise money to pay off his own gambling debts. Then there was the imminent publication of that bloody book, which hung like an albatross around his neck. Presumably to further meet his debt-covering goal, Parker also announced a CBS TV special, to be filmed during one of the tours.

Good news was very thin on the ground that summer, so thank goodness for *Photoplay* magazine, who, in June, awarded Elvis Gold Medal Awards for both Favourite Variety Star and Favourite Rock Music Star. And for the transformative, incandescent, near religious moment that occurred at the aforementioned Rapid City concert during a performance that no one realised was a whisper away from Elvis's last and which is now preserved forever as part of the CBS film *Elvis in Concert*.

Looking so very unwell, it is shocking but not entirely surprising, considering the huge draw that Elvis still was and the money to be gained, that Tom Parker still allowed him to be filmed for the documentary. With hindsight, knowing the level of psychological and physical pain that Elvis was experiencing (he was depressed and addicted with an enlarged intestine, bowel problems, high blood pressure and, oh the irony, an enlarged heart, just some of his ailments), it contains one of, if not *the*, most moving final curtains of all time.

Elvis, bedevilled by demons and as white as his outfit, his once doe eyes cosmetically pinched and small, his hair an unnatural blue-black helmet, is sweating profusely. He looks 'pillowy' (as a doctor once described his bloated appearance) in the Mexican Sundial jumpsuit and requires Charlie Hodge to guide him, teetering like a darted giraffe, to the piano. Concerned-looking

176   Elvis: The King of Fashion

personnel hover tensely in the shadows, ready to catch him should he fall, and exchange relieved glances as he finally sits down to play.

And suddenly, out of nowhere, Elvis transcends into something very close to his former glory.

Not visibly, but vocally.

Surrounded by cables, clutter and cups of Coca-Cola and with Charlie holding a hand mic for him, ready to mimic his boss by singing should he forget his words or can't hit the notes, Elvis delivered a tour-de-force performance of 'Unchained Melody' that reminded everyone in the building of the still unmatched depth, range and power of his voice.

It was a musical damn burst of hurt and regret and a passion for song on a scale that he should not, by then, have been able to reach and it ended with a vocal strength that even Elvis thought he no longer possessed. A force so visceral that it caused him to visibly quake and when he'd done, he beamed like his 19-year-old self, once more finding joy in the realisation that, yes, he really did have the voice of an angel. An avenging one at that.

Having poured his weary heart, and the last of whatever energy reserves he still had in his faltering tank, into his performance, for Elvis, this was symbolically, if not yet physically, the end.

In the July of 1977, his latest single, the aptly titled 'Way Down', was released.

The book *Elvis: What Happened?* was published, stealing the last of his joy and leaving him utterly despondent.

And on 16 August, while back at Graceland with Lisa Marie home for the school summer holidays and preparing to go on tour the following day, Elvis died.

Epilogue

The King is Dead, Long Live The King
The Legacy

'He was unique. He was entrenched in the American, and then global psyche, and there is no other celebrity, performer or notable personage in the world that has, or will ever match him. For three decades, his own life punctuated the lives of humans, and in death … he resonates as much as ever.'

Bernard Lansky, Clothier to the King, 1977

'I just wanted to be as good as Arthur Crudup.'
Elvis to Swedish journalist Borje Lundgren when asked whether he'd achieved all of his ambitions, 1973

'A Lonely Life Ends on Elvis Presley Boulevard'
Memphis Press-Scimitar, 17 August 1977

I ended my final chapter with Elvis's sudden death to emphasise the shock that people felt as the news broke – out of the blue – on 16 August 1977. As with John F. Kennedy and Martin Luther King, people remember exactly where they were when they learned that Elvis had died, because it was equally unexpected and shocking. Even his closest family and friends, all well aware of his weaknesses as well as his strengths, were convinced that he was somehow invincible.

As for Elvis's millions of fans, apart from seeing a few unflattering photos, some speculative, even fabricated stories about questionable aspects of his lifestyle and early snippets from Red and Sonny West and Dave Hebler's book, many, my family included, were unaware of his entrenched medical problems and his corrosive relationship with polypharmacy – or the dangerous misuse of 'cocktails' of prescribed drugs.

Memphis newspaper *The Commercial Appeal* reported that, on the day of Elvis's death, Shelby County Medical Examiner Dr Jerry Francisco had conducted an autopsy and concluded that he died from cardiac arrest with complications that

178 Elvis: The King of Fashion

included 'mild hypertension' and 'coronary disease that had gone undetected'. Later lab reports revealed that fourteen types of drugs were found in Elvis's blood at the time, including 'near toxic levels of codeine, morphine, Placidyl and other prescription drugs'. The local evening newspaper, the *Memphis Press-Scimitar*, also mentioned the drug findings, saying that an 'overdose of depressants' likely caused Elvis to pass out in a slumped 'fetal' position, and that 'he died when the drugs, in combination with pressure from his body weight, brought his respiration to a halt'.

For me, the most affecting revelation was that he was found face down in the thick pile carpet on his bathroom floor. Alone.

Stories and theories abound and some people don't even accept that Elvis is dead, let alone that drugs caused or contributed to his untimely demise, since genetic, accident-based, dietary and other factors exacerbated his poor health. However, Elvis's intentional or misguided over-use of drugs, mainly of the prescriptive variety, is now largely accepted. Whatever the circumstances, the tragedy is part of his legacy, and if there's any positive to be found, then surely, it's that it encourages people to be mindful of friends and family, and of themselves, and to seek help with physical or mental problems sooner rather than later.

Bernard Lansky put Elvis in his first suit. He also put him in his last.

On that 16 August day in 1977, he and his son Hal, who still runs their Lansky Bros. store, were in a coffee shop in Dallas when someone flew in crying, 'Guess what? Elvis died!' They learned the unbelievable news that their friend had been found unconscious in Graceland and had been rushed to hospital, where he was pronounced dead at just 42 years of age.

'You always remember where you were when Elvis died,' says Hal.

> We were devastated. We took the next plane out to Memphis and when we saw him in the casket, we just couldn't believe what we were seeing.
>
> Having dressed him from high school until the day he died, my dad had his measurements in his mind. He chose a white suit, blue shirt and white [possibly striped] tie for him.
>
> Elvis was a decent man, he didn't have a bad bone in his body. He was a practical joker; a Southern gentleman and he was so generous. He wrote cheques anonymously to charities because he genuinely cared, not because he needed the publicity.
>
> His story is a remarkable one – a sad one – but there are so many parts to it.

Dad Bernard attended the funeral of the enigmatic young man he opened his shop door – and a world of possibilities – to in 1952. It felt like the final chapter.

The King is Dead, Long Live The King   179

In fact, it was the start of a new one; the Lansky family never forgot Elvis and have played a pivotal part in keeping his memory alive ever since.

As far as Hal is concerned, Elvis has never really left the building.

As The King's body lay in state by the arch between the lounge and the music room at Graceland, around 80,000 fans lined the funeral route along Elvis Presley Boulevard, towards Forest Hill Cemetery, where he was interred on 18 August, in the same mausoleum as Gladys. After an attempted break-in some days later, the reported purpose of which was to take Elvis's body for ransom, both Elvis and Gladys were moved to Graceland, where they remain today in its memorial garden. Mother and son are surrounded by the graves of other close family members, the most recent being Lisa Marie, who died on 12 January 2023, at the age of 54, reportedly from cardiac arrest and a bowel obstruction.

Shortly before her death, Lisa Marie's eldest daughter, Riley Keough, continued the family legacy by naming her new baby girl Tupelo Storm, in honour of both her grandfather Elvis's birthplace and her late brother, Benjamin Storm.

I grew up with Elvis's films and music and was a teenager when the news of his death filtered into the UK. I remember walking into the house to find my parents staring at the TV in disbelief. Elvis had died.

How could Elvis die? How did he die? He was too young. He was The King. My mum and dad were only a year younger than him. It felt shocking, but, with the luxury of youth, I couldn't equate a sick and troubled man with the smiling, singing, handsome all-American boy I'd watched sail, race, sing, ride and dance his way through the movies of my school summer holidays and whose songs my dad would sing at family get-togethers. Now my children are part of the new generation of Elvis fans and only roll their eyes occasionally when I mention him for the millionth time.

Like his hero, James Dean, Elvis will never have to grow old, he's forever suspended in our memories – however we see him when we close our eyes – a legend both in life and death and one of the brightest, most recognisable stars in the universe.

His life was the ultimate rags-to-riches story, the embodiment of the American dream and proof that we can reach for the sky. In today's cultural narrative, Elvis is omnipotent, more popular than ever, the guy everyone knows by his first name, whose image is instantly familiar and, despite the best efforts of inspired wannabes, impersonators and young pretenders, there has never been anyone to compare to him. Because capturing the essence of Elvis is like trying to capture sunlight in your hands. Yet they try, because they love and admire him, not just for his unmatched musical legacy, but for the person that he was and for the way he held and presented himself with a devastatingly compelling combination of (apparent) self-confidence and genuine humility.

180   Elvis: The King of Fashion

In the glare of the success, the excess, the jewel-encrusted jumpsuits, and the King of Bling years, it is easy to forget that Elvis was once one of the biggest, if not *the* biggest, cultural forces of the twentieth century. Unintentionally, he became the epitome of cool, a defiant music pioneer, a disruptive, dandified anti-hero, who tore up rule books and broke down taboos, tipped entrenched social mores on their heads and had the audacity (not to mention balls) to blur, then cross the entrenched lines between black and white music, style, collaboration – and people.

It's also easy to forget because the consequences of Elvis throwing open closed doors while dressed in black and pink and rocking eyeshadow and showing other artists that they could wear whatever the hell they liked, can be seen everywhere.

Above all, he was human and flawed, at times selfish yet generous to a fault, sometimes on top of the world, at other times wanting to be loved, which he really was, even when he didn't feel it.

Elvis's legacy is immense. A living amalgam of the music instilled in him from birth, his striking looks and, of course, his matchless fashion sense and, at the time of writing (30 July 2023), Elvis is absolutely on fire.

With 145 nominations and forty-five wins during the awards season, director Baz Luhrmann's 2022 *Elvis* movie, with Austin Butler playing, in my opinion, the most convincing and compelling version of Elvis seen on screen, is still attracting accolades and playing at special events more than a year after its premiere. Like Elvis's own films, it appeals to fans of all ages, so is now playing its own role in ensuring that he lives on through generations to come. The film's release has also triggered a wave of contemporary tributes, unsurprisingly with Elvis's iconic style right at the heart of them.

At Lansky Bros.' shop in Memphis, they've always stocked reproductions of garments Elvis wore alongside their modern ranges. However, since sharing their archives and knowledge on how Elvis dressed with *Elvis* costume designer Catherine Martin and her husband, Luhrmann, they now stock *Elvis* movie-themed items.

In the film, the meticulous detail with which Martin recreated Elvis's outfits would turn a doll's house furniture-maker green with envy. She says that Elvis was 'an incredible stylist because he created his own looks' and that his self-created looks (to my mind, when he was at his most adventurous and ingenious stylewise) created his stage persona, the Elvis myth.

'Quite frankly,' she told a *Forbes* reporter, 'Elvis wasn't scared of being a dandy and I think that came from his admiration for so many black performers and having been on Beale Street throughout his youth.'

Studying Martin's work in close-up at Elvis's Graceland mansion in 2023 was a revelation. Along with an already breathtaking display of Elvis's actual

The King is Dead, Long Live The King 181

clothes and stage wear, there was an entire space displaying costumes and artefacts from Luhrmann's film. Martin's sketches, the design minutiae, and the final results are perfection. From the torn knee of the overalls young Shake Rag Elvis (played by Chaydon Jay) wore, through the lavish texturing and pleating of the white, high-waisted trousers and black-lace shirt Butler wears in the film's fairground scene, to his faded Crown Electric Co. uniform and 'Colonel' Tom Parker's Christmas cardigan, complete with leather 'football' buttons, it's as close to being in the film – and to Butler – that a fan can get.

And since it's Graceland, move along some and you're suddenly dwarfed by towering walls of glass cases containing more than a hundred of Elvis's actual jumpsuits – plus belts and boots – in all their glorious detail. There's also an eye-level cabinet with multiple mirrors offering a 360-degree view of the sanctified Mexican Sundial suit adorned with Gene Doucette's exquisite beading. Like all of the suits, it's a work of art but it's so iconic that it conjures up emotive images, not just of Elvis grabbing his guitar and tearing up the house '70s style but also of his heartrending swansong performance of 'Unchained Melody'.

Other peak Elvis wardrobe exhibits include the *Charro!* cowboy movie outfit he accessorised with a beard; his scuffed white '50s stage shoes that show how hard he danced in them; an army uniform; football kit; his first two-piece karate gi-inspired concert suit, and the original *'68 Comeback* black leather suit, which again instantly evokes a legendary performance. And leads us to another legacy connection.

Baz Luhrmann met with *'68 Comeback Special* director/producer Steve Binder to discuss scenes for the *Elvis* film. I asked Steve for his thoughts on the movie and on Austin, who'd just won a Golden Globe.

> I'm glad that Austin won. I understand from Baz that what sold him was Austin's acting abilities. I don't think that the public even knew how great Baz's editing was.
>
> *I* could tell when he mixed Austin's vocals with the real Elvis vocals within the same song, even sometimes a line or phrase from his original vocal. The match was un-noticeable and I thought it was great. The real rock star was Baz and the way he put the whole movie together.

Steve was played by Dacre Montgomery (Billy Hargrove in Netflix's *Stranger Things*), so I asked him if he liked how Montgomery portrayed him. 'I liked Dacre as both a person and an actor,' he says. 'He looked nothing like me yet he caught the essence of who I am. I had lunch with him before they went into production.'

This leads to another link.

182   Elvis: The King of Fashion

Reinventing Elvis: The '68 Comeback, an immensely watchable documentary based on the show, was screened in September 2023 in selected cinemas around the world for one day only to great reviews, prior to its release on Paramount+. Directed by John Scheinfeld, it's no ordinary documentary. If you're going to make a film about Elvis, you should know the world he inhabited, and if said film's about the *'68 Comeback Special*, you need someone who was there, preferably someone who met Elvis. Ideally, Steve Binder.

As luck would have it, Steve made it – along with pal and brother-in-arts, Meteor 17's producer, Spencer Proffer, so it's good. Very good.

With cracking visuals, some unseen footage, a resonant soundtrack and talking heads such as Elvis biographer Alanna Nash, dancers and audience members from the show and Binder himself, it reveals what really happened behind the scenes of what was a mesmerising hour of television and the most watched TV event of the year. Around half of the US's entire TV viewing audience saw Elvis, dressed in the now deified black leather and white suits, deliver some of the greatest performances of his life, surprising the hell out of everyone, rebooting his career, and changing the face of popular culture forever.

'The world is filled with stories about Elvis and his historic *'68 Comeback Special*, but no one has ever told this story the way only I can tell it – because I was there for every moment of it,' says Steve, who delivers delicious nuggets of insider anecdotes throughout.

'I'm so proud of this film because it presents Elvis as he really was and looks at a specific moment in time, when Elvis took control of his life, his career and his legacy. There's never been a television moment quite like this one.'

Spencer Proffer said, 'Steve Binder is one of the most innovative creators in entertainment. To make electrifying paradigm shifts in television, Steve broke moulds with his incredible vision.'

An unassuming industrial unit in Charlestown, Indiana, is the unlikely location of another part of the Elvis fashion legacy and a connection to the *Elvis* movie. B&K Enterprises, a small family firm founded by husband and wife team and Elvis fans Butch and Kim Polston, makes reproductions of Elvis's stage outfits, based on the sketches and designs of his original costume creators.

It all began when Kim asked Butch: 'If you could have anything that The King owned, besides Graceland, what would it be?'

Butch replied, 'One of his jumpsuits.'

'They were pieces of art to me,' he says. 'This is where the story of how we got started actually starts.'

In 1979, after ordering a small jumpsuit for their son from a fellow Elvis fan club member, they decided to decorate it.

The King is Dead, Long Live The King   183

'I took pictures from tribute magazines and purchased small bags of studs, meticulously placing them on it so that our son, Michael, would have a costume for Christmas,' says Butch.

Michael loved it and Kim suggested they could do the same with adult suits and take them to their fan club meetings as conversation pieces. Edna Graham, who made their son's suit, cut four adult versions and the Polstons got to work.

Butch explains: 'We made the Powder Blue, the White Pinwheel, the Red Pinwheel, and the Owl. They were rough copies, but we did our best, applying each stud by hand, through the fabric, and bending each prong over with a screwdriver or a butter knife.'

The suits got noticed and someone advised them to take them to Memphis, where groups of Elvis fans liked to gather. Having low-paid jobs, this was a big ask for the Polstons but it was also their dream to see Memphis, so they literally scraped enough money together, with Butch even digging car batteries out of the mud at a pig farm to claim the deposits, and eventually set off in their clapped-out 1968 Olds Cutlass.

By day two of the trip, with plenty of compliments but little money left for their homeward journey, an Elvis tribute artist happened upon them.

He said our workmanship was wonderful … that he had been doing shows for over a year and paying thousands of dollars for his costumes, which were trash compared to what we made.

Kim and I thought this was strange. Being from a small town in Indiana, we'd never seen anyone pretend to be someone else.

When the Elvis impersonator asked to try on a suit, Butch says he and Kim 'looked at each other, puzzled, like a cow had just kicked us in the face'.

The unexpected visitor offered them $500 for each of the costumes, this at a time when they had 57 cents left to feed Michael and get them back to Charlestown.

Orders came in from other Elvis tribute artists, so they sought and got permission from Bill Belew to reproduce his designs and contacted Elvis's garment craftsmen, Ciro Romana and Gene Doucette, who became good friends. Gene, 'now like a brother', works with the Polstons and together, they're now the world's go-to provider of Elvis-style outfits.

'Gene is one of a kind!' says Kim.

We've been blessed to work with him. He should have a plaque at Graceland, he's gone there with us many times and spoken with the powers-that-be

184   Elvis: The King of Fashion

to answer questions, etc. I think his name should be listed under each suit that he designed for Elvis.

I understand that since Bill Belew was the head costumer, his will always be the name linked with Elvis, but Gene was the hidden secret – and he never got to meet Elvis.

He was like a kid in a candy shop when doing the work, loving every minute of it, but he deserves to be mentioned in history, since his designs are the ones most fans really love.

B&K's Elvis impersonating customers all play their part in keeping the legacy alive. There's the good, the bad and the ugly, but all share a love of Elvis's music and, more importantly for them, his unique style. He is the King of Fashion as well as the King of Rock 'n' Roll, after all, so regardless of whether they sound like him, they really do need to look like him.

Some wear '50s or '60s Elvis gear, but the majority favour the '70s jump-suited look, since, as was the case for their hero, it has the greatest impact.

And while some performers happily pull on a dead raven wig, slap some sideburns on and squeeze into a spangly white onesie, others take Elvis fashion channelling very seriously. And some do a great job of emulating the man who, let's face it, no mere mortal can hope to match, using expensive wigs (costing up to $600); replica jewellery (a copy of Elvis's gold, black sapphire and diamond TCB ring from the original Lowell Hays jewellers costs $7,500) – all of which are deemed worth the outlay.

That's before they buy the elaborately detailed costumes. And where else does your earnest Elvis doppelganger go for authentic duds but B&K?

I ask Kim for a ballpark figure (at time of writing) for a Pinwheel suit and matching belt. 'The Pinwheel with belt is $2,200; if you add a cape, it brings the price up to $2,700. However, the price is determined by how elaborate the costume is and the length of time it takes to make it.'

I ask her about famous folk they've Elvised.

We made three costumes for Miley Cyrus and a pink *Aloha* suit with the cape for Jason Momoa to wear on the *Ellen* show, for Bruno Mars and his band, and an Egyptian suit for Bill Murray to wear on the cover of *Movies Rock* magazine. Our son's a Bill Murray fan and said that if Bill would autograph the suit and return it to us, he'd donate his time to making it.

Bill agreed, so we have the suit on display here. After the cover photo shoot, Bill borrowed it again to open an Eric Clapton concert and he returned it with photos of himself onstage at the concert.

The King is Dead, Long Live The King   185

They've crafted belts for Roseanne Barr and Madonna and made more than thirty costumes for the movie *3000 Miles to Graceland* 'for Kevin Costner, Kurt Russell, David Arquette, Bokeem Woodbine and Christian Slater [and various others], all in six weeks', says Kim.

Other B&K creations include an outfit dipped in brass for the Elvis statue in Hawaii; *Aloha* capes and belts that Graceland presented to President George Bush and the prime minister of Japan; an *Aloha* suit, cape and belt, for President Clinton's presidential library; and costumes for Bruce Campbell in the film *Bubba Ho-Tep*.

Which is why Catherine Martin went to them for Austin Butler's movie outfits. Kim says:

> Catherine went to Graceland and they referred her to us. She came to see us, spending a full day with us, going over the costumes she would need for the movie.
>
> We didn't do fittings directly on Austin, since he was already in Australia. We sent them over and they did them there. They emailed us fitting photos, which is how we do 95 per cent of our orders.

So, latest project? 'We recently finished the movie *Priscilla* [by Sofia Coppola]. Jacob Elordi is playing the part of Elvis.'

Boom, another legacy connection.

And has Butch found that original Elvis jumpsuit?

'Not yet, but still hoping.'

Back to Memphis, the place itself is a living, breathing tribute to Elvis. At Graceland, I marvelled at his personal possessions, including many of the outfits that inspired this book, and at the fact that I could walk through the very rooms and lean on the doorways that Elvis had, too.

At Sun Studio on Union I felt the hairs rise on the back of my neck as I listened to a haunting snippet of Elvis's first ever studio recording, 'My Happiness'; I held Sam Phillips's original studio mic, hoping that some of the talent of the many legends who'd held it might rub off on me, while standing on the exact spot that Elvis did when he recorded 'That's All Right'.

I stood outside the Lauderdale Courts welfare apartment block where Elvis lived as a teenager with no money but plenty of dreams and pictured him shyly playing guitar for his neighbours. I tried to have breakfast at his favourite booth in the glorious time capsule of turquoise, red and cream that is the Arcade Restaurant on South Main, but regretfully, though unsurprisingly, that particular seat was taken.

186   Elvis: The King of Fashion

I wandered the same Beale Street pavements that Elvis had, took a tour of the original Lansky's store with the irrepressible Hal Lansky as my guide and got to peer through the window that Elvis did while dreaming of buying some cool threads.

At Stax Museum on McLemore I delved into the origins of American soul and the story behind Elvis's legendary recording sessions there in 1973. Further exciting connections came to light at the Memphis Music Hall of Fame and the Blues Hall of Fame Museum where the heritage of the music that so inspired his own is beautifully celebrated.

At the Lorraine Motel on Mulberry, I stood by the room and balcony where Martin Luther King was assassinated, an event that dismayed Elvis and which motivated Earl Brown to write the powerful protest song 'If I Can Dream' for him to sing in the *'68 Special.*

Then at the Peabody Hotel on Union Avenue, I saw the RCA contract that Elvis famously signed there (at least his dad did, because Elvis was too young) and stood in its Continental Ballroom, where he was too nervous to dance on his prom night from fear of being ridiculed by his peers. I met the Duckmaster, Kenon Walker, also a showman in a dazzling outfit, who tells tales of both the historic and the duck variety to the crowds who flock to watch the Peabody ducks marching. Kenon trains the resident waddlers to travel in the elevator with him, down to a red carpet that leads them to the foyer's fountain where they swim.

'It's DIT. Ducks in Training,' he says.

> The first march of a new team [ducks are returned to the farm they came from after three months] happens in front of *everybody*. Prayerfully, when the elevator doors open, people either side of the carpet usher them towards the fountain, but if not – I have to be ready to run. I've chased ducks into the gift shop, the ladies room, behind the bar ...

Actor Kenon also answers questions about Elvis and, of course, there's a connection. He's an advocate of St Jude Children's Research Hospital, where Elvis privately donated money and, at one point, a yacht that they could sell to raise funds.

Asked about his most memorable Duckmaster moment, Kenon says:

> I've had so many, but being close to Saint Jude's, when the kids are clear to leave the hospital, often their first trip is here for the duck march. I've had amazing life-changing experiences with them and their families. For a kid who's been through God knows what, to finally be clear to go and

The King is Dead, Long Live The King   187

see the city they've had to visit only for treatment, when they come to the hotel, there's just something that happens.

When I see a family from St Jude's, I know I have to be of service – but in a different kind of way, because of how they're …

He trails off. 'Feeling?' I offer.

'Exactly. This might be their first little piece of joy after the hospital. To see the look on a child's face when they come to march the ducks – it's special.'

The legacy is everywhere.

There are too many actors who've played Elvis to list, but along with those previously mentioned there's Don Johnson (*Elvis and the Beauty Queen*, 1981); Harvey Keitel (*Finding Graceland*, 1998); Michael Shannon (*Elvis & Nixon*, 2016); Jack White (*Walk Hard: the Dewey Cox Story*, 2007), Tyler Hilton (*Walk the Line*, 2005); Val Kilmer (*True Romance*, 1993); and Jonathan Rhys Myers (*Elvis*, CBS min-series, 2005).

In the movie *Blade Runner 2049*, Elvis (played by tribute artist Ben Thompson) appears as a malfunctioning hologram in Rick Deckard's Vintage Las Vegas casino, flickering over the classic fight between Deckard (Harrison Ford) and Officer K (Ryan Gosling) while singing 'Can't help Falling in Love' and 'Suspicious Minds'.

Although Elvis only ever sat for one portrait, he's the subject of many artworks, with artists like Andy Warhol, Gavin Turk and Tommy Kha inspired by him. And he's the star of millions of nik-naks, gewgaws, tree ornaments, clock faces, lamps, garden gnomes, shoes, Monopoly sets, velvet pictures, plates, cups, t-shirts – lots of t-shirts – baby outfits, dog and cat outfits, cookie jars, Barbies, teddy bears … you name it, it's been Elvised. Tom Parker has much to answer for …

And since we're all about Elvis's style legacy, on 13 October 2022, at a New York fashion gala and awards ceremony, bulging with A-listers from the couture and entertainment industries, Elvis was posthumously honoured in the Artists and Icons category.

At Fashion Group International's 38th annual Night of Stars charity event he was awarded the Fashion Oracle Award for 'his pioneering, visionary and enduring style'. The glass trophy was presented by Andy Hilfiger, co-founder of Tommy Hilfiger, and accepted on Elvis's behalf by Joel Weinshanker, Managing Partner at Elvis Presley Enterprises/Graceland.

Our man's still got it.

If further proof were needed of the depth of Elvis's influence and inspiration on today's clebrities, it's the fact that there are too many to mention – but this lot will do for now.

188   Elvis: The King of Fashion

Bruce Springsteen cites Elvis as his hero, saying he was influenced by him from when he first saw him on *The Ed Sullivan Show* in 1956. 'I couldn't imagine anyone not wanting to be Elvis Presley,' he says.

In the 1970s, Springsteen played Memphis as part of a promotional tour for his new album, *Born to Run*; he told chat show host Graham Norton (*The Graham Norton Show*, BBC1) that after the gig, he and band member Steven van Zandt hailed a cab at 3 a.m. to find an all-night diner. The driver told them there was one up by Elvis's house.

'I said, "Elvis's house? You know where Elvis lives? Take us there right now!"' The taxi driver took them to Graceland and, despite a warning that there were 'big dogs' on the property, Springsteen decided that he'd never get another chance to meet his hero and jumped over the wall.

> I walked right up to the front door. I was about to knock … when a security guy came out of the bushes and said, 'Can I help you?'
>
> I said, 'Yes, is Elvis here?' And he said, 'Elvis is in Las Vegas,' so I said to him, can you tell him Bruce Springsteen was here.

Bruce doubted Elvis got to hear about his clandestine visit, and said regretfully that it was the closest he ever got to Elvis.

Lana del Rey wrote a song called 'Elvis' in 2008; it wasn't released but uploaded to her Myspace under the stage name Sparkle Jump Rope Queen. Del Rey says that of all the people that she could collaborate with, Elvis is top of the list. She said she would have loved to sing with him – and to make out with him. On 29 November 2023, Lana got as close to her wish as she could when her friend, Riley Keough, Elvis's granddaughter and now heir to Graceland, asked her to perform there as part of NBC's *Christmas at Graceland* special. Dressed in a brocade, '60s-style mini dress in the colours of Elvis's Mexican Sundial suit, she sang an ethereal and soulful version of 'Unchained Melody'.

Huge fan, U2's Bono (one of the band's drumkits still sits in Sun Studio from when they recorded some of their album *Rattle and Hum* there in homage to Elvis and Sam Phillips), pulled an Elvis impersonator from the crowd onto the stage in Inglewood, California, in 2015 and joked, 'I always wanted to meet you, dude,' then let the awestruck guy, who was dressed in a black Pinwheel suit and draped a powder-blue silk scarf round Bono's neck, sing the intro to 'Can't Help Falling Love'.

'Elvis changed everything, musically, sexually, politically,' Bono told *Rolling Stone*. 'He was not quite a hillbilly, nor yet a drugstore cowboy. He was a Southern – in that word's connotation of rebellion and slow, sweet charm – version of the character Brando created in *The Wild One*.' As Marlon Brando was one of Elvis's big heroes, he'd have happily agreed.

The King is Dead, Long Live The King   189

Liam Gallagher identifies with Elvis. In 2018, he told *Q* magazine, 'I've been singing other people's lyrics my whole life and I own them. Once I get hold of them, I make them something else, like Elvis.' Talking about his 'Wall of Glass' music video, he said, 'I did get to wear a gold St Laurent hooded jacket in one scene which I convinced myself made me look like a modern-day Elvis as he loved to wear gold suits.'

Chrishell Stause, actress and Southern belle of Netflix TV's real estate show *Selling Sunset*'s property sales team, says she loves Elvis so much she names her dogs in his honour. While viewing his former home, the so-called House of Tomorrow in Palm Springs, also referred to as the Elvis and Priscilla Honeymoon Hideaway, for her show she said, 'I am a huge fan of Elvis. In fact, Gracie, my dog, is short for Graceland. I've named all of my dogs after Elvis. I'm from the South. We love Elvis, Jesus and horses.'

Despite a refurbishment, with several King-themed additions, the four-bedroom, five-bathroom house at 1350 Ladera Circle in the Coachella Valley is largely unchanged from when Elvis and Priscilla stayed there, retaining much of the decor that they chose. Elvis rented the place in the lead-up to and after their Las Vegas wedding on 1 May 1967 and he and Priscilla celebrated their engagement there, lounging with friends on a vast curved sofa that hugged the interior stone walls, and then spent their honeymoon and weekends there.

The house is now an important, and very cool example of classic mid-century architecture and, speaking to *The Desert Sun* in 2022, Priscilla said that she and Elvis had 'some wonderful times' there. She recently visited the house and was shocked to see how close it still looked to how she remembered it.

'It was modern back in the day … probably the most modern home in Palm Springs. It's still very modern and still very in,' she said.

In 2023, the house was valued at just under $6 million.

As briefly mentioned in Chapter 7, Canadian singer k.d. lang paid homage to Elvis by using the cover of his first album, *Elvis Presley* (1956), as inspiration for the cover of her own *Reintarnation* album. She told elvisinfonet.com:

I just liked the idea of taking Elvis's album cover, along with The Clash's seminal *London Calling*, as I always used to get compared to Elvis Presley when I was doing country. And so I just thought that that was a tip of the hat to the people who used to call me a Cow Punk.

Of Elvis, she said, 'He had total love in his eyes when he performed. He was the total androgynous beauty. I would practice Elvis in front of the mirror when I was twelve or thirteen years old.'

190 Elvis: The King of Fashion

Singer Harry Styles, an Elvis fan since childhood, explained to *The Howard Stern Show* why he went up for the part of Elvis in Baz Luhrmann's film. 'Elvis was probably the first person I knew besides my family when I was a kid. For that reason, there was something incredibly sacred surrounding him, so I thought I should try to get the part.'

It's said that Luhrmann considered Styles for the role but in the end felt that his considerable celebrity status would have been a distraction. The singer gamely accepted the director's decision, saying, 'If they think the movie's going to be better with someone else then I don't want to do it because I don't want to be the not-as-good version.'

Famous faces, fancy merchandise and faux Elvises all play their part in preserving Elvis's memory, but it's the fans – the old and the new – who, in an almost folkloric manner, really keep it alive through sharing their reminiscences and their photographs – as many have with me – and their anecdotes and amazing facts. And by playing his music, watching his films, watching other people's films and shows about Elvis and reading books about him and talking about him at work, in bars, cafés, churches, on social media, and most importantly, to their children.

So, to all the legacy torch carriers wherever you are, whatever you do and however you do it, in the words of the The King himself:

'Thank you. Thank you. You've been fantastic.'

Appendix

Elvis Filmography

Feature films

1956, *Love Me Tender*, 20th Century Fox. Producer: David Weisbart
1957, *Loving You*, Paramount. Producer: Hal B. Wallis
1957, *Jailhouse Rock*, Metro-Goldwyn-Mayer. Producer: Pandro S. Berman
1958, *King Creole*, Paramount. Producer: Hal B. Wallis
1960, *GI Blues*, Paramount. Producer: Hal B. Wallis
1960, *Flaming Star*, 20th Century Fox. Producer: David Weisbart
1961, *Wild in the Country*, 20th Century Fox. Producer: Jerry Wald
1961, *Blue Hawaii*, Paramount. Producer: Hal B. Wallis
1962, *Follow That Dream*, United Artists. Producer: David Weisbart
1962, *Kid Galahad*, United Artists. Producer: David Weisbart
1962, *Girls, Girls, Girls!*, Paramount. Producer: Hal B. Wallis
1963, *It Happened at the World's Fair*, Metro-Goldwyn-Mayer. Producer: Ted Richmond
1963, *Fun in Acapulco*, Paramount. Producer: Hal B. Wallis
1964, *Kissin' Cousins*, Metro-Goldwyn-Mayer. Producer: Sam Katzman
1964, *Viva Las Vegas*, Metro-Goldwyn-Mayer. Producers: Jack Cummings, George Sidney
1964, *Roustabout*, Paramount. Producer: Hal B. Wallis
1965, *Girl Happy*, Metro-Goldwyn-Mayer. Producer: Joe Pasternack
1965, *Tickle Me*, Allied Artists. Producer: Ben Schwalb
1965, *Harum Scarum*, Metro-Goldwyn-Mayer. Producer: Sam Katzman
1966, *Frankie and Johnny*, United Artists. Producer: Edward Small
1966, *Paradise Hawaiian Style*, Paramount. Producer: Hal B. Wallis
1966, *Spinout*, Metro-Goldwyn-Mayer. Producer: Joe Pasternack
1967, *Easy Come, Easy Go*, Paramount. Producer: Hal B. Wallis
1967, *Double Trouble*, Metro-Goldwyn-Mayer. Producers: Judd Bernard, Irwin Winkler
1967, *Clambake*, United Artists. Producers: Arnold Laven, Arthur Gardner, Jules Levy
1968, *Stay Away, Joe*, Metro-Goldwyn-Mayer. Producer: Douglas Laurence
1968, *Speedway*, Metro-Goldwyn-Mayer. Producer: Douglas Laurence
1968, *Live A Little, Love A Little*, Metro-Goldwyn-Mayer. Producer: Douglas Laurence
1969, *Charro!*, National General. Producer: Harry Caplan
1969, *The Trouble with Girls*, Metro-Goldwyn-Mayer. Producer: Lester Welch
1969, *Change of Habit*, Universal. Producer: Joe Connelly

Documentary films

1970, *That's The Way It Is*, MGM. Director: Denis Sanders
1972, *Elvis On Tour*, MGM. Directors: Robert Abel, Pierre Adidge

Bibliography and Sources

Books

Allen, Steve, *Hi-Ho Steverino!*, Barricade Books, 1994

Alverson, Keith, *Strictly Elvis*, eponstage@charter.net

Anrias, David, *Through the Eyes of the Masters*, Routledge & Kegan Paul, 1947

Binder, Steve, *ELVIS '68 Comeback: The Story Behind the Special*, Printer's Row/Thunder Bay Press, 2021

Cash, Johnny with Carr, Patrick, *Cash: The Autobiography*, HarperSanFrancisco, 1997

Dundy, Elaine, *Elvis and Gladys*, University Press of Mississippi, 2004

Dunleavy, Steve (from conversations with Red and Sonny West and Dave Hebler), *Elvis: What happened?*, Ballantine Books, 1977

Greil, Marcus, *Mystery Train: Images of America in Rock 'n' Roll Music*, Plume Books, 2015

Guralnick, Peter, *Last Train to Memphis: The Rise of Elvis Presley*, Little, Brown, 1994

_____, *Careless Love: The Unmaking of Elvis Presley*, Little, Brown, 1999

_____, *Sam Phillips: The Man Who Invented Rock and Roll*, Little, Brown, 2015

Hutchins, Chris & Thompson, Peter, *Elvis Meets the Beatles*, Smith Gryphon, 1994

Juanico, June, *Elvis In the Twilight of Memory*, Little, Brown, 1997

Lansky Bros., *Clothier to the King*, Beckon Books

Mason, Bobbie Ann, *Elvis*, Viking, 2003

McReynolds, Alistair, *Kith and Kin: The Continuing Legacy of the Scots-Irish in America*, Ulster Scots Agency, 2013

Nash, Alanna, *Elvis Aaron Presley: Revelations from the Memphis Mafia*, HarperCollins, 1995

Pearlman, Jill, *Elvis for Beginners*, Writers & Readers Publishing, 1986

Physician's Desk Reference, Medical Economics Inc.

Presley, Lisa Marie & Presley, Priscilla and other family members, *Elvis by the Presleys*, Century/Random House, 2005

Presley, Priscilla with Harman, S., *Elvis and Me*, Berkley Publishing

Thompson, Charles C. & Cole, James P., *The Death of Elvis: What Really Happened*, Ballantine Books, 1977

Wallis, Hal, *Starmaker: The Autobiography of Hal B. Wallis*, Macmillan, 1980

Whitmer, Peter, *The Inner Elvis*, Hyperion, 1996

Other Sources

Newspapers and magazines
Associated Press
Billboard (www.billboard.com)
Far Out
Good Housekeeping magazine

Bibliography and Sources   193

Jacksonville Magazine
Look
Memphis Press–Scimitar
Movies Rock
Photoplay
Q magazine
Rolling Stone
Time
The Commercial Appeal
The Humes High Class of '53 Yearbook, credit Rose Howell-Klimek
The New Yorker (www.newyorker.com)
TV Guide
TV Radio Mirror
United Press International (UPI)
Variety (www.variety.com)

TV/film/documentaries/radio
Baz Luhrmann interview with Sam Bell (www.youtube.com/watch?v=LrFCyNMvZWk)
Daisy Jones and the Six, Amazon 2023
Elvis, Warner Bros. (2022)
Elvis: In His own Words, MGM interview with Bob Abel
Elvis On Tour, MGM documentary
Elvis: The Man Who Shook Up the World, Channel 5 documentary (www.channel5.com/show/elvis-the-man-who-shook-up-the-world)
Elvis: The Rise and Fall of The King, Channel 5 documentary (www.channel5.com/elvis-rise-and-fall-of-the-king)
Elvis Presley on film and television, Wikipeida television and film credits (en.wikipedia.org/wiki/Elvis_Presley_on_film_and_television)
George Klein's Memphis Sounds with Red West, 2011 (https://www.youtube.com/watch?v=KulDWSqtLwU)
Late Night Show, David Letterman with Liberace (https://www.youtube.com/watch?v=_JZLWnkLupo)
Louisiana Hayride radio KWKH broadcast 16 October 1954
Elvis: That's The Way It Is, MGM documentary
The Wizard of Oz, MGM, 1939
3,000 Miles to Graceland, Warner Bros., 2001
Elvis (Singer Presents), now known as the *'68 Comeback Special*, NBC, 3 December 1968

Elvis on TV
Aloha from Hawaii, main satellite broadcast, 14 January 1973, followed by various video broadcasts. (NBC and RCA)
Elvis in Concert, 3 October 1977. (Posthumous broadcast, CBS)
Teenage Dance Party with Wink Martindale, WHBQ-TV, interview 16 June 1956
The Dorsey Brothers' Stage Show, 28 January, 4, 11 & 18 February, 17 & 24 March 1956. (CBS)
The Ed Sullivan Show, 9 September, 28 October 1956, 6 January 1957. (CBS)
The Frank Sinatra Timex Special: Welcome Home Elvis, 12 May 1960. (ABC)
The Milton Berle Show, 3 April, 5 June 1956. (NBC)
The Steve Allen Show, 1 July 1956. (NBC)

194   Elvis: The King of Fashion

Photos and images
Alverson, Keith, photographer, email: eponstage@charter.net
B&K Enterprises
Bell Clawson, Ardys (Jacksonville Historic Society www.jaxhistory.org)
Hammond-Kincaid, Teri
Lansky Bros. (www.lanskybros.com)
Library of Congress (www.loc.gov)
National Gallery of Art NGA Images (www.nga.gov)
The TCB Ring (www.lowellhaysjewelers.com)
www.commons.wikimedia.org
www.wikipedia.org
www.loc.gov

Websites
Bill Belew's Early Days Beechwood Entertainment Productions/B&K
Elvis Presley Worldwide (www.facebook.com)
Enterprises/DUMAS (www.youtube.com/watch?v=qwQta7gVp3s)
Globetrotting with Trey: *The Elvis Travelogues* (www.youtube.com/
    watch?v=m8MwCcqVNCM)
Historic Memphis (www.historic-memphis.com)
Lansky Bros. (www.lanskybros.com)
Louisiana Hayride (www.youtube.com/watch?v=bLaPnpjw-pc)
Marty Wilde (www.martywilde.com)
Spa Guy (www.youtube.com/@SpaGuy)
www.elvisblog.net
www.elvis.com.au
www.elvisconcerts.com

Podcasts
Revisionist History, Malcolm Gladwell podcast (www.omny.fm/shows/revisionist-history/
    analysis-parapraxis-elvis)

Albums
London Calling, The Clash
Reintarnation, k.d. lang

Index

20th Century Fox, 89, 110, 191
'68 Comeback (*Singer NBC-TV Christmas Special: Elvis*), viii, xvi, xvii, xviii, 40, 88, 120–35, 137, 144, 181–2, 186, 192–3

ABC TV, 109
Abel, Bob, 14, 25, 27–8, 52, 63, 137, 150, 193
Aberbach (Hill & Range), Jean and Julian, 79, 81, 135
Abilene, 164
Alabama, 162
   Mobile, 145, 160, 166
Alabama Avenue, Memphis, 28
Aladdin Hotel, Las Vegas, 119
Albuquerque, 151
Alden, Ginger, 173
Ali, Muhammad, 158
Allen, Steve and *The Steve Allen Show*, 86–8, 109, 192–3
Aloha from Hawaii, TV show, ix, 17, 111, 139, 155–6, 158, 159, 184–5, 193
Amarillo, 163
American Sound Studio, Memphis, 135–6, 149
Anaheim, 160
Anderson, Nancy, 12–13
Ann-Margret, 114–15
Arcade Restaurant, Memphis, 185
Arizona, 160
   Phoenix, 160
      Veteran Memorial Coliseum, 145
Arizona, USS, 111–12, 127, 155
Arkansas, xvi, 75, 100
   Fort Chaffee, 100
Arnaz, Desi, 38
Arnold, Eddy, 72
Arquette, David, 185
Asheville, 158, 166, 168

Asia, 157
Assembly of God Church, (First), 5, 14–15
Atlanta, 160, 166, 171
Auburn, 162
Audubon Drive, Memphis, 83, 92
Australia, 185
Axton, Estelle, 162
Axton, Mae, 72, 76, 79,

Baity, Jack, 152
Ball, Lucille, 38
Ballard, Mayor James L., 91
Baltimore, 150
Bardwell, Duke, 165
Barr, Roseanne, 185
Baton Rouge, 163, 171, 175
BB King, 2, 21, 49, 55
Beale Streeters, 21
Beale Street, Memphis, ix, xiii, xv, 1–2, 18, 21–2, 35, 38, 43–4, 46, 55–6, 89, 180, 186
Bean, Orville, 5, 9–10
Beatles, The, 115–17, 192
Belafonte, Harry, 122
Belew, Bill, 40, 126–30, 140–4, 148, 155–7, 183–4, 194
Bell, Sam, 14–17
Bell Clawson, Ardys, viii, xv, 76–7, 194
Bernero, Johnny, 57
Beverly Wilshire Hotel, Beverly Hills, CA, 109
Biloxi, 78
Binder, Steve, viii, xvi, 105, 121–32, 137, 181–2, 192
Black, Bill, 54–63, 67–9, 74, 81, 83, 85–9, 98–9, 108
Blackwood Brothers, 12, 14, 22–3, 46, 52, 103
Blancett, George, 29

196 Elvis: The King of Fashion

Bland, Bobby Blue, 1
Bloomington, 163, 171
Blossoms, The, 132
Bluebirds, 105
Blue Hawaii, film, xvi, 109, 111–12, 158, 191
Blue Moon Boys, The, 63, 66, 68, 75
Bond, Eddie, 53
Bono, 188
Booker T. & the MGs, 162
Boston, 150
Bova, Joyce, 148
Brando, Marlon, 24, 39, 93, 109, 188
Brenston, Jackie, 47
Brewer, Teresa, 28
Brewster, Revd. Harper, 52
Brooks, Jane Ellen, 52
Brown, Earl, 127, 130–2, 186
Brown, Leroy, 17
Buck dancing, 7
Buffalo, 150–1, 171
Burton, James, 137
Bush, President George, 149, 185
Butler, Austin, x, 1, 36, 42–4, 88, 126, 131, 138–9, 156, 180–1, 185

Cadillac, x, 12, 44, 75, 78, 94, 105, 168
California, 36, 84, 111, 116, 160–1, 173, 188
Campbell, Bruce, 185
Canby, Vincent, 115–16
Carolina, 65, 158
Cash, Johnny, 37, 49, 68, 121
Catholic Immaculate Conception High School, Memphis, 114
CBS, 38, 81, 126, 175, 187, 193
Chanel N° 5, 78
Change of Habit, film, 120, 136, 191
Charleston, ix, ix, xvii, 166–7
Charlestown, Indiana, 182–3
Charlie's Records, Memphis, 22
Charlotte, 151, 162, 170
Charro!, film, 110, 136, 181, 191
Cher, 143
Chicago, 96, 152
Chisca Hotel, Memphis, 23, 55
Cincinnati, 150, 160, 170
Circle G Ranch, Mississippi, 118–19, 134

Clambake, film, 118, 191
Clapton, Eric, 184
Clark, Petula, 122, 126
Clarke, Dr Charles, 101
Clash, The, 82, 189
Claypool, Bob, 172
Clearpool, Memphis, 63
Cleveland, 150, 163, 166
Clinton, President Bill, 185
Clooney, George, 10
Cohn, Nudie, 95, 118, 130
College Park, 164
Columbus, 163
Continental Ballroom, the Peabody, Memphis, 29–31, 186
Coppola, Sofia, 185
Costner, Kevin, 185
Coward, Noel, 96
Crown Electric Company, 52, 54, 64, 181
Crudup, Arthur (Big Boy), 21, 23, 54–5
Cruise, Tom, 35
Curtis, Tony, 27
Cyrus, Miley, 184

Dallas, 150, 166, 178
Davis Junior, Sammy, 109
Davis, Oscar ('The Box office'), 72–4
Dayton, 151, 164
Daytona Beach, 72
Dean, James, 24, 93, 109, 179
Del Rey, Lana, 188
Denver, 146, 160, 170
Des Moines, 163
Detroit, 145, 151, 164
Diamond, Neil, 136
Dion, Celine, 143
Diskin, Tom, 74
Dorsey Brothers, Jimmy and Tommy, 38, 81–2
Double Trouble, film, 118, 191
Doucette, Gene, 156, 174, 181, 183–4
Dundy, Elaine, 7, 192

Eagle's Nest, Memphis, 63–4, 68, 72
Early, Cole, viii, 61
East Tupelo Consolidated school, 11
Easy Come, Easy Go, film, 118, 191
Eckstine, Billy, 54

Index 197

El Paso, 153, 171
Elordi, Jacob, 185
Elvis, film (2022), x, xiv, 1, 4, 15, 35–6, 42–5, 174, 180–2, 185, 190
Elvis in Concert, film, 175–6
Elvis Presley (first album, 1956), 82–3, 97
Elvis Presley Boulevard, Memphis, 179
Elvis Presley Worldwide (Facebook), ix, 177, 179
Epstein, Brian, 117
Esposito, Joe, 113, 117, 157
Evansville, 152

Fashion Group International (Night of Stars), 187
Fields, W.C., 90
Fike, Lamar, 19, 72, 95, 98–100, 102, 105, 136, 143
Finkel, Bob, 121–5
Flaming Star, film, 110, 191
Florida, viii, 31–2, 72, 76, 83, 86–8, 129
    Jacksonville, viii, 76–8, 87, 129, 151, 166, 193, 194
    Miami, 109, 145
    Tampa, 83, 145, 166
    Theatre, 87–8
Follow That Dream, film, 112–13, 191
Foley, Red, 13
Fontana, DJ, 70, 81, 85–6, 89, 98, 108, 129
Ford, Harrison, 187
Forest Hill Cemetery, Memphis, 103, 108, 179
Fort Dix, 107
Fort Homer Hesterly Armory, 83
Fort Hood, 101
Fort Wayne, 152
Fort Worth, 101, 152, 163, 171–2
Fortas, Alan, 99, 129
Francisco, Dr Jerry, 177
Frankie and Johnny, film, 116
Fun in Acapulco, film, 114
Fuqua, Lonnie, ix, 158–9
Fury, Billy, 98

Gable, Lether, 9
Gallagher, Liam, 189
Gator Bowl, Jacksonville, Florida, 77

Geller, Larry, 115, 138–9, 146, 170, 172, 175
General Randall, USS, 103
Germany, 98, 103–107, 113–14
    Bad Nauheim, 103
    Bremerhaven, 103
    Munich, 105
    Wiesbaden, 107
GI Blues, film, 111, 191
Girl Happy, film, 115, 191
Girls, Girls, Girls!, film, 111, 191
Gladwell, Malcolm, x, 52, 194
Gleaves, Cliff, 99
Glover, Lillie Mae, 1
Golden Globe, 44, 181
Goldenberg, Billy, 127, 130–1
Gooding, Marion, 87–8
Gordon, Roscoe, 57
Gosling, Ryan, 187
Graceland, Elvis Presley Boulevard, Memphis, ix, xiii, xvii, 19, 38–41, 44, 51, 59, 64, 78, 94–5, 100–104, 107, 114–15, 118–19, 124, 149–50, 152, 155, 157, 162, 164–6, 169–71, 174, 176, 178–83, 185, 187–9, 193
GRAMMY Award, 45, 165
Grand Ole Opry , 21, 68
Gratz, H. Tucker, 111
Great Depression, 9, 13, 75
Green Street, Tupelo, 14–15
Greensboro, 151, 162, 166, 171
Grimes, Oleta, 12–13
Groom, Arthur, 24
Gunter, Arthur, 78
Guralnick, Peter, ix, 15, 27, 49, 65, 164, 170, 174, 192

Halberstadt, Alex, 48
Hamilton, Roy, 149, 169
Hammond-Kincaid, Teri, ix, xvii, 167–8, 194
Hampton Roads, 151, 162
Hancock, USS, 84
Handy, W.C. and Club Handy, 1
Hanks, Tom, 42, 131
Harford, Margaret, 116
Harrison, George, 117
Harum Scarum, film, 115–16, 191

198 Elvis: The King of Fashion

Hawaii, xviii, 104, 112, 155–9, 173,
   185, 193
   Bloch Arena, 112
   Honolulu, xvii, 112, 128, 153, 158
   International Centre Arena, 158
   Pearl Harbor, 111
   Waikiki, 158
Hawkins, Hoyt, 72–3
Hayes, Isaac, x, 162
Hays, Lowell, 145, 166, 173, 184
Heard, Dick, 136
Hebler, Dave, 164, 171–3, 192
Hendrix, Jimmy, 122
Hess, Jake, 46
Hi-Hat Club, Memphis, 53
Hilburn, Lorisa, 51
Hilfiger, Andy and Tommy, 187
Hill, Eddie, 72
Hilton, Tyler, 187
Hodge, Charlie, 105, 129, 157, 164, 175
Holly, Buddy, 70
Hollywood, xvi, xviii, xix, 80, 82, 89, 91,
   93–7, 99, 109–11, 113–14, 116, 121,
   135–6, 139, 153
Howe, (Dayton Burr) 'Bones', 123
Howell-Klimek, Rose, 22, 193
Howlin' Wolf (Chester Arthur Burnett), 2,
   21, 49
Hughes, Howard, 149
Humes High School, Memphis, 19, 20, 22,
   25–9, 56, 67–8, 99, 193
Humperdinck, Engelbert, 142
Huntsville, 166

I Love Lucy, TV show, 38
Imperials, The, 137
Indianapolis, 151, 164–5, 174
Inglewood, California, 188
International (Hilton) Hotel, Las Vegas, ix,
   126, 135, 137, 143, 146, 158
   Hilton Gold Attendance belt, 139, 143,
   146, 151–2
It Happened at the World's Fair, film,
   114, 191

Jackson, 166
   State Fair, Coliseum, 167
Jackson, Bull Moose, 21

Jackson, Dorothy, 26
Jailhouse Rock, film, xviii, 24, 41, 45, 53, 64,
   96–9, 122, 142, 191
Jay, Chaydon, 181
Jaycee (Ten Outstanding Men of the
   Nation) Award, 4, 149
Jenkins, Scott, 27
Joel, Billy, 171
John, Elton, 143, 171
Johnson, 170
Johnson, Don, 187
Jones, Tom, 142
Jordanaires, 72, 89, 91, 101, 108
Juanico, June, 20, 78, 99, 192

Kansas, 18, 150, 163, 170
Katz drugstore, Memphis, 66, 68
Keisker, Marion, x, 44, 48, 50–3, 60,
   62, 64–5
Keitel, Harvey, 187
Kennedy, John F., 177
Kennedy, Robert 'Bobby', 124
Kentucky, 138
   Louisville, 138–9, 150, 163
Keough, Benjamin Storm, 179
Keough, Riley, 179, 188
Keough, Tupelo Storm, 179
Kid Galahad, film, 112, 191
Kilmer, Val, 187
King, Martin Luther, 124, 130–1, 177,
   186
King Creole, film, 99–101, 191
Kirkham, Millie, 138
Kissin' Cousins, film, 115, 191
Kissinger, Henry, 149
Klein, George, 26, 53, 67, 99, 136, 140,
   172, 193
Knoxville, 65, 151, 162
Krogh, Egil, 149
KWKH radio, 68

Lacker, Marty, 25, 95, 99, 117, 135
Lake Charles, 166
Lakeland, 166
Lamar-Airways, 66
Landeau, Jon, 120
lang, k.d., 82, 189
Lange, Hope, 111

Index 199

Lansky, Bernard, ix, xiii, xvi, 1–3, 35–43, 89, 177–8
  Bros. (Lansky's), Memphis, ix, xiii, xiv, xv, xvi, 2–3, 18, 23, 25, 29, 33–46, 51, 59, 64, 77, 89, 91, 96, 177–80, 186, 192, 194
Lansky, Guy, 2, 35, 64
Lansky, Hal, ix, xiii–xiv, xv, 2, 35–7, 39–45, 64, 77, 91, 179
Lansky, Julie (granddaughter), ix, 2, 35, 42–4
Largo, 171
Las Vegas, xviii, 40–1, 65, 92, 110, 113–15, 119, 126, 134–52, 159–60, 162–5, 168–9, 172–3, 187–9, 191
Lauderdale Courts, Memphis, 20, 28, 52, 126, 185
Lawford, Peter, 109
Lee, Kui, 158
Leek, Ed, 51
Leiber & Stoller, 53, 96
Lennon, John, 116
Leonard's Barbeque, 22, 30
Letterman, David, 92
Lewis, Jerry-Lee, 37
Liberace, 92, 140
Little Richard (Richard Penniman), 2, 22
Little Rock, 151
Live a Little, Love a Little, film, 109
Locke, Dixie, 37–8, 46, 52–3, 58, 62–3, 66–8, 75, 78
Loew's State Theatre, Memphis, 23–4, 93
Logan, Horace 'Hoss', 69
Long Beach, 153, 170
Lopez, Jennifer, 143
Lord, Jack and Marie, 157
Lorraine Motel & National Civil Rights Museum, Memphis, ix, 186
Los Angeles, 146, 148, 163
Louisiana Hayride, 38, 68–9, 73, 137, 193–4
Louvin Brothers, 12, 70
Love Me Tender, first film, 89, 92–4, 115, 191
Loving You, film, 94–5, 97, 191
Lubbock, 70, 153, 171
Luhrmann, Baz, xiv, 1, 15–16, 35–6, 42–5, 88, 131, 139, 156, 174, 180–1, 190, 193
Lulu, 98
Lundgren, Borje, 177

Macon, 151, 166
Madison Square Garden, xix, 89, 125, 134, 151–2
Madonna, 185
Malone, Dwight, 25
Mansfield, Rex, 105
Marcus, Greil, 133, 169, 192
Mars, Bruno, 184
Martin, Catherine, 41–2, 44–5, 126, 180–1, 185
Martindale, Wink, 193
Mason, Bobbie-Ann, 12, 23, 70, 82, 87, 104, 192
M.B. Parker machinist shop, Memphis, 29
McCartney, Paul, 117
McComb, 167
McCuen, Brad, 65–6
McEvoy, Cathy, 141
McEvoy, Jim, 141
McGuire air force base, Fort Dix, 107
McKeen, William, 80
McLemore Avenue, 52, 186
McReynolds, Alistair, 192
Memphis, viii, ix, x, xi, xiii, xv, xvi, xix, xx, 1–2, 15–28, 31–9, 42–4, 46–9, 55, 58–60, 63–70, 83, 88, 90–1, 93–107, 110, 113–14, 124, 130, 135–7, 141, 145, 148–9, 162–3, 166, 168, 171, 175, 177, 178–80, 183
  Baptist Memorial Hospital, 166, 175
  Blues Hall of Fame Museum, 186
  East Trigg Baptist church, 22
  Ellis Auditorium, 52, 72, 74, 108
  First Assembly Church, 52, 66
  Methodist Hospital, 101–102
  Music Hall of Fame, 186
  Tourism, 37
  University, 136
  University Press of, 192
Mexican Sundial jumpsuit, xvii, 174–5, 181, 188
MGM, 6, 14, 25, 28, 96, 114–15, 123, 137, 191, 193
Michigan, 31, 169
Midler, Bette, 143
Midsouth Coliseum, 162
Milam School, Tupelo, 13
Miller, Trey, viii, 76–7, 194

200 Elvis: The King of Fashion

Milton Berle Show/Milton Berle, 38, 82, 84–6, 126
Milton, Little, 49–5
Milwaukee, 152, 163
Minneapolis, 150
Minnesota, 164
Mississippi, 2, 4–5, 10, 21, 23, 46, 49, 78, 81, 90, 118, 167, 192
Mississippi-Alabama Fair and Dairy Show, 12, 90
Mississippi Slim, 12
Moman, Chips, 135–6
Momoa, Jason, 184
Monroe, 162, 166
Monroe, Bill, 57
Montgomery, 162
Montgomery, Dacre, 181
Moore, Mary Tyler, 120
Moore, Scotty, 54–61, 63, 67–70, 74, 81, 85–6, 89, 98–9, 108, 129
Moore-Munson, Betty Jean, 26
Morrison, Sam, 65–6
Muhoberac, Larry, 137
Municipal Auditorium, New Orleans, 87–8
Murfreesboro, 162, 166
Murray, Bill, 184
'My Happiness', 51

Nash, Alanna, 19, 25, 72, 78, 139, 182, 192
Nashville, 52, 68, 101, 108, 112, 114, 135, 158–60
Country Music Hall of Fame, 52
NBC, xviii, 38, 120, 155
Neal, Bob, 46, 59, 74, 79, 90
Nelson, Gene, 6
Neostyle Nautic sunglasses, 139, 146, 148
Nevada, 173
New Frontier Hotel, Las Vegas, 92
New Haven, 166
New Orleans, 87, 99
New York, viii, xvi–xvii, 36, 38, 79, 81, 87–9, 95–6, 103, 115, 125, 128, 141, 150–1, 187
Hilton, 151
Newman, Paul, 10
Niagara Falls, 163, 166

Nichopoulos, George C. ('Dr Nick'), 138, 147, 161, 163, 166, 168, 170, 172, 174–5, 192
Nixon, President Richard, 148–9
Norfolk, 166
Norton, Graham, 188

Oakland, 146, 153
Oceania, 157
Odessa, 171
O'Dwyer, Jenny, x, 45
O'Grady, John, 170
Oklahoma, 146, 160, 166, 171
Old Saltillo Road, Tupelo, 5
'Old Shep', 13, 27, 28, 90
Omaha, 163, 170
Oregon, 173
Oscars (Academy Awards), 44
Overton Park (Levitt) Shell, Memphis, viii, 28–9, 35, 58–9, 62–3, 66–7, 128

Page, Frank, 69
Pakes, Bob, 79
Palm Springs, 119, 171, 173, 189
Paradise, Hawaiian Style, film, 115, 191
Paramount Pictures, 85, 89, 94, 99, 109, 111–12, 182, 191
Parchman Farm Prison (Mississippi State Penitentiary), 9–10
Paris, 105
Café de, 105
Hotel Prince de Galles, 105
Lido, 105
Moulin Rouge, 105
Parker, Col Tom (aka Colonel or The Colonel or Andreas Cornelis van Kuijk), xvi, 11, 35–6, 42, 73–81, 86–7, 92–100, 106–25, 121–5, 130–40, 143, 154, 158–9, 161, 164–6, 170–5, 181, 187
Parker, Junior, 21, 53, 57
Peabody Hotel, Memphis, viii, x, 29–32, 35, 43, 48, 79, 186
Pearlman, Jill, 20, 192
Pepper, Gary, 108
Perkins, Carl, 37, 49
Perugia Way, Bel Air, CA, 116
Philadelphia, 150, 163, 171
Phillips, Dewey, xv, 23–4, 55–6, 63, 66

Index   201

Phillips, Jerry, 48, 57
Phillips, Sam, x, 22–3, 35, 47–62, 64–5, 74, 79, 97–8, 113, 128, 185, 188, 192
Pittsburgh, 160
Polston, Butch and Kim (B&K Enterprises), x, 140, 156, 182–5, 194
Polston, Michael, 183
Pontiac, 169
Poplar Avenue, Memphis, 20
Poplar Tunes, Memphis, 22
Porter, Bill, 108
Portland, 146, 160
Presley, Clettes/Cletes (née Smith, Gladys's sister and Vester's wife), 11, 64
Presley, Gladys Love (née Smith, mother), 5–19, 23, 39, 44, 56, 58, 67, 75, 77–9, 84, 90–1, 94, 97, 100–106, 110, 115, 117–18, 142, 179, 192
Presley, Jesse Garon (stillborn twin brother), 7–8, 19, 24
Presley, Lisa Marie (daughter), 104, 119, 124, 136, 147–8, 161–2, 164, 166, 173–4, 176, 179, 192
Presley, Minnie Mae (grandmother), 12–13, 94, 100, 102, 173
Presley, Patsy (cousin), 11
Presley, Priscilla (née Beaulieu, wife), 43, 75, 106–107, 113–23, 124, 128, 136, 141–2, 147–52, 154, 160–1, 164, 170, 185, 189, 192
Presley, Vernon Elvis (father), 5–7, 16, 18–19, 23, 35, 58, 67, 78–9, 90–1, 94, 97, 100, 103–104, 110, 114, 161, 171, 173–4
Presley, Vester (Vernon's brother), 5, 11, 14, 64, 94
Priscilla, film, 185
Prisonaires, The, 48, 50, 53
Proffer, Spencer, viii, 123, 182
Providence, 163, 171
Prowse, Juliet, 109

Rabbitt, Eddie, 136
Rainbow skate rink, Memphis, 66
Rapid City, South Dakota, 174–5
RCA, 35, 65, 79, 81–2, 84, 88–9, 95, 101, 108, 135–6, 162, 169, 186, 193
    Studio B, 101, 108, 162
Redding, Otis, 162

Reeves, Jim, 65
Reinventing Elvis, 2023 documentary, viii, 182
Rhys Meyers, Jonathan, 187
Richard, Cliff, 98
Richfield, 166
Richmond, 151, 162, 171
Roanoke, 151, 162
Robertson, William V. 'Red', 83
Romano, Ciro, 155, 183
Romero, Alex, 96
Roosevelt, Franklin D., 13
Roustabout, film, 115, 191
Russell, Kurt, 185
Russwood Park, Memphis, 88

Sahara Tahoe Hotel, Nevada, 150, 160, 163–5, 170, 174
Salt Lake City, 150, 163
San Antonio, 151, 164
San Bernardino, 153, 163
San Diego, 84, 146, 160, 170
San Francisco, 146
Santa Monica, 160
Sarnoff, Tom, 120
Scheff, Jerry, 137
Scheinfeld, John, 181
Schilling, Jerry, 26, 117, 148–9, 159, 171
Schutt, Frank, 79
Scrivener, Mildred, 28
Seattle, 114, 146, 160, 170
Shaft, film, 40, 162
Shake Rag, Tupelo, 15, 143
Shannon, Michael, 187
Sharecroppers, 5–6, 14, 84
Sharp, Nancy, 110
Sholes, Steve, 65, 101
Shreveport and Municipal Auditorium, 68, 166, 171
Siegel, Don, 110
Sinatra, Frank, 88, 109, 121
Sinatra, Nancy, 109–10
Skinner, Frank, 91
Slater, Christian, 185
Sleepy-Eyed John, 63
Smith, Billy (cousin), 19–20, 102, 117, 167, 174–5
Smith, Bob (Gladys's father), 6

202   Elvis: The King of Fashion

Smith, Doll (Octavia, Gladys's mother), 6
Smith, Rev. Frank, 14
Smith, Gene (cousin), 20, 99
Smith, Johnny (uncle), 14
Smith, Lorraine (wife of Travis Smith), 20
Smith, Travis (Gladys's brother), 9, 20, 94
Snow, Hank, 54, 65, 74, 90
South Bend, 164
Spears, Britney, 143
Speedway, film, 119, 191
Spehar, Kathie, 146
Spinout, film, 11, 191
Springfield, 166
Springsteen, Bruce, 188
Sri Daya Mata, 115
St Jude Children's Research Hospital, Memphis, x, 88, 186–7
St Louis, 96, 145, 160, 170
St Paul, 164–5
Stage Show, TV show, 38, 81–2, 86, 193
Stallings, Billy, x, 30–1, 162
Stanley, Dee, 110
Starr, Ringo, 117
Statesmen Quartet, 22–3, 46
Status Quo, 98
Stause, Chrishell, 188
Stay Away, Joe, film, 118, 191
Stax Museum, Memphis, x, 162, 186
Stewart, Jim, 162
Stoker, Alan, 52
Stone, Mike, 150
Streisand, Barbra, 126
Studio 50, New York, 81
Styles, Harry, 190
Sullivan, Ed/*The Ed Sullivan Show*, TV, xiii, 38, 87–90, 115, 152, 188, 193
Sun Studio (Sun Records; Memphis Recording Service), Memphis, x, xx, 22, 35, 42, 48–57, 81, 98, 114, 136, 185, 188
Super Fly, film, x, xiii, 40
Sweet Inspirations, 137, 168

Taurog, Norman, 109
TCB, 137, 146, 166, 173, 184, 194
Tennessee, 65
   State Penitentiary, 50
Terre Haute, 166

Texas, 39, 70, 101, 144–5
   Houston, 144–5, 150, 162, 166, 172
      Astrodome, 144
The Trouble with Girls, film, 136
Thomas, Rufus, 53, 55, 162
Thompson, Ben, 187
Thompson, Howard, 111
Thompson, Linda, 152, 161–2, 166, 169, 171–3
Thornton, Big Mama, 53
Tickle Me, film, 115, 117, 191
Tipler, Gladys and Jim, 64
Torian, Charlie Jr., 59
Tubb, Ernest, 12
Tucson, 153, 171
Tulsa, 152, 162, 171
Tupelo, Mississippi, 4–21, 25, 27, 33–5, 46, 75, 81, 90–4, 179
   Fairgrounds, 12, 14
   Hardware Co., 13
Turner, Ike, 2, 47
Tuscaloosa, 150, 166
Tutt, Ronnie, 137, 170
Tyler, Judy, 97

Uniondale, 160, 166
United Artists, 122
United Paint Co., Memphis, 20

Valentino, Rudolph, 115
Van Zandt, Steven, 188
Virginia, 65
Viva Las Vegas, film, 114–15, 191

Walker, Kenon (the Peabody Duckmaster), x, 186–7
Walker, Opal, 66
Wallis, Hal, 82, 85
Walters, Barbara, 106
Warner Bros., 35, 193
Washington, DC, 98, 131, 147–9
   Capitol Hill, 147
   Lincoln Memorial, 131
   Spokane, 98, 160, 170
   White House (and Oval Office), 130, 148–9
Waters, Muddy, 1, 21, 25, 55
WDIA Radio, 21–4

Index 203

Weinshanker, Joel, 55, 187
Weisbart, David, 110
Welch, Raquel, 160
Welles, Orson, 149
WELO Radio, 12
West, Red, 18, 26–7, 31, 79, 95, 112, 159, 164, 170–3, 177, 192–3
West, Sonny, 149, 159, 170–3, 177, 192
Westmoreland, Kathy, 168
WHBQ Radio, 23, 55
White, Booker (Bukka) T., 1
White, Governor Hugh L., 10
White, Jack, x, 51–2, 187
White, Morning Dove, 6
Whitehaven, Memphis, 94
Whitman, Slim, 58
Whitmer, Peter, 6, 192
Wichita, 152, 164
Wild in the Country, film, 111
Wilde, Kim, 98

Wilde, Marty, x, 97–8, 194
Wilkinson, John, 137, 152
Williams, Nat D., 1
Willis, Ellen, ix, 141–2
Wilson, Regis, x, 29–32, 35, 37, 105
Winchester Avenue, Memphis, 20
Witchita, 152, 164
Wizard of Oz, film (1939), 18
WMPS Radio, 22, 46
Wolfson Park, Jacksonville, Florida, 76
Wood, Anita, 99
Wood, Natalie, 91
Woodbine, Bokeem, 185
WREC Radio, 48
WSM Radio, 21

Yandell, Paul, 70–1

Zoolander, film, 81

Dear Reader,

We hope you have enjoyed this book, but why not share your views on social media? You can also follow our pages to see more about our other products: facebook.com/penandswordbooks or follow us on Twitter @penswordbooks

You can also view our products at www.pen-and-sword.co.uk (UK and ROW) or www.penandswordbooks.com (North America).

To keep up to date with our latest releases and online catalogues, please sign up to our newsletter at: www.pen-and-sword.co.uk/newsletter

If you would like a printed catalogue with our latest books, then please email: enquiries@pen-and-sword.co.uk or telephone: 01226 734555 (UK and ROW) or email: Uspen-and-sword@casematepublishers.com or telephone: (610) 853-9131 (North America).

We respect your privacy and we will only use personal information to send you information about our products.

Thank you!